# SAMUEL RAMEY

## AMERICAN BASS

by

## Jane Scovell

Illustrations by
Amy Sarah Appleton

GREAT VOICES
11

BASKERVILLE
PUBLISHERS

Copyright © 2009 Jane Scovell

Baskerville Publishers, Inc.
2455 Halloran Street
Fort Worth, Texas 76107
www.baskervillepublishers.com

All rights reserved, including the right to reproduce this book or portions thereof in any form whatsoever without permission in writing from the publisher.

Library of Congress Cataloging-in-Publication Data

Scovell, Jane, 1934-
Samuel Ramey, American bass / by Jane Scovell ; illustrations by Amy Sarah Appleton.
p. cm. — (Great voices ; 11)
Includes index.
ISBN 978-1-880909-76-8 (alk. paper)
1. Ramey, Samuel. 2. Basses (Singers)—United States—Biography. I. Title.
ML420.R2817S36 2010
782.1092—dc22
[B]
2010006282

Manufactured in the United States of America
First Printing, 2010

*for*

*my grandchildren*

*Charlotte, Ben, Isabelle, & Kate*

# CONTENTS

| | |
|---|---|
| CD- Contents | vii |
| Foreword by Marilyn Horne | ix |
| Preface | xi |
| Origins | 1 |
| Be it ever so Humble | 4 |
| On the Road | 24 |
| Wonderful Town | 40 |
| Samson's Song | 62 |
| Sam's Song | 71 |
| The Song Continues | 85 |
| Star Turns | 100 |
| Well Met | 125 |
| Ya Gotta Have a Gimmick | 145 |
| An Ending | 170 |
| A New Beginning | 173 |
| Ecco il suo Mondo | 183 |
| Sound Bites from Sam Ramey | 193 |
| Epilogue | 255 |
| Chronology | 257 |
| Discography | 267 |
| Index | 275 |

# CD CONTENTS

1. Sibilar gli angui d' Aletto — G. Handel
   From <u>Rinaldo</u>
2. Tutto e' disposto.... Aprite un po quegli occhi — W. Mozart
   From <u>Le Nozze di Figaro</u>
3. Il di gia cade .... Deh ti Ferma quei numi furenti — G. Rossini
   From <u>Semiramide</u>
4. Uldino! Uldin!.... Mentre gonfiarsi l'anima.... Oltre quell limite — G. Verdi
   From <u>Attila</u>
5. Elle ne m'aime pas — G. Verdi
   From <u>Don Carlos</u>
6. Ecco il mondo — A. Boito
   From <u>Mefistofele</u>
7. Le Veau d'Or — C. Gounod
   From <u>Faust</u>
8. Vous qui faites l'endormie — C. Gounod
   From <u>Faust</u>
9. Impossible Dream — M. Leigh
   From <u>Man of La Mancha</u>
10. Ol' Man River — G. Gershwin
    From <u>Showboat</u>
11. Embraceable You — G. Gershwin
    From <u>Girl Crazy</u>
12. Just Another Rhumba — G. Gershwin
13. Charlie Rutlege — Charles Ives
14. I Bought Me a Cat — Aaron Copland
15. Ching-a-ring Chaw — Aaron Copland

*"Although nature has gifted us all with voices, correct singing is the result of art and study."*
*...Aristotle*

# FOREWORD

## BY
## MARILYN HORNE

I love going to the opera. I always have and I still do. Even in the days when I was very busy singing myself, I'd go for the sheer joy of being at a live performance—it was my version of the busman's holiday. That's why, back in the fall of 1979, I eagerly accepted an invitation from my friend Matthew Epstein, an Artists Manager, to attend a New York City Opera production of Rossini's *Le Comte d'Ory*. One of Matthew's artists was in the production and as soon as the curtain went up, the plot, as is often the case when Matthew is involved, began to thicken. Matthew knew that I was preparing to record Rossini's *L'Italiana in Algeri*, and he also was aware that finding a suitable bass was a big challenge. Singing Rossini is hard enough for sopranos, mezzos, tenors, and baritones, but it's murder for a bass to get around all the notes. The minute I laid eyes and ears on Sam Ramey, I knew I'd discovered a bel canto goldmine. I should say that Matthew had discovered a goldmine, and led me to it. Sam gave a delightful comic performance. He looked great, sang brilliantly, and we hired him for *L'Italiana*.

Through the years Sam and I have sung together many times on discs and on stage. In the beginning, I played mother hen and took him under my wing. For example, I called his attention to the fact that although he'd made a lot of recordings, all of them were complete operas. Obviously the record companies needed him in the casts so I suggested that he use that as leverage to get his own solo albums. I can't take complete credit for the result, but check his discography to see what happened. The point is you didn't have to repeat yourself with Sam. He got it. He gets everything.

Sam would be in my dream cast of almost any opera but especially those written by Rossini. In works like *Semiramide,* we would get into what amounted to vocal duels on stage. We'd stand toe to toe and challenge each other, phrase after phrase, embellishing like crazy. It was exhilarating for us and, I think, for audiences, too. Quite frankly, I cannot imagine anyone ever singing Assur's *gran scena* in *Semiramide* better than Sam. In the role of Arsace, I had some pretty grand things to sing, myself. However, it is my opinion that Assur's mad scene, which runs nearly twenty-five minutes, contains the opera's greatest music. Everything is packed into it, including exciting coloratura, dramatic recitative, and gorgeous cantilena. I loved the way Sam did it. I loved it so much that whenever we performed *Semiramide*, I would stand in the wings during his mad scene just to hear him.

He has been a dear friend and colleague for three decades. Truly, I consider myself the luckiest mezzo on the face of the earth to have had the privilege of listening to, and of singing with, Samuel Ramey.

New York City, 2009

# PREFACE

This biography contains some 75,000 words, possibly more words than Sam Ramey has uttered in his life; he lets his singing do the talking. On stage, Sam dazzles; off stage, he tends to keep to himself. He seems to prefer listening to speaking, yet if you engage him, he is thoroughly engaging. In a way, Sam embodies the Superman/Clark Kent dichotomy. Like Superman, Sam's singing was faster than a speeding bullet, his stage presence was more powerful than a locomotive, and he was able to leap octaves with a single bound. That superhuman side of Samuel Ramey can be verified by listening to the accompanying CD. On the human side, like Clark Kent, Sam is unpretentious, thoughtful, smart, and funny, all of which you will discover when you read this book.

Jane Scovell

# Acknowledgments

Thank you to the many people I interviewed, most of whose names appear in the book. In addition, I want to thank Billy Appleton, Lucy Appleton, Mikki Ansin, David Beer, Michael Lonergan, Patricio Corillo Lopez, Laura Marshall, Marion Rosenberg, Eliza Thorne, and Charlene Trimper.

Special thanks to: Beth Bergman for her creative insight. Todd Shuster for his guidance and gallantry.

I am very grateful to Shelley Welton for her astute editorial contributions and, for her friendship.

I would like to acknowledge Ron Moore and his staff at Baskerville Publishers, especially Fanchee Ann Whitaker. Baskerville's Great Voices Series should be declared a National Treasure.

Finally, I want to thank Sam Ramey for being so forthright about his art and his life.

# SAMUEL RAMEY

## AMERICAN BASS

# ORIGINS

Once upon a time America's small towns were pretty much alike and, whether situated in the North, South, East, or West, they possessed standard elements. First and foremost was the main street, usually called just that. Main Street was the center of activity, and on and around it stood the public buildings: a town hall, a sheriff's office, a one-engine fire station, and perhaps a courthouse. A general merchandise store took care of most needs from underwear to hardware, and was flanked by other mercantile establishments: a drugstore, a grocer, a plumbing and electrical supply store, and, almost certainly, an auto repair shop. There was a library, a movie theatre or two, and a building in which Rotarians, Elks, Odd Fellows or Masons met. Railroad tracks wound around or through the town and a hospital was somewhere in the vicinity. Citizens worshipped in Protestant churches of various denominations or in a Catholic church, but rarely in a synagogue, and never in a mosque. Small towns had a scant selection of restaurants, none of which was gourmet and one of which inevitably was a diner. Most small towns had a public hall called the Grange, the War Memorial, or the Opera House. Despite the lofty title, opera houses seldom housed grand opera; they were venues for a variety of entertainments, including vaudeville, traveling theatrical shows, and itinerant soloists. While not every small town had a full complement of these elements one characteristic was shared by all—everyone knew everyone, if not by sight, then certainly by name. It is also a fact that many of these communities were named for a real person. Colby, Kansas is such a town.

In 1882, J.R. Colby, a homesteader, and his wife Mary arrived in western Kansas and settled in Thomas County. Mr. Colby had "visions of establishing a town" and, by 1884, secured a patent. In 1885, after a land rush brought in settlers, a town was founded on his property and named for him. Colby, located at the intersection of Kansas Highway 25 and Interstate 70, 220 miles east of Denver, Colorado, and 375 miles west of Kansas City, Kansas, is known as the "Oasis on the Plains." Not too long ago, if you drove into that oasis, you passed a sign on the interstate that read: "Colby, Home of International Opera Star Samuel Ramey." The juxtaposition of those words seems oddly out of place in such an isolated rural setting, and yet the legend is true. Colby's native son did become an international opera star.

In the early days of his career, Sam Ramey was discussing fees and fame with Marilyn Horne. He asked the iconic mezzo what to expect. "Put it this way," she answered. "If you compare singers to car rental companies, sopranos and tenors are Hertz, mezzos and baritones are Avis, and basses are definitely Budget." Horne was right. Operatically speaking, Hertz and Avis do align with names that resonate, names that operaphiles delight in reciting, endlessly. Budget basses, on the other hand, come down to a precious two, Feodor Chaliapin and Ezio Pinza. More than a century ago, Chaliapin achieved stratospheric celebrity. At $2,000 per performance, he was the highest paid artist of the Metropolitan Opera's 1908 season, a season in which Enrico Caruso also sang. In the mid-twentieth century, Ezio Pinza attained phenomenal renown in opera and then became a Broadway legend. Chaliapin and Pinza are the super bassos and even if you expanded the Budget list to include acknowledged artists such as Cesare Siepi, Boris Christof, or Nicholai Ghiaurov, none had the full Chaliapin/Pinza clout. Of note, all these men were from European locales that are about as far away as you can get from a prairie town smack in the middle of the USA. How then to explain Samuel Ramey's ascension to the basso pantheon?

America has produced exceptional indigenous basses, among them James Morris and Jerome Hines. And, were we to skip over the Canadian border, George London surely would pass muster. But Colby's Samuel Ramey, like Chaliapin and Pinza, transcends the Budget label. Ramey looms large throughout the world. He has appeared on nearly every major opera and concert stage across the globe and has worked with every major conductor from Abbado to von Karajan. He is the most recorded bass in history and his recordings have garnered major prizes, from Grammys to Gran Prix du Disc awards. He was twice awarded the prestigious Abbiati Prize for the best performance on the Italian operatic stage, and was presented with the coveted Rossini Medal for his many appearances at Pesaro's renowned Rossini Festival. Formal recognition came from his home state when he was named "Native Kansan of the Year." Soon thereafter, the French Ministry of Culture awarded him the rank of Commander in the Order of Arts and Letters. All told, Samuel Ramey is definitely not in Kansas anymore. Still, despite his worldwide prominence, he has never lost that homespun, country boy quality that comes directly from his small town Midwestern roots.

Jane Scovell

# Be it ever so Humble

Samuel Edward Ramey was born in the Thomas County Hospital on March 28, 1942 and after all these years, still refers to himself as an 'accident.' He probably has that right since fifteen years separated him from his nearest sibling. The three first tier Ramey offspring, Leonard born in 1922, Rebecca Darlene born in 1925, and Joseph born in 1927, were part of the adult world by the time Sam came along. His siblings, along with his parents, were rather taken aback at his arrival. His sister, who goes by the name Darlene, remembers that their mother was embarrassed by the whole thing and kept quiet about her pregnancy—until she could no longer hide the fact. Supposedly, their father was "over the moon."

Besides being a late child, Sam was marked in another way; he was born with a clubfoot. At the age of six months, his leg was placed in a cast and when the cast was removed both feet were put into a pair of boots attached to each other by a metal bar. He wore that contraption for two years and although he remembers nothing of this it had to have been terribly confining. Once the brace was taken off Sam got moving and never stopped. He was a very active little boy and according to his sister "prone to wander away from the house and get into mischief in the neighborhood." Sam's mother found it difficult to deal with her son's wanderlust. To keep him close, she would tie one end of a long rope around the trunk of a tree and loop the other end around Sam's waist. The rope kept him tethered still he had enough slack to move freely within the confines of his own backyard. The procedure became ritual but in time he was given a choice. One morning, his mother readied him for play and as he scampered toward the backdoor she called out,

"All right, Sam, are you going to stay in the yard or shall I get the rope?" Halfway through the door he turned, paused, and answered, "Better get the rope, Mom." Samuel Ramey's practical nature had been set.

Both Ramey parents, Grace Irene Mallory and Robert Guy Ramey, were Kansans of, respectively, Irish and French stock. The Mallorys were a bit more prosperous than the Rameys. Grace was born in 1900 into a family of wheat and corn farmers whose property lay a few miles south of Colby. Sam loved his mother's stories about her childhood, especially her vivid descriptions of farm duties, which included gathering in the cows for milking. As one of the older siblings in a family of nine children, Grace was expected to look after the younger ones yet despite her babysitting responsibilities and many farm chores, she managed to graduate from high school. Her future husband only completed eighth grade. Robert Guy Ramey, always called Guy, was born in 1897 in Linda, Kansas—a town that no longer exists. He, too, came from a large family whose ancestry was well documented. In the late 1990s, Sam Ramey sang with the Indianapolis Symphony and was introduced to Lolly Ramey, an assistant to the Symphony's music director. She told Sam that her father had traced the surname back to three brothers who came to America with Christopher Columbus. While Sam does not claim any such heritage, it makes a good story. Grace, the family historian, did track down her husband's ancestry if not to the Pinta, the Nina, and the Santa Maria at least back four or five generations. Over the years Sam has had a few note-worthy encounters because of his surname and, give or take a couple of vowels, with one gentleman in particular. The most memorable instance of this specific mistaken identity took place in Washington D.C. where Sam, as a member of the Artists Selection Committee of the Kennedy Center Honors, occasionally attended the award ceremonies. During one visit Sam, his wife Lindsey, and his friend Sherrill Milnes were at a pre-award reception at the White House. Sam and Lindsey were chatting with Milnes and his wife when they spotted Stephen Spielberg standing by himself. They decided to go over and talk to him. Milnes spoke first.

"I'm Sherrill Milnes and I enjoy your work very much, Mr. Spielberg." Spielberg smiled and said "pleased to meet you." Then Sam spoke.

'Hi, Mr. Spielberg, I'm a big fan of yours, too. I really love your work. My name's Sam Ramey.' Spielberg's face lit up. He grabbed Sam's hand and started shaking it.

"Oh, how great to meet you. My kids love your movies. They watch them all the time on DVDs." Spielberg went on and on until the embarrassed singer broke in. "Excuse me Mr. Spielberg I'm Sam Ramey the opera singer not Sam Raimi the movie director."

Another time, after a matinee performance in San Francisco, Sam went to a restaurant, gave his name to the maitre d' and as he was shown to a table heard buzzing all around him. "...See that guy over there, did you hear him give his name? That's Sam Raimi. Who? You know, the one who directed *The Evil Dead*." No sooner was Sam seated than a man, armed with a sheet of paper and a ballpoint pen, came rushing over. Pushing the autograph paraphernalia in front of Sam he asked, "Are you Sam Raimi the director?" And when Sam answered, "Nope, I'm Sam Ramey the opera singer," the man pulled away the paper and pen, turned, and went back to his table. "It just doesn't stop," Sam laughs, "and it got worse after Raimi did the *Spiderman* films. People actually called and left messages on my answering machine asking if I were casting and could they make appointments to read for parts." Sam has learned to take the Raimi/Ramey confusion in stride and remains confident that the confusion is one-sided. "I'm sure nobody's ever asked Sam Raimi if he's the opera singer."

While Sam's childhood memories are positive he is understandably vague about his siblings. They simply were not around. At the time Sam was born, Leonard was serving in the Navy. Later, Leonard and his wife, Idalu, settled in St. Louis, Missouri. Sam was a two-year-old when Darlene married Joe Alcott, an Air Force serviceman. After his discharge, Alcott became a civil engineer and was employed by Mobil Oil. The Alcotts were moved around oil-rich areas from Oklahoma to New Mexico to Texas. They eventually retired to Lubbock in the Texas Panhandle where Darlene, now widowed, still lives. (Lubbock's most famous citizen, Sam is quick to point out, was Buddy Holly whose museum is the town's big attraction.) Joe Ramey, the closest in age to Sam, left high school and joined the Navy near the war's end. After the war he finished his education and became a civil engineer. He and his wife Flora lived for a while in Lawrence, Kansas and eventually settled in Albuquerque, New Mexico where they reside today. Joe Ramey remembers occasional baby-sitting stints for his little brother. "My mother would ask me to keep an eye on him while she and my father went out. My high school buddies usually came over to keep me company and we'd play a little poker. Sam hung around the table taking everything in. He caught on to poker awfully young. Sam always had a lot of friends. One time I came home and found him playing with a bunch of neighbor kids. Sam's hands were tied behind his back and there was a noose hanging around his neck. A couple of the boys were marching him towards the big tree in the backyard. I didn't know whether they were about to string him up or what! I broke that game up fast. I have to say I was kind of glad I dropped in when I did!" According to Darlene, "although Sam saw more of me than he did of Leonard and Joe, we were so much older it was like two families." Darlene and Joe remember Sam as an impish kid as does Joe's wife, Flo Forney, who grew up a few doors down from the Rameys. Sam would sneak over to the Forney's house, hide in the bushes, and then jump out to throw fistfuls of dirt through the open windows before high tailing it for home. She also recalls Mrs. Ramey shouting, "SAMMY, SAMMY, where are you? Come home!" at all hours of the day. "From what my mother told me I knew Sam was into everything," laughs Darlene Alcott. "When Joe and I came home on vacations we could see how ornery he was, which was understandable because of my parents' advanced age. You couldn't get mad at him, though, he was so darn cute. I always used to say my little brother was an *only* child. But he was a blessing and we all just loved him and spoiled him like anything."

Sam recalls his childhood and youth in a characteristically terse, droll manner. He is forthright and at the same time guarded—shielding as well as revealing.

"I never felt lonely when I was growing up because there were lots of kids in the neighborhood and we were a large extended family. My mom had brothers and sisters but my dad's family were all boys, eight of them, and Dad was somewhere in the middle. The Mallorys kind of stuck around Colby, but my dad's brothers spread out all over the country. I actually had two or three Ramey uncles I never even met. The Mallorys were in the vicinity but they were scattered and we had to travel to see them. We'd get in the car on a Sunday and drive out to visit an aunt or uncle. The next Sunday, we'd pile into the car and go off in completely the opposite direction to see some other set of relatives, and then do the same thing all over again the next Sunday. I honestly can't recall an occasion when the entire family was together.

"We were a meat and potatoes family and there was always plenty of good meat because my dad was a butcher. I'm pretty sure my dad had to leave school to go to work and I guess he kind of floundered for a while. I know that he had a series of odd jobs like delivering milk until he became a meat cutter—that's the trade he was in when I came along. My dad was good with people. He had a way of making everyone smile and he was a popular guy. Folks would go out of their way to come to the store where he worked. We didn't have much money but I never consciously gave it a thought. It wasn't until I got to high school that I began to notice that other kids had certain things I didn't, like a lot of my classmates had their own cars. I could get the family car just about any time I wanted but that was different from having one of my own. Anyway, we always seemed to have enough money for whatever was *really* needed, food, clothes, and things like that.

"The summer after I was in the fourth grade my dad took a job in a grocery store in Winona, a much smaller town than Colby. We were there for two years and then we moved sixty or seventy miles away to Quinter. My dad had heart problems and while we were in Quinter he had his first heart attack. The doctors told him that he'd have to take things easy. That meant he couldn't continue lugging those huge sides of beef in and out of the locker room, so he had to give up butchering. I was thirteen when it happened and it scared me. But I was sure everything would be okay.

"We moved back to Colby where my dad did a bit of meat cutting for a while. Eventually, he stopped butchering and became the deputy sheriff of Thomas County. Not the kind of deputy sheriff you see in the movies or on television shows; it was a desk job. My dad stayed in the office and manned the radio when the sheriff was out on patrol. Wherever we lived and whatever he did, my dad was well liked. My mom was too, but she was a little less outgoing. She didn't work while I was growing up—I mean, she didn't have a paying job. She did do volunteer work for the county historical society and she was good with figures. After my dad passed away she ran for county treasurer. She went from door-to-door meeting people and asking them to vote for her. They did. She was elected, and held the office for two terms. By the way, both my parents were registered Democrats, which was unusual in our neck of the woods. They even voted for Adlai Stevenson as opposed to Dwight Eisenhower. That was quite something considering that Eisenhower was raised in Abilene, Kansas. My folks were down-to-earth people and, except for a few deviations such as their allegiance to the Democratic Party, traditional mid-Westerners. One thing's for sure, strong feelings weren't shown at home. My parents didn't talk much and about some things they never spoke at all. Their silence was sometimes spooky. We had a huge bible that was kept on a table in the living room in which the family's births, marriages, and deaths were recorded. I looked through it one time and was amazed to discover that my parents had had another child, a girl born between Leonard and Darlene. She died in infancy. *Nothing*, not a single word, ever was said about her. If I hadn't accidentally come across the information, I never would have known she existed. My folks just didn't talk about things. Occasionally, their silence could hurt. I especially remember the time we were forced to return to Colby because of my dad's health. I was in the middle of my first year of high school and one day, without any advance warning, my parents told me we were moving back, and that was that. I know they didn't mean to upset me but I really was thrown for a loop. I was used to living in rather small places, in Winona there were about nine kids in my class and in Quinter there were twenty. Colby was the largest town in the area with a population of a whopping four thousand. I had fifty-four classmates at Colby Community High School and for a while I was terrified. Looking back, I can see the humor in the situation; I mean, thinking that I was moving to a BIG city. Why I've sung in front of an audience of more people than Colby's entire population. I sure didn't notice it then but Colby really was a small town;

we couldn't even get television broadcasts. I spent my childhood and teens listening to the radio, great stuff like *The Lone Ranger*, *Fibber McGee and Molly*, *The Shadow*, *Jack Benny*, and *Amos and Andy*. By the time we moved back to Colby, some folks did own television sets but they had to put up 200-foot antennas to get reception. Booster stations were added when I was a senior in high school and an antenna was placed on top of the grain elevator. The antenna brought television to everyone, except us. We didn't have a set at home and I had to go over to friends' houses to watch. Really, I was radio-raised."

Although television was a novelty in western Kansas, Sam made his first appearance on the small screen before his return to Colby. In the seventh grade, in Quinter, he and a few other children were taken to a local television station in Hayes, Kansas to participate in a broadcast. Darlene happened to be visiting her parents at the time and, because there was no television set at home, she and her mother went to the grocery store where Guy Ramey worked to watch Sam. "The picture was grainy and the sound was tinny but there was my little brother singing a solo. His voice still hadn't changed, I remember that."

Back in Colby, Sam got used to the size of the high school and settled in to 'big city' life. His best friend, Steve Hedden, also was in musical studies. Sam sang and Hedden played the trombone. Sam stayed with music and became a performer; Hedden took the academic route and recently retired as Dean of the College of Fine Arts at the University of Kansas.

"Sam and I were very involved with music. In this day and age they'd probably call us music nerds," laughs Hedden. "Sam was a star of the vocal department and I was kind of a shining light in the instrumental department. Summers we went to music camp together, and during the school year we participated in district and state music contests. They called them 'festivals' to play down the competitive factor. If you got a one rating in the district contest, you were eligible for the state contest. Both of us usually got through the district competition. Typically, my parents would drive us to the state festival where Sam and I would compete in our respective division. Back then a lot of pressure was put on kids from rural backgrounds to find a vocation that would sustain them, and music was not the top choice. If you were interested in music, you were advised to get a job as an educator rather than a performer. Good career advice wasn't easily come by, either. We didn't have particularly strong guidance counseling at Colby Community High in those days; it was up to individual teachers to do mentoring. Both Sam and I were fortunate in finding strong advocates; his was Kay Paterson, the choir director. Sam sang a lot of classical music but he never said anything about wanting to sing in opera. Quite frankly, I don't think he knew anything about it. He liked pop, and his role model was Pat Boone. In fact, Sam wore the kind of white suede shoes Boone sported, which was quite a fashion statement. Not many guys in Colby Kansas wore white suede shoes but Sam carried it off. We were good buddies and some of my happiest memories are of the two of us 'dragging' Main with Sam behind the wheel of his family's car. We'd shoot down from the A&W stand at one end of Main Street to the Rainbow Drive-In at the other, waving at our friends gathered on the sidewalks. Those really were far simpler days."

Junior year, Sam got together with his classmates, Paul Ackerman, and Phil Harrison, to form a trio. Ackerman played the piano, Harrison played bongo drums, and Sam sang. They performed at proms and dances and their repertoire included popular songs of the day. "We played in the trio to impress the girls but they weren't overwhelmed," recalls Ackerman. "The school athletes were the cool guys not musicians. My wife, Betty, was in the cool set back then and I was sort of on the fringe of it. Aside from the trio,

Sam and I never ran around together. He'd hang around with us from time to time and while he may not have been in the super cool set, he never was bullied or picked on by the ones who were in it. He was a good easy guy and nice to have around. Truly, I don't think you could find anyone in Colby, back then or now, who'd have anything bad to say about Sam Ramey." Sam acknowledges that he was never in the cool set but adds that, while he did not set the world on fire, socially or academically, he was an okay student—not dumb but not highly motivated, except in music and sports.

In Colby, sport was king but music was a notable consort. The town took great pride in its cultural activities and music topped the list. Vicki Secrest, born and bred in Colby, was a freshman when Sam was a senior at Colby Community High. They sang in the chorus together and she played oboe in the orchestra for the *Mikado* production in which Sam starred. "Music was a big part of everyday Colby life," she reminisces. "My grandfather went on the road a lot, and when he came back he always brought the latest sheet music. We'd put it right on the piano and play and sing. That wasn't unique to our house, either; it went on in lots of homes in Colby. We weren't in thrall to television in those days. We looked to live performances for inspiration, especially the ones presented by the Community Concerts series. I remember hearing the Vienna Boys Choir and Ferrante and Teicher, the duo pianists, in person! Really, Community Concerts set the tone for our town."

In the mid-Twentieth century, Community Concerts revolutionized the performing arts in America and set the tone for a great many towns and cities. At the end of the 1920s, live performances, vaudeville, minstrel shows, and soloists, were dying out. The public still wanted them but the cost of presenting them had zoomed and so had the deficits. Around 1927, two groups, one in a few eastern states, and another in the Great Lakes area, came up with the same plan at the same time. The idea was to raise the money and *then*, hire the performers. It turned out that communities were more than willing to subscribe to a series of concerts without even knowing what they would be seeing, a system which insured that artists would be paid. Eventually the idea grew into Community Concerts, the country's largest and most enduring network of performing arts presenters. At last, ordinary people had the chance to see, in the flesh, extraordinary artists—legendary musicians such as violinists Jascha Heifitz and Yehudi Menuhin; pianists such as Vladimir Horowitz and Rudolf Serkin; ballet companies ranging from the Ballet Russe to the Joffrey; full symphony orchestras including the Minneapolis and St. Louis Symphonies; choral groups such as Robert Shaw and the DePauer Infantry Chorus. And Community Concerts abounded in great singers, people like Jussi Bjorling, Dorothy Kirsten, Robert Merrill, Leontyne Price, Paul Robeson, Bidu Sayao, Cesare Siepi, Richard Tucker, and Leonard Warren, to name just a few. Community Concerts was an inspiration to generations; those who were privileged enough to attend the concerts will never forget them. No matter how many times television trots performing artists before our eyes, it is never as awe-inspiring or as thrilling as being in the actual presence of greatness. Community Concerts added immeasurably to the musical life of the country but even if it never had come into being, Sam remembers that music was in the air.

"Music always was a part of my life. My whole family sang—my brothers and sister, and my mother. Matter of fact, my brother Leonard was a bass and I always thought he had a better voice than I did. All of us sang in the church choir and my mom used to sing hymns when she was cleaning up the house. We were Methodist and serious churchgoers—every week I went to church, Sunday school, and choir practice. My first voice teacher was a fellow church member named Jones. I was still a boy soprano and sang tenor in the choir when I worked with her. Mrs. Jones didn't teach me anything technical but whatever she did, she didn't hurt the development of my voice. While I was studying with her, my mother decided we needed a piano at home so she borrowed one. She tried to get me to take piano lessons but I wouldn't and within a short time the piano was returned. I never played an instrument. Well, that's not quite true, I did play the snare drum but only because my older brother's drum set was around the house and I picked it up. Mostly, I sang. The funny thing is, as far back as the second grade, I sensed there was something strange about my voice. I had this kind of vibration and I was very aware that I sounded different from the other kids. When I got up to do solos, I'd try to stifle it. I had no idea that the 'strangeness' was a natural vibrato. I later learned that vibrato is characteristic of classical singing and it happens when a sung note rises and falls rapidly in barely perceptible changes in pitch. It produces a kind of tremulous, pulsating effect. And if you use it right, it gives the voice its color, or timbre. Popular singing generally calls for a straight or "white" sound and that was what I was after. For a long time, I struggled to smother my natural vibrato, fortunately, I didn't succeed.

"My folks always knew I had talent. Other people began to recognize it about the time I entered junior high in Quinter. My voice changed between the eighth and ninth grades. I don't remember going through any 'process.' I just woke up one morning, jumped out of bed, and there it was. Anyway, back then being musical wasn't such a big deal. Sports was everything and I mean *everything*. Everybody went to the games and if you were good, and lucky, you could get an athletic scholarship to a state university. I went out for football when we still lived in Quinter but I wasn't any good at it and I was so-so in basketball. Baseball was my game. I was on the junior high team in Quinter. After we moved back to Colby, I played in the summer league sponsored by the American Legion One year, we won the area tournament and I'm pretty sure I was named one of the All Stars. Ironically, I had to play in a summer league because the Colby high school didn't have a team. Like I said, I wasn't any big shot letterman but I was an okay athlete, good enough for the junior high sports coach to drop by the grocery store one day to talk to my father. Later, my dad told me the details of their meeting.

'You know, Mr. Ramey,' the coach said, 'your son Sam is a good athlete. I just don't understand why he wants to waste his time with all that music stuff when he could be playing out on the field. I think he should forget about the music and concentrate on sports.'

'Well, Coach,' my dad answered after a bit, 'my son likes music and if that's what he wants to do, that's what he's going to do.'"

And Sam did what he wanted to do. His active participation in sports waned but music remained a vital part of his school days. He consistently landed leading roles in Colby Community High School's musicals. He played the Scarecrow in the *Wizard of Oz* in his junior year, and in his senior year, he was Nanki-Poo in *The Mikado*. He got the top roles because he had the best voice; it was also the lowest voice. Leading roles generally are written with tenors in mind; the teachers, however, wanted Sam enough to transpose down the parts. He loved music but, eventually, Sam had to make a decision about his future. Sophomore year, for want of a career focus, Sam decided to follow in his brother Joe's and his brother-in-law Joe's footsteps and become a civil engineer. "I had no idea what civil engineering was, but I figured that it had to be okay since the two Joes were doing it. Meanwhile I took a chemistry course, hated it, and barely passed. When the two Joes advised me that engineers are required to take a lot of chemistry, I immediately decided civil engineering, whatever it was, wasn't for me.

"I was trying to figure out what I could do when I had a

piece of good luck. I was singing in the Colby High School chorus and the choral director and music teacher, Kay Paterson, 'spotted' me. She was impressed with my singing and offered to give me private voice lessons. She was a good teacher and I was an enthusiastic student and by senior year I determined to make music my career. I told Miss Paterson and she was pleased, so much so, she threw in some extra lessons on music theory. Unlike chemistry, I enjoyed singing and it came easily to me. I had a 'natural' voice and thanks to Kay Paterson I learned to read music. I admit I did have a brief dream of becoming another Pat Boone or Elvis Presley, but my sister told me that if I wanted to make it in show business I had to have a gimmick. Although I never figured out a gimmick, I never gave up liking pop stuff. I was in the audience at Madison Square Garden in June 1972 when Elvis made his first and only New York appearance. That was one of the most exciting nights of my life!

"When I said I was going for a career in music, I didn't mean I was going to be an opera singer. I knew nothing about opera. I hadn't even heard one, let alone seen one. My only contact with opera came through the Ed Sullivan TV program. He used to have Metropolitan Opera stars like Rise Stevens, Roberta Peters, Robert Merrill, Cesare Siepi and Jerome Hines on his Sunday night variety show. I was sort of fascinated by the singers, but I didn't really like what they sang. I preferred the music on the Lawrence Welk Show. Welk had a guy named Larry Hooper who had a voice so low he could sing notes that were off the piano, like at the end of that old chestnut, *Rocked in the Cradle of the Deep*. Hooper sang *dee-ee-ee-ee-eep* moving down the scale and ending up below sea level. The sound reverberated in your ears and made you dizzy. That's what I wanted; I wanted to have a voice like Larry Hooper's.

"For the last couple of summers that I was in high school I went to the Kansas State Music Camp which was sponsored by Kansas State University. When it came time to go to college, I decided to apply to KSU, figuring that they knew me from my work at the camp. I got a small scholarship that paid for my tuition. As I recall, the tuition was $104 a semester. I guess it would be in the $2500 range today. One morning, I got up early, gathered my things, said goodbye to my parents, and took a Greyhound bus for the 300-mile ride to Kansas State University. I was floored by the size of the place; it was like Colby Community High School in quintuplicate. My dorm mate was another first year music student, a bass horn player. He was an okay guy but soon after I moved into the dorm, I ran into Doug Brush who'd been at music camp with me. Doug wasn't a music major, but he did sing in the college choir. He'd been recruited into Kappa Sigma fraternity and asked me over to the frat house for dinner. I went a couple times and was too dumb to realize that I was being rushed. I was, and I joined. I moved into the fraternity house, which was a lot smaller and more congenial than the dormitory. Unfortunately, I became a little too congenial for my own good. I joined the school choir and enthusiastically participated but I neglected everything else. Fraternity high life took its toll and, scholastically speaking, my freshman year was headed for disaster. My grades kept falling and falling. Then, while I was on tour with the choir, I received an urgent message from my brother telling me to call home immediately. I called back and my brother said I had to come right home.

'But I'm on tour, I can't leave,' I protested.

'Dad died,' said my brother. 'Get home.'

"The train ride back was miserable. All I could think of was I'd never see my father again. I kept going back over so many things, those times where, in his own quiet way, my dad stood up for me. I was scared, really scared not only for myself, but for my mother, too. She'd be alone now. I can't remember much about what happened after I got home, just a general feeling of deep sadness. My mom was sad but strong, too. She urged me to get back to school and a few days after the funeral I returned to Kansas State. I found it even more difficult to concentrate on my work. Somehow, I managed to squeak through the first year. Sophomore year I wasn't so lucky and by the end of the second semester, I was in big trouble. I flunked everything but music. My scholarship was cancelled and I returned to Colby, shamefaced. I'd never felt so lost in my life. I couldn't cope with the idea of returning to Kansas State so I decided to take the next year off and try to get my feet on the ground.

"For all the bad stuff that went down at KSU, one really great thing happened. I was introduced to opera. In my freshman year, I worked with a voice teacher named William Fischer and we concentrated on arias. The first one he gave me to work on was *non pui andrai* from *The Marriage of Figaro*. I didn't have a clue how to sing it. Mr. Fischer suggested that I go to the library and listen to opera recordings. For some reason, instead of going to the library, I went to a record store. I looked through the bins and came across an LP of Ezio Pinza singing operatic arias; *non pui andrai* was one of the selections. I didn't know who Pinza was, but I bought the record, took it back to the dorm, and played it, and played it, and played it, over and over again, not just the aria I was studying, but each and every one of the selections. I couldn't get enough of Pinza. I was fascinated with his singing. His voice resounded in my brain. No kidding, he opened up those incredible pieces of music to me. I began going to the library to listen to operatic recordings and I didn't just stick with Pinza, either. I also listened to Chaliapin, Siepi, and Georgio Tozzi. I realized that each of them brought something different to the same aria. I learned, then, that you don't have to imitate any one person or style. As long as you respect what's written by the composer, every singer has a right to his, or her, own interpretation. From the moment I began to study opera, it intrigued, excited, and sustained me. And, believe me, I really needed something to hang onto when I left KSU."

Back in Colby, fatherless, in academic limbo, and short of funds, Sam searched for employment. In past summers, he had worked for Sam Lunsway, a building contractor and a good friend of the family. Indeed, Sam Ramey was named after the contractor who was like a big brother to him. The older Sam always came through for his namesake and when young Sam sought his help, Lunsway immediately put the college dropout to work on various construction sites. That summer, Sam honed his carpentry skills. After the building season ended, he took a job as a haberdashery salesman in Bernard's Clothing, a local men's store.

During the year that Sam took off from college, his fascination with recorded music continued. He began buying records, obsessively. He joined a record club and amassed hundreds of LPs featuring complete operas, arias, anything and everything vocal that was available; he still has them. Besides buying and listening to records, Sam became involved with a local theatre group and appeared in a few one-act plays. Ron Loch, the director of the acting company and a knowledgeable opera buff, owned an even more extensive collection of opera on LPs than Sam. Sam and his fellow actors often gathered at Loch's apartment to listen to those recordings. Aware of Sam's avid interest in singing, Ron Loch suggested that the haberdasher cum singer apply to the summer program at the Central City Opera in Colorado. Sam liked the idea and decided to go for it. He contacted Central City Opera and was sent an application form. The selection process required an audition tape, as well as paper work, and Sam set about putting together his submission. The big question was, what should he sing? One of the LPs he owned, *The Ezio Pinza Collection*, contained songs and arias that the great basso had featured in his recitals. Sam took it out and listened with renewed interest. "There were two pieces I thought I could handle pretty well, "Sarastro's *in diesen heil'gen Hallen* from Mozart's *The Magic Flute*, and Flagier's *Le cor* (*The Horn*) a French art song. The Mozart was kind of solemn and stately while the Flagier piece was a bit more bravura. I thought they made a good contrast and would really show off my voice. I hired a pianist and we went over to the local radio station where I hired a sound engineer. We made a tape and I sent it off to the head of the Central City chorus. Honestly, I didn't have much hope that anything would come of it but it was worth a try. Lo and behold, they hired me! In the summer of 1963, at age 21, I headed west to begin my operatic career."

Central City Opera is the fifth-oldest opera company in the United States. The Opera House itself was built during the gold rush days of the late 19th century when Central City was known as "the richest square mile on earth." In due time, the mines played out, and both the opera house and the town fell into disrepair. In the early 1930s, the theatre was restored to its former 550-seat glory and a live production of Dumas's, *Camille*, starring Lillian Gish, inaugurated Central City's annual six-week festival of theatre and opera. Each season, the music festival presents established opera singers and a chorus, composed of young hopefuls, in two operatic productions. The summer Sam arrived, the operas were Verdi's *Il Trovatore* and Mozart's *Don Giovanni*, and both were double cast. Norman Treigle of the New York City Opera was one of the two Giovannis. Spiro Malas, also a NYC Opera member, alternated in the role of Leporello, and Sherrill Milnes played Masetto. Sam had found his element.

"Central City was a revelation to me. The minute I arrived I knew I was home. It was that simple. First, I had the opportunity to sing in opera and my thoughts went something like, 'Hey, this is fun. I want to do this! I want to be an opera singer.' Sure, I was just a chorus member but, at the end of the season, chorus members also participated in a program of opera scenes. I was assigned the role of Figaro and sang in the sextet, *Riconosci in questo amplesso*. It blew my mind to be making music like this. Second, I had the chance to watch and listen to Norman Treigle—maybe that should be put first, I'm not sure. I'd watch from the wings every time he performed and believe me, Treigle was something to see. I met him that summer but I really didn't get a chance to talk to him that much; I just kind of admired him from a distance.

"A lot of people in the chorus were from Wichita State University and I had a great time with them. We'd sing in the opera and after it was over we'd go to a local bar and sing all night. The Wichita gang thought I was good and encouraged me to go on with singing. They really wanted me to go to their school. When Harrison Boughton, the choral director at Wichita State, came out to Central City, my fellow choristers urged him to listen to me. I did a little audition for Mr. Boughton and I guess he was impressed.

'Why don't you come to Wichita State this fall,' he suggested.

'Okay,' I said."

Harrison Boughton, now retired and professor emeritus, regards the 'discovery' of Samuel Ramey as a highlight of his teaching years. "I knew the potential. He was a combination of exceptional talent and determination. Sam was determined that he was going to sing professionally." For Sam, the prospect of changing academic venues was heaven sent. He did not need much prodding to make the switch and for good reasons. First and foremost, Wichita State had an opera program, which Kansas State did not; moreover, Sam knew that the Wichita program was "excellent." And, there was another, more personal incentive. Sam felt that his reputation at Kansas State was tarnished; he wanted a fresh start, a tabula rasa. He filled out the necessary applications and mailed them before he left Central City for home. Not long after his return, he received a letter from Wichita State informing him that he had been accepted in the musical study program. "I was plenty happy," he recalls, "and so was my mother. I couldn't wait to get there! Even thinking about it all these years later, I really can't make a big enough deal about my summer at Central City. There's absolutely no question that my operatic life began in that little mining town in Colorado. It was the turning point because, while I was there, I appeared in an opera for the first time. The fact is, I actually *appeared* in an opera before I ever even *saw* one."

Jane Scovell

# On the Road

"I enrolled at Wichita State in 1963, I was able to transfer a few credits, but basically, I had to start from scratch. I took a lot of music theory and other related subjects and I did very well. I was a better student because I was doing what I wanted to do and I liked what I was doing. It wasn't all smooth going, though. I had a bit of trouble passing the piano-proficiency requirement. Years later, after I'd made my career, one of the department heads told a writer for *Opera News* that at Wichita I was a 'great vocal athlete but a lousy musician.' Hmmm. He also said that I 'spent more time working on the chorus girls in the dressing room than studying my music.' Hmmm. Whatever he said about me, I know that I really enjoyed performing in the operas. We did one complete production a year and sometimes, a program of scenes in the spring. The first full production was Offenbach's *Tales of Hoffman*. In that opera, one singer usually takes on all the four major bass parts, Lindorf, Coppelius, Dapertutto, and Dr. Miracle. However, to give as many students as possible a chance to perform, four different basses were assigned to the quartet of villains. I sang Dr. Miracle and that was my first complete operatic role on the stage. The next year, I was Don Alfonso in Mozart's *Cosi fan tutte*, followed by my appearance as Bottom in Benjamin Britten's *Midsummer Night's Dream*. Then came a rarely performed work by Haydn, *Infidelity Foiled*, in which I sang the role of Nanni. I made my last undergraduate appearance at Wichita State as Sir John in Verdi's *Falstaff*.

What a terrific part that is. I loved playing him and over the years often thought about doing *Falstaff* professionally. I wish I had, but I didn't.

"I did quite a bit of singing while I was at Wichita. One time, just for the fun of it, I entered a competition sponsored by a local women's club. Those competitions were very important to the community and taken very seriously by the ladies as well as the performers. The ladies were championing culture and we singers were delighted to have any opportunity to sing. A club in Quinter contacted me and asked if I would come there for a recital. I was thrilled to have the opportunity to sing in one of my 'home towns,' and immediately accepted. There was one problem—I didn't have an accompanist. I told the woman who spoke to me that I'd love to come to Quinter but that I didn't have a regular pianist or anything like that.

'Oh, that's not a problem,' she answered, 'we've got someone here. Do you remember Vicky Bolen?'

'Vicky Bolen? Sure I remember her, but she's a kid. She was in grade school when I left Quinter.'

'Well, she's in high school now, and a really good pianist. I'm sure she can do it.'

"I said it would it would be fine with me, but I couldn't believe it. Little Vicky Bolen? She was in the fourth grade when I was an eighth grader. I only knew her because of her big brother. He was a star athlete in the high school and coached our junior high baseball team. I never thought of Vicky as anything but a kid. Anyway, I sent the music to her and then I drove out to Quinter to see her. WOW! She'd grown up real good. She was a very attractive young woman and, I soon discovered, a good pianist, too. I sang, she played, and we had a few dates before I went back to Wichita State. I liked Vicky a lot, but I had to get back to my studies. I didn't know when I'd see her again. Then, as the saying goes, fate stepped in.

"Vicky was always more interested in ballet than piano

and she'd been on the lookout for a good dance school. About the time she played for me she found one in Wichita. Instead of finishing her senior year in Quinter she went there to study ballet. Later on, she got her high school diploma through a correspondence course. I had no idea that Vicky was in Wichita until we ran into each other on the street. Pretty soon we were dating, seriously. I was crazy about her and asked her to marry me. She accepted, and we were married in a civil ceremony at the local courthouse. She was eighteen and I was almost twenty-two and because we were so young, we weren't sure that our families would approve. We decided to keep our marriage a secret, at least for a while. Ha. Sam Lunsway happened to be passing through Wichita the day after our wedding. He dropped into a coffee shop for lunch, picked up a local newspaper, and was flabbergasted to read that I'd gotten married. Vicky and I had no way of knowing that a wedding announcement would be published in the paper. When Sam saw it he immediately called my mother. Mom knew Vicky and liked her and was okay with it. Mrs. Bolen knew and liked me, too, but I think she probably would have preferred more of a traditional wedding for her daughter. Anyway, she accepted it. It just goes to show how hard it is to keep things secret, especially a marriage.

"Vicky and I moved into a small apartment and I remember how really nice it was being with someone. She went to ballet school and, believe it or not, I took some ballet classes myself. I can't say I could have had a career as a dancer but learning how to control my body movements helped me quite a few times when I was on the operatic stage. I remember a particular *Semiramide* at the Met that really tested my balance. I had a terrific mad scene near the end of the opera. I made my entrance at the top of a long flight of stairs and began the aria as I descended. Well, I wore these big boots with a fairly tall heel and as I took the first step down, one of the heels caught and snapped off. I got to the bottom and walked around on tiptoe, kind of *en pointe*, for the entire mad scene just to keep from listing from side to side. That wasn't the only test but it's one that sticks out in my mind.

"Married life with Vicky became kind of routine, in a good way. She was doing her thing and I spent half my time at school and the rest of the time working. My first job was as a salesman in the shoe department of a large specialty store. Next, I took a factory job in the Manning Clampitt Meat and Chile Company. Manning put out steaks and other cuts and sold them to schools and restaurants but that wasn't all; leftover scraps were used to make chili. The factory had a room with two huge vats into which all the scraps and fat were dumped. I arrived at Manning's at the crack of dawn to deliver the meats. After making the deliveries, I returned to the factory to help make the chili. Two of us, the 'chef' and I, worked in the chili room. The chef poured spices and flavorings into the scrap-filled vats and, when the stuff was all mixed up, he'd scoop it out and put it into one-pound aluminum containers. The containers were placed on racks in the freezer and left overnight. My job was pretty specific. While the other guy cooked, I'd pull the racks out of the freezer, knock the little blocks of chili out of the aluminum containers, and take them to be packaged. Not exactly rocket science. To this very day, if you go to Wichita, you'll find packages of Manning's Chile on the shelves. They call it 'brick' chili because of its shape, and I don't know of anyplace else where chili is made that way.

"For the next year I continued working at the meat factory and going to classes. I was studying languages, Italian and German, but for some reason, I wasn't taking French. Maybe I was planning to concentrate on the Italian/German repertoire, I simply don't remember. Meanwhile, Vicky was studying and working. She taught dance classes and gave piano lessons, too. All in all, everything was going fine. Really, I felt like one lucky guy, especially when a great opportunity to sing opera came up.

"In the summer of 1964, the University of Tennessee inaugurated a music festival in Gatlinburg, Tennessee, a small town next to The Great Smoky Mountains National Park. The property was a gift to the University from a man named R.L. Maples and his wife, Wilma. They gave it for the express purpose of helping the young people of the state and providing the university with an opportunity to further the arts in that region. The location was a perfect summer site for what, I'm sure, the University hoped would become an Aspen-like venture. The plan was to bring in college students, conduct classes, and put on operas and musical comedies in an outdoor Greek-style amphitheatre. A Wichita faculty member was hired to stage the operas and a bunch of us students decided to give it a try. Vicky and I stuffed our belongings into a car and drove off to Gatlinburg for the summer. Vicky worked in the box office and I sang. We did *Tosca, The Bartered Bride, The Mikado* and *Oklahoma.* I got the lead in *Oklahoma,* I played Kezal in *The Bartered Bride*, and I was Angelotti in *Tosca*. (Morley Meredith was Scarpia, the big bass-baritone role.) That summer was another invigorating 'let's put on a show' experience, like an old movie musical with some opera thrown in. The more singing I did, the more secure and happy I was in my choice of a profession.

"At the end of the summer, we returned to Wichita and I was on a real high. I was so fired up I didn't notice that Vicky had become kind of withdrawn. I mean she was sweet and kind, but not really there. Finally, I asked her straight out if everything was okay. She admitted that she was unhappy, mostly because she felt hampered in her career. She told me she'd gotten all she could from the ballet school and, as far as she was concerned, Wichita had nothing more to offer. I was sympathetic and told her to see if she could find something more satisfying. She began looking around and discovered what she wanted, in Salt Lake City. She told me that the dance department at the University of Utah was fantastic and what's more, if she went to Salt Lake she'd have a chance to perform with the Utah Ballet. I hadn't expected her objective to be so far away. Although I knew other couples did it, the idea of living separately bothered me. But I figured she had as much right to pursue her dream as I did. It would be just plain selfish to hold her back. I said okay and tried not to think about it. Why worry? We'd been happily married for nearly two years. I was content and assumed that she was, too. We were still a couple when she left and she vowed that's what we'd remain. I buried myself in my studies and various projects so as not to feel the loneliness."

After his wife left for Utah, Sam tried out for the Metropolitan Opera's National Council Auditions. Since its first try-outs in Minneapolis/St. Paul in 1954, these auditions have been held annually in fifteen regions of the United States and Canada. The purpose is to discover exceptional young talent and to give that talent a chance to be heard by representatives of the Metropolitan Opera. Within the fifteen regions there are forty-five districts, each of which allows singers to enter at the local level; district winners go on to the Regionals. The victorious Regional participants compete in the National Semi-Finals in New York out of which some ten singers are chosen to appear in the Grand Finals. The roster of artists who have received awards is impressive and includes such luminaries as Renee Fleming, Susan Graham, Thomas Hampson, Ben Heppner, Jessye Norman, Frederica von Stade, Deborah Voigt and Dolora Zajick. Sam won the District competition but that was as far as he got. His first pass at the Met was, indeed, a pass. Sam feels it might have been because his voice was 'late' in maturing. At the same time, however, he did audition successfully for the Santa Fe Opera's summer program in New Mexico.

The Santa Fe Opera is another innovative summer company that tosses big names and young hopefuls together.

When John Crosby founded the company in 1956, his aim was to offer American singers the chance to learn new roles with plenty of rehearsal time. Up to then, aspiring American singers went to Europe to get their training. They signed on with small government-subsidized companies and sang anything they were offered. With a few notable exceptions, Beverly Sills being one, an American artist almost *had* to go to Europe to prepare for his or her career. In addition, opera singers were supposed to have "fancy" names. Consequently many singers studying overseas assumed exotic European ones, a practice in vogue for generations. Today, if you so choose, you can become famous with the name, plain or fancy, with which you were born. She never changed her name yet Marilyn Horne is a good example of what was expected of American singers in the mid-twentieth century. Horne's journeyman years were spent in the coal-mining town of Gelsenkirchen in Germany's Ruhr Valley where she sang everything from Mimi in *Boheme* to Marie in *Wozzeck*. Since the sixties, the proliferation of music training schools and summer festivals in America has allowed subsequent homegrown talent to flourish at home.

Sam spent the summer of 1966 in Santa Fe, and found it as stimulating an experience as his stay in Central City. He had the opportunity to sing and he made good friends. But it was while he was in Santa Fe that his personal life floundered. Not long after he arrived in New Mexico he received a letter from his wife asking for a divorce. She gave no reason, and begged him not to fight it. Sam was heartbroken. With hindsight he felt that, in spite of her assurances that they would remain a couple, Vicky wanted a divorce when she left for Utah and simply could not say it to his face. Although he loved her, and believed that she still loved him, Sam acceded to his wife's request and a divorce was granted. It was an amicable parting. They remained on good terms and saw each other whenever she visited Wichita. Inevitably, they lost personal contact but, through friends, Sam kept up with her activities for many years. Vicky Bolen went on to achieve her goals. She became a teacher, ran a dance company, and among other accomplishments, founded the ballet department at the University of Tennessee at Knoxville.

In many ways theirs had been an ideal union, two attractive, intelligent, and talented young people who got along together and encouraged each other. On paper it was fine, yet almost from the beginning, Sam sensed something amiss. They were on the same wavelength in every aspect, except for the physical. From the manner in which she shied away from intimacy, he sensed what his wife could not put into words or perhaps did not even realize. As it turned out, Sam had intuited correctly. A few years ago he was appearing at the Paris Opera, when a message appeared on his website. The sender of the email introduced herself as Vicky Bolen's former business partner and the executrix of her estate. Vicky, she wrote, recently had died of cancer. They had been together for many years, she explained, and in going through her late partner's effects she had come across a manila envelope containing letters, articles, and pictures, which Vicky had saved from her married days. She asked if Sam wanted her to send him the envelope and if so would he send a mailing address. Sam immediately responded. Shortly thereafter the envelope arrived and its contents remain a last link to his first love.

"So there I was in my third year at Wichita and still in the same apartment that I'd shared with my ex-wife. I missed her terribly, yet I knew it was important for me to get on with my life. I started seeing people and dating. It wasn't easy because a lot of girls didn't want to have anything to do with a 'divorced' man. I got a job as a copy boy with the local newspaper, the Wichita Eagle-Beacon and, once again, I had to start work early in the morning. This time though, it wasn't to deliver chili. I was responsible for pulling out copy from the wire machines and distributing it to the various editors. I actually enjoyed it. I liked being right where the news was coming in. I had steady employment, was doing well in school, and slowly getting over my divorce. I also was looking forward to going back to Santa Fe. In those days if you were accepted one year, you were expected to return the next. But there was a problem; a war was going on in Vietnam. While I was opposed to it, and politically active, I didn't belong to the SDS or anything like that. I did take part in anti-war demonstrations, and I got into plenty of arguments with people who kept throwing up the 'threat of communism' as an excuse for us to be in Vietnam. It really bugged me the way people threw 'patriotism' around to justify any course of action no matter how right or wrong—it still bugs me. I wanted to finish college before I was called up, and in order to get a student deferment, I had to have a certain amount of academic credits. I didn't have enough. I had to take summer courses in order to qualify, which meant I couldn't go back to Santa Fe. The draft board kept deferring me until they discovered that I was about to turn 26—the cut off age. Automatically, my name went to the bottom of the deferment list and just before Christmas, the Colby draft board ordered me to go for a physical. I went home for the holidays, had my physical, was classified 1-A, and told that I'd probably be inducted by February. I went back to Wichita and waited for the inevitable. Amazingly, I never was called up and I just couldn't figure out why. The only possible reason I ever came up with had to do with my hospital records. I know they were attached to my draft papers and I know those records went all the way back to my childhood and included information about my clubfoot. I've always assumed, somehow or other, that long ago condition kept me out of active service. Look, despite my personal feelings about the Vietnam War, I would have served my country if I had been called, but I wasn't."

"In my senior year I made up my mind what I was going to do after graduation. I think I knew from sophomore year where I was headed. Arthur Newman, my voice teacher, was a charter member of the old City Center Opera Company in New York and had appeared with the company for many years. He talked about New York all the time and I loved hearing his stories. Listening to him, I decided that after I got my degree I would 'go east.' My goal was to sing at the New York City Opera just like my teacher. Coincidentally, while I was at Wichita State, I got a preliminary taste of the New York City Opera in action. I saw an announcement in the paper that the company was doing *Tales of Hoffman,* with Beverly Sills, Placido Domingo, and Norman Treigle, in San Antonio, Texas. In a flash, I decided to make the 600-mile trip. I told Mr. Newman and he urged me to go backstage and say hello to Beverly Sills for him. I remember thinking to myself, 'wow, I'm going to meet a real live opera singer.' I drove down to San Antonio with a bunch of friends and we arrived just in time for the performance. It was terrific and afterward we went backstage. I didn't have the nerve to say anything to Treigle, but I introduced myself to Beverly Sills. She was lovely and really unassuming. When I gave her Mr. Newman's greetings, she smiled and said, 'wait a minute.' She got a piece of paper and a pen, wrote a note, and asked me to take it back to my teacher. I did and he showed it to me. It read, 'No note, no letter, no Xmas card, no nothing. Why don't I hear from you? Love, Bev.' The words were warm and unpretentious, just like Sills."

In the early 1980s, after Sam Ramey became an operatic headliner, *The Wichita Eagle* interviewed Arthur Newman. Newman reported that he was not surprised at his former pupil's success. "In any group of 25 or 50 students, you find some not so good and some that are pretty good, and, sometimes, perhaps once in 500 or 1000, you find the one who has something special—like Sam. He just had a superior quality about him. He looked good, had an inner poise, and was very at home on stage. Vocally, he had an unusual facility and talent for going from very low to very high." His teacher was further impressed by Sam's "remarkable intelligence, great musicality, natural aptitude for languages, and great memory." In Newman's opinion, even as a student, Sam Ramey already was a singer/actor with a natural instinct for performing. As for Sam, he was inspired by his teacher and wanted to follow in his footsteps.

"My sights were set on the New York City Opera. I honestly never gave a thought to the Metropolitan. City Opera was tops because that's where Arthur Newman sang. He was a great teacher and I really owe him a lot. He taught me so much and I'm particularly grateful that he emphasized the importance of scales and vocalizing. We used *Vaccai's Practical Vocal Method*,[1] which is kind of the bible of bel canto. Bel canto just means 'beautiful singing' and refers to the Italian technique of the late 17th century to the early 19th century. Bel canto emphasizes flexibility and, while I always had that in my voice, working with Vaccai helped to further develop my skill. Those kinds of exercises and that repertoire keep the voice healthy, light, and flexible, and that's why I kept a certain amount of the bel canto in my repertoire throughout my career. Believe me, it paid off.

"I received my Bachelor of Music in the summer of 1968. My mom came down to the graduation along with Vicky's mother. They knew each other and had remained friends. I had no idea what Mrs. Bolen thought about my breakup with her daughter because the subject never came up. I guess she was okay enough with it to come to my graduation. After graduating I planned to go to New York City, but I was in no rush. I stuck around Wichita for a while mostly because the music department asked me to stay on and take a few more courses. They had an ulterior motive, *Falstaff*. They wanted me to do it and that was okay with me. I

---

[1] Nicola Vaccai (1790-1848), Italian composer and singer whose Metodo practico de canto, written in 1832, teaches the Italian legato style

stayed on, took a couple of courses, and sang Sir John. When that was over, did I immediately take off for New York? Nope. I further postponed my eastward trek by taking on a job, doing what I liked best—singing.

"While I was doing the *Falstaff*, a tenor friend in Wichita told me about a small group called The National Opera Company based in Raleigh, North Carolina. Once known as the 'Grass Roots Opera,' the NOC was a troupe of strolling singers that went on the road performing around the Southeast. The company sounded like something I'd like so I decided to try and join up. I sent them a tape and they wrote and told me that they had to hear me in person. Fine, except I didn't have the money to get there. I called my sister and asked if she would loan me enough for an airline ticket to Raleigh. She sent a check right away. To save money I took a flight from Wichita to Chicago and from Chicago to Raleigh. I had a short layover so I stuck around the airport. I went to the gate to check in when a bunch of big, I mean *big*, bodyguard-size, guys walked into the gate area and began looking the place over. I figured somebody important was coming. I was right; a minute later in walked Muhammad Ali. I was a huge fan of Ali, both for his boxing skills and his stand against the Vietnam War. He'd been banned from boxing for his conscientious objections and to support himself was traveling around giving speeches against the government's policies. Ali was on his way to Raleigh to give one of those speeches. I wanted his autograph. I rummaged in my pockets for a piece of paper. The only thing I could come up with was my checkbook. I ripped out one of the checks and went over to him. 'Mr. Ali, could I have your autograph?' I asked. The champ took the check, signed it, and handed it back. I still have that check somewhere.

"I arrived in Raleigh, sang an audition, was hired, and for the next six months toured the Southeast with The National Opera Company. A.J. Fletcher, a wealthy Southerner who owned the Capitol Broadcasting Company in Raleigh, was the founder of the NOC. Fletcher came from the mountains of Western North Carolina and was one of fourteen children of a Baptist minister. Apparently, he had seen a touring musical company in his youth and it bowled him over. He was so carried away, he'd tried to become a singer, himself. Well, his business career took off, he was a prominent lawyer as well as a television-broadcasting pioneer, but his singing didn't. Still, he was so excited about opera he decided to create his own company. In that way, he'd be helping young singers by having them perform in a professional group. At the same time, opera in English would be brought to audiences that might never have had a chance to hear live performances. Fletcher established an endowment fund to subsidize the opera company and when the fund's assets grew quicker than company's needs, he established a foundation. He died in 1979 and, believe it or not, as recently as 2000, his foundation donated $10,000,000 to start an Opera Institute at the North Carolina School of the Arts. It's thanks to people like Arthur Johnston Fletcher that the arts continue to flourish in our country.

"There were twelve of us in the National Opera Company, ten singers, a music director and a technical director. In size it might have been more 'grassroots' than 'national.' We started out in Raleigh where the NOC owned a big, old house and a smaller house next to it. Some of us stayed in the little house and some in the big one. The big house had a large formal living room where we rehearsed. Photos of all the singers who'd been with the company lined the living room walls. Arlene Saunders's picture was prominently displayed but I didn't recognize any of the others. In our group, there were three sopranos, two mezzos, two tenors, two baritones, and one bass (me). The repertoire was Donizetti's *Don Pasquale*, Rossini's *L'Italiana in Algeri* and Offenbach's *La Perichole*. I did all the *L'Italianas* and split the two *Dons*. *L'Italiana* specifically calls for a basso; the other roles were for bass-baritones. Surprisingly, there weren't that many cuts in the operas; *Pasquale*, in fact, was nearly complete. It's hard to believe but sometimes we'd turn around those operas and do all three in a single day— a morning for one, a matinee for the second, and an evening performance for the third! Anyway, just before we left Raleigh for the road, Mr. Fletcher gave the company a terrific send-off. He threw a big party at his home and invited friends and constituents. One of them was Jesse Helms, the future five-term Republican Senator from North Carolina and a leader of the Christian Right. I believe Helms got his start as a commentator and political analyst on one of A.J. Fletcher's radio stations. (I've tried not to hold that against Mr. Fletcher.) During the party I was standing with a few of my colleagues, one of them, David Couzyn, was a baritone from South Africa. Helms came over, introduced himself, and chatted cordially. He noticed David's accent and asked if he were from England. David said no, he was from South Africa. There was a pause and then Helms replied, 'So you're from South Africa. Well, I have to say you South Africans sure know how to handle your blacks!' I wish I could say I punched him in the nose, but I didn't. We all just looked down at the floor. I'll never forget that crack, though.

"The tour lasted from January to May of 1969 and it was a terrific experience. When the company was started Mr. Fletcher sometimes sang with the group, but by the time I got there he'd stopped. Occasionally, he'd travel with us and sit in the audience while we performed. Most important for me, A.J. Fletcher was a bass and he *loved* basses. The company really bonded, we were like a family. I can't honestly say that the standard was of the highest order but we had a few really good singers and we were well received everywhere we went. Sometimes I wonder if I ever had quite as much fun singing in the great opera houses of the world. Maybe I was more *thrilled* being on the stages of the New York State Theatre, the Metropolitan, Covent Garden, La Fenice, La Scala and the Paris Opera, but for sheer joy, I promise you, being a member of the National Opera Company was right up there.

"When the tour ended I said my goodbyes, made arrangements to see my friends in the near future, and took a bus from Raleigh to Wichita. I planned to go to New York in the fall and figured I could find some summer work to tide me over. I didn't find a job so I packed up everything and went back to Colby. I didn't stay there long, either. I didn't even unpack. My mom was glad to see me, but she agreed that I had to move on. Like always she pushed me forward. My mother was always hopeful that someone in the family would go into music. I was doing it but I think my whole family thought I was crazy. Hey, I must have been crazy to go to New York to become an opera singer. Anyway, to this day I'm so grateful for my mom's support and my dad's, too. It makes a big difference when your parents encourage you to go for it, whatever *it* is.

"I crammed all my stuff into nine big boxes and took the boxes down to the Greyhound Station. I sent them ahead to New York where they'd be held till my arrival. I don't think you'd dare do that today. About a week after I'd shipped my possessions, my mother drove me to the Greyhound station. We got out of the car and stood side by side on the curb as the bus pulled up. I started to step on board when mom reached out and took my arm. I turned to look at her.

'Sam,' she said kind of softly, 'I'm scared.'

'I am, too,' I answered. She hugged me close, and walked away. I don't think either of us looked back.

"I didn't go straight to New York; I went to St. Louis where my brother Leonard and his wife lived. They picked me up and I stayed with them overnight. We had a nice visit and the next morning they drove me back to the station where we said our goodbyes. I saw so little of my brother and that's why I made the stop. I just wanted to connect with him before I took off, and I was glad I did.

SAMUEL RAMEY: American Bass

"I arrived in New York City in June of 1969. I had fifty dollars in my pocket, no job, and no prospects, but within a few years I would make my debut at the New York City Opera, and within a few months I would meet the woman who became my second wife."

Jane Scovell

# Wonderful Town

When Samuel Ramey arrived in the summer of 1969, New York City was lumbering through disastrous times. From the mid-sixties on, financial crises, a decline in manufacturing, a waning job market, a falling real estate market, and soaring crime rates fueled by drug trafficking sent people pell-mell into the suburbs. Yet even as New York fought to avert insolvency, its cultural life braved on. Opera was a vital part of that life. Then, as now, two disparate companies dominated the operatic scene—the Metropolitan Opera and the New York City Opera. The former opened its doors on the southwest corner of Broadway and West Thirty-Ninth Street in 1883 in an era when New York cultural life was determined along class lines. The city's foremost opera house, the venerable Academy of Music on Fourteenth Street, was established in 1854 by New York's socially elite. The Academy of Music, aptly described by Edith Wharton as "small, shabby and sociable," was a closed book. Consequently, when a group of wealthy opera loving gentlemen, including Vanderbilts, Astors, Morgans and Roosevelts, found it impossible to obtain the best box seats, and, in some instances, were denied admission to the Academy's Board of Directors, they built their own concert hall, the Metropolitan Opera House. One might be tempted to say that, despite their eminent names and their present day status, the Met was founded by a bunch of disgruntled social climbers.

The original Met was dubbed "The Yellow Brick Brewery," a playful dig at the building's stolid exterior. Inside, a classic horseshoe-shaped auditorium provided a splendid setting for those rich enough to be seated in the plum area known as the "Diamond Horseshoe." For the less affluent, sight lines throughout the rest of the house offered a profusion of partial views. While the stage was adequate, the backstage was woefully inadequate. The dressing rooms were tiny and too few, and storage space was limited. Indeed, in the mid-twentieth century, pedestrians walking along Seventh Avenue during opera performances had to thread their way through scenery flats that were put out into the street and propped up against the theatre's back wall. This was one of many reasons for the Metropolitan's eventual move to Lincoln Center in 1966.

The New York City Opera Company gave its first performance in 1943, not in a house especially built for it, but rather, in the Mecca Temple on West Fifty-Fifth Street between Sixth and Seventh Avenues. Erected in 1923, the Moorish-style Temple had been home to an offshoot of the Masonic Order, the Ancient Arabic Order of the Nobles of the Mystic Shrine, aka the Shriners. Slated for destruction in the early Forties, the building was saved by Mayor Fiorello LaGuardia and City Council President Newbold Morris, and re-opened in 1943 as the city's first performing arts center. Both the New York City Opera and the New York City Ballet were created there. Some two decades later the opera and ballet companies moved into the New York State Theatre, which stands adjacent to the Metropolitan Opera House and across the plaza from Avery Fisher Hall at Lincoln Center.

From the start the relationship between the Met and the City Opera was based on socio-musical snobbery and their proximity at Lincoln Center did nothing to alleviate the situation. The Met was an upper class, world class, opera house presenting international stars in operas sung in the original languages. Conversely, La Guardia and his contingent envisioned their creation as "the people's opera company," a repertory group of American singers performing works, for the most part, translated into English. While City Opera's policy altered over the years the principles remained the same. "Foreigners" were added to its ranks but they were young performers on the rise, not established stars. In 1968, it was one of those young singers, the Hispanic tenor, Placido Domingo, who broke through the Met's unspoken sound barrier. Heretofore, others had quietly crossed over but either were siphoned into the chorus or allotted secondary roles. Ironically, Domingo made his Met debut long before that of City Opera's acknowledged superstar, Beverly Sills. In spite of Sill's spectacular triumph at the State Theatre in Handel's *Julius Caesar* (1966), General Manager, Rudolf Bing barred her from his Met. His snobbish obduracy kept the Brooklyn-born diva out of the swanky opera house for nearly a decade. Sills did not appear at the Met until 1975. Not until 1984, nearly a decade later, did the Metropolitan again, albeit grudgingly, grant access to a homegrown City Opera star. In the summer of 1969, that future star had just arrived in, and, as he relates, had been totally dazzled by, New York.

"My first impression of New York City was, WOW!!!! It was big beyond my wildest imaginings. I was just glad someone was coming to the bus station to get me because no way could I have gotten around on my own. One of the singers from the National Opera Company met me and was kind enough to let me stay at her apartment for a couple of weeks till I found my own place. After I settled in, the first thing I did was to pick up my worldly goods at the Greyhound Station. I was pleased and relieved to find that all but one of the boxes made it from Colby. The missing carton contained my make-up kit and my typewriter neither of which were essential at the moment. It wasn't like losing the clothes off my back. Next, I went about looking for work. In those days *The New York Times* had a popular advertising campaign for its want ads. Posters of different men and women, with big smiles on their faces and with "I Got My Job through The New York Times" written above or below them, were plastered on buses and billboards. I actually *did* get my job through the *Times*. I answered an ad and was hired as an advertising copywriter by Academic Press, a small house specializing in scientific and medical textbooks; years later Academic Press was absorbed by Harcourt, Brace, and Jovanovich. I wrote book flap copy, and while the salary was small, $105 a week, it was enough for me to live on, frugally. Now that I was employed I began making the rounds looking for singing engagements. At the same time I reconnected with friends from Wichita State. One of them, a tenor named Don Junod, offered to let me stay in his apartment. I thought I'd be more comfortable rooming with a guy so I moved into his place on 73rd Street just west of Columbus Avenue. I wanted a place of my own but until I could afford it I was very grateful for the generosity of my National Opera and college friends.

"All of us singers would get together in the evenings at one or another's apartment and talk about what we were doing or, in most cases, what we were trying to do. We all wanted to sing. We had a strong network. In those days there were a couple of agents in New York who booked singers into church and synagogue choirs either as soloists or choir members. I wonder if these agencies still exist. I was put in touch with an agent and began my quasi-religious singing career. I sang in a lot of churches and a lot of synagogues and for a long, long, time. I started out in Queens, and then I heard about an opening in a church in the Lincoln Center area. I tried out and joined the choir of The Broadway United Church of Christ, which shared facilities with St. Paul the Apostle. The church was on Columbus Avenue across the street from Fordham University. It was a lot easier for me to get there than taking the subway out to Queens.

"I began singing with the United Church's choir in the fall of 1969 and stayed for four years. It was not your run-of-the-mill Sunday choir. The United Church had a good organist/choir director, Wally Klauss, and, musically, we did fantastic things. The church had a better than average budget so a couple of times a year a full orchestra was brought in. We performed a lot of cantatas, oratorios, and requiems, and I also got some solo work. I sang the bass aria from Bach's *Ich Habe Genug* and I had a great time with a Vaughan Williams song cycle. As far as liturgical singing I was totally ecumenical and spent equal time in synagogues, especially the Metropolitan Synagogue, which shared space on East Thirty-Fifth Street with the Universalist Unitarian Community Church of New York. The Universalist Unitarian Community Church and the Metropolitan Synagogue were a good combination; the church was sort of left wing liberal and the synagogue was so reform it was almost Presbyterian. Most synagogues hid their choirs in a loft or behind the altar, not the Metropolitan. The eight members of the choir marched right down the center aisle at the beginning of the service and sat right up on the stage. It really was like show business. Not only were we center stage we only had to sing on Friday nights not Saturday mornings. I had a great time being a 'choirboy' in New York City and only stopped when I became too busy doing opera.

"Vocally speaking everything was moving forward but one thing was for sure, I needed a voice teacher. I had no interest in going back into formal education to get a Masters Degree; I just wanted one-on-one instruction. I checked with my friends and all of them seemed to be studying with a teacher named, Herta Sperber. I went to talk to Ms. Sperber and ended up studying with her. She was a good teacher and yet, from the start, I felt that she had the wrong idea about me. Maybe it was because she was Viennese and partial to German operas. Whatever the reason, she thought I was perfect material for a German dramatic baritone. She wanted me to work on Wotan and stuff like that. I thought I was a bass-baritone or a basso cantante and I wasn't interested in the German repertoire. (As it turned out, during my career I did hardly any singing in German. I did the Nazarene in *Salome* in my early City Opera days, and, though it really doesn't count, I once sang Prince Gremin in a German language version of *Eugene Onegin*.) There was something else, too. I believe that the singer/teacher relationship has to be a personal one, not clinical like going to the doctor or to a class. Some people would disagree saying you don't want to get personally involved with your teacher. For me it's the only way, it has to be like family. In that respect I never really connected with Herta Sperber. It kind of bugged me but I stayed with her for a while. I knew I'd have to make a decision, eventually.

"Another thing got to me. I'd come to New York from a world where I was appreciated and my talent was acknowledged, kind of a big fish in a little pond. Now I was the opposite, a minnow in an ocean. It was tough and there were a couple of occasions when I seriously considered packing it all in. I'm not kidding. I was ready to give up singing. I admit I was very naïve about what was going to happen when I got to New York. Somewhere in the back of my head I thought that all I had to do was call up the people whose names Arthur Newman had given me, and sing for them. They would be impressed and then everything would fall into place. I did sing for a few of them like Thomas Martin who was associated with the City Opera. I'm not sure what his position was but I know that he and his wife, Ruth, translated librettos into English for occasional Met performances. When I sang for him he was polite but not terribly encouraging. He wasn't the only one. In general the few people I contacted seemed to be 'underwhelmed.' No one said to me anything like okay you've got talent but you should do this or that to bring it out. Frankly, nobody gave a damn. In my opinion that's what was wrong with the system then and perhaps even now. Even if it's just a smile or a nod of the head, the smallest recognition can make a big difference. Young artists need encouragement and I've tried to keep that in mind whenever I've been asked to listen to aspiring singers."

Sam continued to work at his day job at Academic Press and to take on various singing jobs whenever they arose. His social life primarily revolved around his fellow singers. Late in the summer of 1969 he went to a party given by Janice Stinson, a friend from Wichita, who had been living in New York for over a year. She worked at RCA and one of the guests at her party was a fellow worker, Carrie Tanate Newton, a striking woman of Eurasian parentage. Carrie's Filipino father and her German mother met and married in San Francisco. Subsequently, they moved to New York City. Carrie was born in Yorktown, a section of the East 70s predominantly populated by German-Americans. Carrie Newton, like Sam Ramey, had been divorced after a brief first marriage. At the party, Janice Stinson, as had been her intention all along, introduced her two friends to each other.

"I remember walking in the door and seeing Sam," Carrie Ramey recalled in a 1986 interview. "At the time his hair was very blond and he was really skinny and I thought, 'hmmm, not bad.' Obviously drawn to each other, Sam and Carrie found a lot to talk about. At the end of the evening he walked her home. As they strolled along Sam told her that he was living with a friend but looking for a place of his own. She, in turn, said that she was going to Europe for the month of August and needed someone to water her plants. Would Sam be interested in 'sitting' her apartment? He said, "Sure." They went out together a few times and after she took off for Europe, he moved in. She returned in three weeks and he stayed put. Carrie Newton and Sam Ramey were married on the morning of January 10, 1970 in the chapel of the United Church of Christ. A small group of friends joined them for a wedding breakfast at Janice Stinson's apartment. In the beginning everything was low-key. Their marriage, however, was the start of a spectacular partnership, a working relationship from which he would emerge as a celebrated artist. The bride soon discovered that her husband marched to his own drummer and the beat had been fixed back in Kansas. "When I first met him Sam was very reserved. He didn't talk much. He could go a whole night without saying a word. People would ask me if there was something wrong with him. He got much better but whenever he was studying a role he would become withdrawn and quiet. We'd walk down the street and his lips were moving but he wasn't saying a word. I knew he was going over his part. Who knows what other people thought." Carrie Ramey was a perfect helpmeet. More outgoing socially she gave Sam the security of a solid home base. Moreover, since she had no career aspirations of her own, all her efforts were centered on him. Sam had his job but spent most of his time studying and singing. Carrie soon realized that when it came to his career, her husband was far too "worried about what others would think." He preferred "not to make waves." She advised him to "put himself first," and if it made waves, so be it. A Midwesterner had come face-to-face with a New Yorker. Carrie Ramey took over the day-to-day management of their lives and looked after the general picture while her husband focused specifically on his singing. Later, when his career took off, she booked all the travel arrangements and living accommodations. She always traveled with him. Sam preferred to stay in rental apartments rather than hotels and left it to her to find them. If not totally symbiotic, their relationship was very close to it; they were almost never apart. "It was always Sam and Carrie, it was never just Sam," commented one long time business acquaintance. One of Sam's erstwhile agents called them "SamCare" and in an updated version of "Cash and Cary," (the sobriquet applied to the union of heiress Barbara Hutton and movie star Cary Grant) publicist, Cynthia Robbins, dubbed them "Cash and Carrie."

In the summer of 1970, Sam and Carrie took a delayed honeymoon in Europe. They went to the opera in Vienna and in Salzburg where Nicolai Ghiaurov was appearing in *Don Giovanni*. The Rameys saw the *Don Giovanni* but not at the Festspielhaus where ticket prices were sky high; they attended a more affordable performance at the Marionette Theatre. After their return, Carrie continued to work at RCA while Sam kept up at Academic Press and pursued his career. One problem persisted—which direction would or should that career take? Sam could sing in all three bass categories *cantante*, *buffo*, and *profondo*, but he had to make a choice. The bass voice, as defined in the Grove Dictionary of Opera, is "the lowest male voice, normally written for within the range F to e' which may be extended at each end." Under the bass umbrella come those three major categories. The basso profondo is the lowest; lowest that is if you do not factor in the Russians. Russian Liturgical music has produced the *basso profondo assoluto*, someone capable of singing as much as an octave lower than norm. The *basso profondo* sound is described as deep, cavernous, and resonant, and in the case of the *assoluto* plunges to the sepulchral. The *basso cantante* is a lighter, more lyrical voice usually with a somewhat higher range. *Basso buffo* means 'comic' bass and is used to describe roles that do not necessarily call for lyrical, elaborate singing but do require comic timing and vocal flexibility. The bass-baritone is the hybrid of the bass and baritone voices, singers who can produce some of the low notes without the complete extension and are able to sing comfortably in the higher range. For basses the *cantante* roles are the most taxing because they are in the highest range. Much of the Wagnerian repertoire lies in that tessitura, the direction in which Herta Sperber was herding Sam. He, however, loved Italian and French operas and was loath to limit himself to the Teutonic. He talked the matter over with his wife. She encouraged him to follow his instincts and seek a new teacher. A chord sounded in his brain.

Before he arrived in New York, Sam had seen an article in *Opera News* about Paul Plishka, a young American bass. Plishka, less than a year older than Sam, already had made his Metropolitan Opera debut and in the article gave a good deal of credit to his voice teacher, Armen Boyajian. Sam also heard that name during his touring days with the National Opera Company. One of the baritones had gone to New York City to sing for Boyajian and came back singing the teacher's praises. At the time Sam made a mental note of the name, Armen Boyajian. Nonetheless, when he got to New York Sam claims he was "kind of roped in" to becoming Herta Sperber's student which, given Sam's nature, was understandable. His friends were studying with her, and she was highly recommended, so why scramble to find someone when he could take what was at hand and save time and bother? The problem with Herta Sperber arose not with her pedagogy, she was an excellent teacher, but with her desire to typecast him. Fortified by Carrie's directive to follow his instincts, he made the decision to leave. However, he did not have the heart to inform Sperber in person nor could he bring himself to tell her the real reason. Consequently, he wrote a letter informing her that he did not make enough money to continue lessons. Graciously, Sperber offered to lower her fee. Confronted with her kindness, Sam got cold feet and started to back down. Once more his wife stepped in. She felt that Sam was resisting because he was afraid that his Wichita State friends, who were studying with Sperber, would be mad at him if he left her. It took a bit of doing but Sam became convinced that there was no other way. He stopped seeing Sperber and almost immediately another opportunity arose. Sam discovered that one of the tenors in the Metropolitan Synagogue choir was studying with Armen Boyajian. Sam boldly asked his choir mate to inquire if Boyajian would listen to him sing. The tenor asked and the teacher said yes. Thus, on Election Day of 1970, Samuel Ramey met with Armen Boyajian for the first time. For the second time that year, Sam embarked on a long and fruitful association.

The word "dapper" might have been coined to describe Armen Boyajian, the ebullient vocal teacher with whom Sam worked for more than three decades. And behind Boyajian's debonair façade resides a first class musician and teacher. Despite the exotic sound of his name, Boyajian was born in Paterson, New Jersey where his parents had settled after fleeing from their native Armenia. Early on, Armen evinced musical talent and was good enough to be admitted to the Juilliard School of Music, not, however, as a vocalist; Boyajian was a pianist. He studied at Juilliard for a year and then switched to Montclair Teachers College in New Jersey. Although he had achieved a measure of success on the piano, Boyajian was keenly aware of the vicissitudes of the performing life. He decided to seek a teaching degree; something to fall back on should his playing career stall. While his academic environs changed, his solo piano career continued to flourish. Among other engagements Boyajian frequently appeared with the New Jersey Symphony where his specialty was Gershwin's *Rhapsody in Blue*. As he puts it, "every summer festival it was Boyajian and the *Rhapsody in Blue*." In the winter of 1951, also in his words, "Bingo! It happened!" What happened was Boyajian's first visit to the Metropolitan Opera. He paid the $2 standee fee for a performance of *Aida* with a cast featuring Zinka Milanov, Fedora Barbieri, Mario del Monaco, George London, Cesare Siepi, Jerome Hines, Lucine Amara and, in the small role of the Messenger, James McCracken. In baseball terms, this was the operatic equivalent of Murderers' Row, the New York Yankees' 1927 batting lineup. Boyajian left the performance on such a high that, a few days later, he returned to the Met. Once again he stood outside for four hours, to stand inside for four hours, to see *Aida*. Just as before, he was completely wiped out. For a grand total of $4 Armen Boyajian had stumbled upon what would become his life's work.

"I got so hooked on opera I think that I must have gone nearly every night that first year. And oh, what wonderful things I saw: Leonard Warren in *Rigoletto*, Rise Stevens in *Carmen*, Bjorling in *Boheme*, artists like that, great singers in great operas, one right after another. I stood in the same spot on the side of the old Met, which had this horseshoe shape. I was close enough to actually see what the singers were doing diaphragmatically and structurally. Then I'd go home and practice what I saw. I didn't have a great voice but imitating what those artists were doing helped me to understand what went into singing. I was besotted with singing and soon opera began to conflict with my 'pianistic' thing. I was scheduled to play the Rachmaninov *Second Piano Concerto* with the New Jersey Symphony. I knew when I finished that engagement my days as a concert pianist would be over. I was a convert to singing.

"I began working at several prominent vocal studios in New York City. One teacher could not play the piano herself so she hired me to accompany her students. She paid me by the hour and I sat there all day, playing when necessary, and watching and listening as she taught. I was fascinated. I'd go home and try out what I'd see her do with her students. From the get-go I was only interested in teaching. I didn't want to be a singer myself because I knew I didn't have a great voice. But I learned how to build a voice from nothing and actually made it work for me. It emboldened me. When I played operatic scores during lessons I had to sing out musical cues. I gained confidence and soon I was singing quite forcefully. The teacher would look over at me and say, 'Hmmm, very good, very good.' She was amazed that I could play and sing so well. Little-by-little I got the courage to start coping with the singers themselves. And it all happened in the standing room line at the Met.

"All sorts of singers stood in the line. They'd huddle together talking with each other and someone invariably would say, 'Gee, I need a pianist for an audition.' Or, 'I need a pianist to work with on a score. Does anyone know a pianist?' Well, as soon as they found out that I was a pianist, a few of them asked me to work with them. I'd go over to the singer's apartment and accompany him or her for an hour or so, and make suggestions about what they were doing. The suggestions proved to be very helpful. Eventually they began to regard me as a teacher and things kind of steamrolled from there."

While studying and soloing, Boyajian earned extra money by accompanying up-and-coming artists; one of the first was Beverly Sills. At that point in her career, Sills was paid around $250 a recital, out of which she paid her accompanist $75 or so. "Not big money," recalls her erstwhile accompanist, "but every little bit helped." Boyajian accompanied a number of artists and though none of them became as famous as Sills, each had something to offer. Simply by accompanying them, he learned a lot about singing. So much so that, in 1956, delighted with the vocal business, Armen Boyajian started his own "little" company, the Paterson Lyric Opera Theatre. In the beginning it was more a "workshop" than anything else. Productions were given in public schools and local colleges, and the singers did their own costumes and scenery. As a rule, the operas were performed with piano accompaniment. However, if enough money became available, Boyajian would hire and conduct a small orchestra. Aside from the occasional orchestra members, nobody, including the impresario-cum-conductor, got paid. "Money never entered into it," laughs the Lyric Opera's founder. "It was all done for love and for experience." The experience proved fruitful, indeed, for a few company members who went on to sing at the New York City Opera and the Metropolitan. Along with producing operas, Armen Boyajian started teaching, and his reputation began to build as his singers' careers took off. He never formally studied to be a voice teacher, never took a course in vocal pedagogy, and never received a certificate let alone a degree. Of his academic deficiencies, Boyajian laughingly comments, "It should make me a charlatan but I guess I'm not, otherwise Juilliard would not have offered me a teaching position. That was in the eighties, and while I was honored, I declined. I just didn't want to have the added worry of fitting into curriculums and things like that. I work better in my private situation."

By the early 1970s, singers were making the pilgrimage to Paterson to work with Boyajian. Encouraged, he crossed the river, found a large apartment on West End Avenue, and opened a studio in New York City. Because he could not afford the rent on his own, he sublet two rooms to two different gentlemen. For thirty years Armen Boyajian maintained professional offices in New Jersey and New York commuting back and forth across the Hudson. In 2000, his New York landlord decided to go co-op, and offered Boyajian an "astronomical" amount of money. "My thinking was even if no one came out to New Jersey to study with me I'd have enough to live on for the rest of my life. It was an offer I could not refuse and it turned out just fine. The commute didn't faze the majority of my students and they continued to study with me. I really was flattered."

For half a century, Armen Boyajian has reveled in his career choice, with one minor squawk. In the film world George Cukor was labeled a woman's director because of his skill at working with female stars such as Greta Garbo and Katharine Hepburn. In the opera world, because of Samuel Ramey and Paul Plishka, Armen Boyajian became identified as a bass specialist. "Listen," Boyajian laughingly protests, "I'm a voice teacher not a bass voice teacher. I do enjoy the bass voice but I enjoy all voices and all challenges. And I've taught plenty of sopranos and mezzos and tenors, too. Believe me I'm not complaining. I've had a ball. It will never cease to amaze me how beautifully things worked out."

That first encounter between Samuel Ramey and Armen Boyajian was not an earth-shattering experience by any means. In later years, Boyajian confessed that he was not bowled over by what he heard on November 3, 1970. "Sam had a nice quality to his voice. It was healthy, and he didn't push, but it was 'dull' and it lacked zip, vitality, and presence. However, every now and then he'd hit a vowel with a certain resonance that the rest of the vowels didn't have. I'd think to myself, that voice could do more; there are possibilities here. I heard sounds that were good but I've heard lots of singers who had something special and nothing ever came of it. God doesn't always give great singing qualities to intelligent people. Some of the greatest voices I ever heard were in the heads of non-artistic, non-musical, non-intellectual people who never did anything. Sam had the gift, and he also had musicality and intelligence. The seeds of what Sam would become were there, for sure, but his voice needed to be fine-tuned and centered. Eventually he would achieve artistry but when he came to me, it all boiled down to 'technique.'"

Simply put, a solid vocal technique is based on an individual's ability to sing all the vowels softly and loudly, slowly and quickly, so that the tone coming out has the right degree of vibrato; furthermore, until every single note has the correct degree of vibrato throughout the range, on every single vowel, it's not being done right. Sam's initial discrepancies in technique, things which could be learned, were more than made up for by other qualities immediately apparent to Boyajian, those *seeds*. But it would take a while for them to sprout. Later, after Sam's career skyrocketed, Boyajian shrugged his shoulders and said, with sincere amazement, "Every bass needs a gimmick and Sam's gimmick is his strong physical presence and his security, brilliance, and flexibility in high tones. But, oh God, if you'd ever told me at the beginning that Sam would get to where he got, I wouldn't have believed it." Sam's recollections go along the same lines. "When I sang for Armen that first time he listened and then said something like, 'Well, it's a good voice; I can see real potential but there <u>are</u> things that we have to work on, so we'll start to work.'" And work they did.

Once a week, Sam ended his day at Academic Press and immediately went to Boyajian's West End Avenue studio. Other than his choir singing, Sam had no musical engagements, which gave Boyajian the freedom to work with him unimpeded. Bit by bit, vowel-by-vowel, Boyajian lifted Sam's voice and got it ringing. The "mouthy thing," Boyajian's term for mashing the vowels, was replaced with resonance. It was not an overnight process; it took a solid year of doing nothing but vocal exercises. The months rolled by, and Sam desperately ached to sing something, anything, other than scales, but Boyajian was resolute. One afternoon, Sam came to the studio, took his place by the piano, and was ready to begin his scales when Boyajian handed him a sheet of music. "Okay," said the teacher, "your voice is where I want it. You've got it out of that 'uhh' [*back of the throat*] position. Let's work on an aria for next week. Why don't we try to sing a bit of it, now?" The aria was *il lacerate spirito*. Affectionately known as the bass national anthem, *il lacerate spirito*, Fiesco's aria from Verdi's *Simone Boccanegra*, is mother's milk to the lowest male voice. That afternoon as they worked on the "bit," Sam barely could contain his excitement. After the lesson, he raced home, ran into the apartment, and shouted out to his wife, "I got to sing part of an aria, today!" whereupon they opened a bottle of wine and drank a toast to Boyajian, Verdi, and themselves. For Sam, the moment that he was given that scrap of an aria to sing was "like being let out of prison." (The role of Fiesco, however, did not become part of Sam's regular repertoire. He sang it only once, in a San Francisco Opera production.)

At their next session, Boyajian was delighted to hear Sam's voice immediately move "out of the 'uhh' and into the right position." The painstaking practice had paid off. Reassured that Sam's technique was now spot on, the teacher felt they could move forward. "Next week, we'll work on two arias," he told his delighted student. And so the lessons continued, with Sam gleefully tackling aria upon aria. At the same time he began auditioning for various musical establishments and events; one of them was for the Rockefeller Foundation. Sam asked the Foundation to send him the critiques, which he calls "a big mistake." The best notice he received read, 'may have talent.' In light of Sam's future accomplishments the Rockefeller assessment bore similarities to the famed evaluation of Fred Astaire's screen test: 'Can't act. Can't sing. Balding. Can dance a little.' On a more positive note, the Little Orchestra Society hired Sam to sing in Benjamin Britten's *The Prodigal Son*. In order to appear with the Society he had to join AGMA, the American Guild of Musical Artists. Sam now was working if not steadily at least with enough engagements to keep him occupied.

Meanwhile, Armen Boyajian's Paterson Lyric Opera Theatre was preparing for a major event, a production of Gounod's *Faust* in which Paul Plishka was scheduled to sing his first Mephistopheles. Everything was in readiness, the high school auditorium was booked, the scenery was being built, the costumes were being fitted, and Boyajian was preparing the chorus for a performance on April 17, 1971. Shortly before rehearsals began, Plishka called Boyajian to tell him that he just had been offered an engagement, a *paying* engagement. Plishka did not say, "I can't sing with you," he simply presented the situation. "Of course, you've got to take it," was Boyajian's immediate response. "Don't worry about the *Faust*, just take the paying job." By doing the right thing for Plishka, Boyajian had created a dilemma for himself. Mephistopheles is a demanding role and requires great singing combined with effective acting. "I had this *Faust* ready to go and no bass. I mulled it over, trying to figure out what to do. I couldn't cancel the performance but who was I going to get to take over for Paul? I couldn't go out and hire anyone because we had no money, and believe me, there were no potential Mephistopheles lurking around the company. I was making a mental list of possibilities and all of a sudden I thought of Sam. He was coming for a lesson and I remember thinking, do I dare? Should I take a chance? It was not the logical choice for a first full role for someone studying with me. Colline in *Boheme*, Zuniga in *Carmen* would be the natural path, not a behemoth like Mephistopheles. But I knew that prior to coming to me Sam had sung a lot with this North Carolina group. Of course, his voice was in that 'uhh' position then but he'd worked his way out of it with me. And French was good for him. And he did have this wonderful sound. But could he act? Well, I could show him a few things about acting, but was he really capable of handling it? Frankly, based on what I saw during our lessons I didn't expect much. I kept going over things, detail by detail, until finally I thought, what the heck, whatever else, it'll be interesting."

Sam arrived at the studio and before they began the lesson, Boyajian spoke.

"I've got something to ask you, Sam."

"Yuh?"

"I've got a crisis on my hands and I was wondering, if I wanted you to sing *Faust* with my Paterson group, do you think you could do it?"

After a long pause, Sam answered, "Yeh. I don't have anything else to do. I guess I could do it. Yep, I could do Wagner. Sure."

There are two full bass parts in *Faust*, Mephistopheles, the Devil, and Wagner, a friend of the heroine's brother.

Mephistopheles is a leading role and appears throughout the opera; Wagner is finished after the first act. Sam, being Sam, naturally assumed that he was being offered the comprimario role.

"No, Sam, I don't mean Wagner, I'm talking about Mephistopheles, I want you to sing him."

According to Boyajian, Sam's eyes widened, and his jaw fell open as he stammered, "Me...Me...Mephistopheles? You want me...me...me to do Mephistopheles? With your company?"

"I think you should try it."

Again, a long pause ensued before Sam replied, "Well, if you think I can do it, I'll give it a try."

They began preparing straight away.

Boyajian swears that singing the French language helped develop the brilliance that became a trademark of Sam's voice.

"I'd worked with Sam in the Italian, it was good and getting better, but it made the voice go a little more dullish. The French was something else. There's a certain twanginess and nasality in the French which he got right away. The role actually helped his voice. Even so, I was nervous about the end product. When I told the *Faust* cast that Paul couldn't do it, the chorus members took it particularly hard. Paul was big star to them and having a 'name' singer in a small company added a special quality to any production. They got excited when someone important or scintillating appeared with us. Now, everyone was dejected. All I heard were complaints like, 'this is going to be a disaster without Plishka' or 'maybe we should postpone it.' The mood was glum. I was nervous myself. Sam was very laid back and very low key, hardly what you'd call scintillating. I could just imagine the reaction when he walked in. I could hear them saying, 'this shlump is going to play the Devil?' At the next rehearsal, I told the scenic designer and the stage director that a new Mephistopheles would be joining us. I remember saying, 'we need someone who'll sing for nothing, so be nice to him.' Those were my very words, BE NICE ...to the Devil?

"We were rehearsing in the high school auditorium and when Sam arrived no one paid much attention. You might say he blended into the surroundings. We started working on the first act and got to the place where Mephistopheles has his big aria, *le veau d'or*. A lot of people don't like *Faust* but even those who hate the opera realize that when that aria's done right, it's the very devil itself. It takes a certain voice to do the *veau d'or*; you have to have a combination of animal excitement and brilliance to bring it off. It all has to be done through the instrument even the snarling and barking that comes with it. I was quaking in my boots, believe me. Anyway, Sam ambles over and stands in front of the chorus, most of whom are rolling their eyes to the heavens. Honestly, at that point even I didn't know what to expect. What we got was a miracle! The minute Sam opened his mouth, I knew the voice was right in! And he acted the part as well. The pure physicality was amazing. He was alive, and using his hands and his body to put it over. No one had to tell him what to do; it was like he'd been doing it all his life. He tore into that aria and when he finished, the chorus burst into applause. People came running up to me crying, 'oh, he's great,' 'he's fabulous' 'where did you find him?' Who knew there was a natural devil in this guy waiting to break loose? Up to then I had no idea what was lurking behind this blank exterior, this low-key fellow. I saw for the first time Sam's split personality and, believe me, the difference between the off stage and on stage Sam is positively schizophrenic, absolutely two different people. In the beginning you had to pry the words out of him in conversation but when he was on stage he was as outgoing and confident as anyone you'd ever see.

"Over the years he's found his tongue a little more but it used to be a chore to get him to talk. I'll never forget his first radio interview with Bob Sherman, a popular host on a New York classical music station. I went along to accompany Sam and sat with him during the interview. Sherman would throw a question at him; Sam would give the answer, and then, silence. Sam answered the questions intelligently but that was it, which doesn't add up to a sparkling interview that was being broadcast into thousands of homes. So, after a few more short questions and long silences, I took it upon myself to 'amplify.' I wound up talking for the entire hour. I never would have done it if it hadn't been necessary. Look, he was always a great listener but he wasn't a talker. He got a lot better but conversationally speaking Sam still cuts to the chase. I have to tell you the first time I heard Sam tell a joke, I nearly passed out."

From the moment Sam sang at the *Faust* rehearsal, the production was all about Samuel Ramey. Well, not quite, there was a hitch. Thanks to his engagement with the Little Orchestra Society, Sam was a member of AGMA. It was illegal for union members to work with non-union companies and The Paterson Light Opera Theatre was non-union. The situation had arisen often enough for Boyajian to find away around it; any AGMA artist appearing with his company received a false name. It became a regular procedure and occasionally resulted in amusing consequences. Perhaps the best known occurred when Marisa Galvany, a soprano with the New York City Opera, sang with the Paterson Opera as 'Clara Zamboni.' Speight Jenkins reviewed the performance for the *Daily News* and was so impressed with Galvany's singing that he wanted to give her credit. In his review Jenkins wrote, "the soprano Clara Zamboni, who bears a striking resemblance to Marisa Galvany...." Boyajian loved it. "What a hoot," he exclaimed. "Honestly, we made up more darned names for people. Really, I can't count the number of pseudonyms we created for Paul Plishka alone." Now, it was Sam Ramey's turn.

On April 17, 1971 opera attendees at the Paterson Lyric

SAMUEL RAMEY: American Bass

Opera Theatre's production of Gounod's *Faust* heard a rising young bass sing his first Mephistopheles. The name listed in the program was *Samson Rameaux*.

Jane Scovell

# Samson's Song

Samson Rameaux's debut as Mephistopheles was a triumph. *Faust*, in fact, was so well received, additional performances had to be added. On the strength of the Gounod work's success, The Paterson Lyric Opera Theater was graduated from the no-frills high school auditorium to grander facilities at William Paterson College. Mephistopheles became the first of a number of noteworthy roles that Sam created in the four years that he appeared with Armen Boyajian's company. He did his first Don Giovanni, his first (all four) villains in *Hoffman*, his first Henry VIII in *Anna Bolena*, his first Colline in *La Boheme,* and his first Basilio in *Il Barbieri di Siviglia*. All of the roles were selected by and performed under the watchful eye of his teacher. Later, the New York City Opera would put Sam into the identical roles in nearly the same order. Whatever motivated Armen Boyajian, City Opera followed the same trajectory. "Having Sam sing in my company was an ideal situation, a terrific way for me to watch him in action. After each rehearsal I could go to him and say, you forgot to do that or, maybe you should try this, or maybe don't do that, and in this way he homed in." For the next few years Sam kept busy homing in on his singing and keeping himself afloat financially. He had his nine-to-five job at Academic Press, his work with the Paterson Lyric Opera, plus the various church choirs—but only two out of three were paid positions. By the winter of 1972, Boyajian felt Sam was ready for general auditions, including those held by the Metropolitan Opera. He told his pupil to "go for it." Sam, his ability proven, was ready for the big time, which meant he had to have an agent.

"I knew if I were going to audition I needed representation, especially for the Met. It's like the old Hollywood conundrum, an actor can't get a job if he doesn't have an agent and he can't get an agent if he doesn't have a job. I didn't have an agent so I started writing to agencies and auditioned for a few of them. Actually I had an agent in mind, someone I really wanted. I knew about him through Brent Ellis, a singer friend of mine. Brent was a baritone and we'd been apprentices together in Santa Fe. He already was in New York when I arrived and all he talked about was a guy named Matthew Epstein. Brent was one of Matthew's first artists. I wrote to Matthew Epstein at the Shaw Concerts Agency. I wrote *twice*, but I never got an answer. At the same time, I wrote to City Opera asking to audition for them. In those days, they'd hear anybody; you just had to write a letter. They telephoned and told me to come down to Lincoln Center. I went to a cattle call in the basement of the State Theatre. If you got past the basement tryouts, the next step was a stage audition. Sure enough, a few months later I got a second call asking me to come and sing on the stage. I think I did something from *Figaro,* probably *se vuol ballare.* Brent Ellis was at the audition along with his agent and he introduced me to him. I told Matthew that I would like to have him represent me. I never heard back from City Opera and I never heard anything from Matthew Epstein. I did hear from a few agents, including Placido Domingo's representative at the time, Gerard Semon. Semon said he'd be interested in adding me to his roster. There was a catch, though. I had to pay him a monthly retainer of $200 and there were no guarantees. No way could I afford that. Without any representation, I entered the New York Region Met Auditions and was one of the finalists. I got $2000 for reaching the finals but I didn't win; Christine Weidinger got first prize, which in those days included a Met contract. Even though I lost out on the top prize, I was pretty pleased. I was $2000 richer and I'd sung on the stage of the Metropolitan Opera. In 1986 I appeared with Christine Weidinger in Hamburg. While talking about our past experiences she remarked, 'It's a long way from the Met auditions, isn't it, Sam? I won, and came over here, and you went on and had a great career.'

"Around that same time I auditioned for a small summer opera company just north of Baltimore and was hired by the Harford Opera to sing Colline in *Boheme*. The performances were given in a school auditorium with two pianos providing accompaniment. We singers were put up in a huge old house not far from the school but in the middle of nowhere. None of us knew each other and it was kind of like the *Big Brother* television show. It wasn't fancy or anything but I was glad to be singing. I liked it enough to return the next summer to do *Trovatore*."

Eager to hone his craft, Sam decided to supplement his teaching lessons with Boyajian. He began studying with a coach who maintained a studio in the Ansonia apartment hotel. The Ansonia, a Beaux-arts landmark on New York's Upper West Side, has a long entertainment history, musical and otherwise. Diverse inhabitants have included Enrico Caruso, Igor Stravinsky, Theodore Dreiser, Florenz Ziegfeld, Jack Dempsey and Babe Ruth. As for Sam studying with someone else, it is not unusual for a singer to employ both a teacher and a coach. A teacher has a solid knowledge of the body's physical structure and clearly understands what must be done physically to build the voice and to produce the desired sound. A coach helps the singer learn the music and concentrates on repertoire, musicality and vocal effects. A voice teacher does not necessarily play the piano and may not be able to accompany a student but he or she knows all the exercises the singer needs to practice. A coach is a pianist. The line between teacher and coach is a fine one, yet it exists. Armen Boyajian started out as a coach, and then crossed the line. "I knew a lot about the repertoire and could play most of it and I knew the literature. I also had an idea of the voice and where it should start to get to certain notes. Truly, unless you know the mechanism, something about the body, and something about the diaphragm and the passageway that gets the voice up and out, you should not be teaching. Coaches can talk interpretation, and they can talk diction, and by the way coaches can be very good with Italian or French, really a lot better than me, but they should not transgress into the teacher's territory. Bottom line, coaching can involve everything other than the actual production of the voice." Sam's coach did not cross that line. She helped him, technically, and was responsible for getting him one of his earliest professional jobs, an engagement with Sarah Caldwell's Opera Company of Boston.

Tales of her peccadilloes, most of which are verifiable, can obscure the fact that Sarah Caldwell was a major innovator on the American operatic scene. Born in Maryville, Missouri in 1924, Caldwell was raised in Fayetteville, Arkansas. A child prodigy, she gave recitals on the violin by the age of ten. She was graduated from high school at the age of fourteen and from Hendrix College in 1944. She attended the University of Arkansas and the New England Conservatory of Music for postgraduate studies. In 1946, she received a scholarship as a violist at Tanglewood's Berkshire Center where, in 1947, she branched off into opera by staging Vaughan William's *Riders to the Sea*. For nearly ten years she was chief assistant to Boris Goldovsky, head of the Berkshire Center's opera department. Caldwell moved to Boston in 1952 to head Boston University's opera workshop and in 1957 established her own Opera Company of Boston. In 1976 she became the first woman to conduct the Metropolitan Opera and subsequently appeared on the podium for the New York Philharmonic, the Pittsburgh Symphony and the Boston Symphony Orchestra. Caldwell was the General Director and resident conductor of her Boston

Jane Scovell

group until it folded in 1991. She died of heart failure in 2006.

Under Caldwell's aegis, the Opera Company of Boston staged an extraordinary number of American premieres: Schoenberg's *Moses and Aron*, Prokofiev's *War and Peace*, Berlioz' *Les Troyens* and *Benvenuto Cellini*, Luigi Nono's *Intolleranzo*, Alban Berg's *Lulu*, and Rogers Sessions's *Montezuma*. Despite its remarkable artistic achievements, the company failed to achieve the tiniest measure of financial security. Caldwell paid no attention to alarums voiced by her Board of Trustees regarding the company's fiscal state and, with disturbing frequency her productions had to be rescued from creditors by an infusion of last minute funds. In one widely publicized incident, thousands of dollars were crammed into brown paper bags and arrived at the theatre for distribution just before the curtain almost did not go up. On another occasion, an advertised production of Verdi's grandest of grand operas, *Aida*, was replaced by *La Finta Giardiniera (The Pretend Gardener)*, a delightful, small-scale, Mozart work. While substitutions are not uncommon, ticket holders, eagerly awaiting an expansive trip down the Nile did not discover until they arrived at the theatre that they were being led down the garden path. Nor were artists immune to the Opera Company of Boston's quirky pecuniary dealings. Joan Sutherland, paid to sing three performances of *La Traviata*, was infuriated when she walked on stage for the dress rehearsal and found herself standing before a packed house of paying customers eagerly awaiting a bona fide performance. To her credit, after being apprised of the situation, Sutherland sang out rather than marking.[2] Not all singers are that gracious. Sam remembers a late 1970s production of *La Boheme* in which he appeared with Luciano Pavarotti. "When we got to the final dress we saw

---

[2] In opera rehearsals, singers may choose to *mark*, that is, to sing half-voice (sotto voce), in order to save themselves for the actual performance.

a full house seated in the auditorium and we were told that tickets had been sold. Luciano refused to go on until the audience left. They had to clear the house and refund all the money. Look, he probably had his reasons, but I felt bad for all those people out there."

Sarah Caldwell's treatment of creditors, subscribers, audiences, board members and stars was cavalier. And, she could be downright brutal when it came to minor cast members, a fact Sam Ramey discovered soon after he arrived in Boston.

"Sarah Caldwell used my coach as a source to fill in the small parts in her Boston productions. One day the coach called me at Academic Press to tell me that she'd just recommended me to Caldwell for the role of Dr. Grenville in *Traviata*. I jumped at the opportunity. Of course it meant I had to go up to Boston for a while which also meant I'd have to take off from work. Luckily, my boss, John Vance, the head copywriter, was a big opera fan. He'd always given me a break when I had to go to auditions and he'd even come out to New Jersey to see me perform. This time he gave me a humungous break, a leave of absence. I went up to Boston in April of 1972 where I had the mixed blessing of working with the notorious Sarah Caldwell.

"I arrived in the city and checked into a hotel. The performances were weeks away but all of us in the small parts began rehearsing immediately. We spent a minimum of twelve hours a day in the theatre. Sarah would move us around, telling us where to go and what to do, and we'd go over it many times. Then she'd stop. Naturally we assumed that the action had been set. It never was. She'd come back, have us go through what we'd learned, and then she'd say, "No" and move us around again. I couldn't get over the way Caldwell improvised. It was like she was playing with paper dolls, not human beings who needed, rest, food, and occasional trips to the bathroom. Okay, maybe I'm exaggerating, but it sure seemed like that. Another thing I remember, she opened up all the cuts, big time. She even put back the cabaletta after *di provenze il mar,* Germont's great second act aria, which had been scuttled by most opera houses, including the Metropolitan. I didn't even know that cabaletta existed till I heard it sung in Boston. Today it's the opposite, everything's been opened up, which is fine in most cases but it does tend to extend the length of the performance. Basically, I don't think I ever met a bit of judicious cutting I didn't like, except perhaps when it comes to what I have to sing. Just kidding. I gave points to Sarah Caldwell for trying to adhere to the composer's original work, but she sure wore us out with the *Traviata* preparations. By the time the leads, Beverly Sills, Stuart Burrows, and Peter Glossop arrived, three days before the opening, I felt as though I'd given a year's worth of performances.

"At the *Traviata* dress, we got to Violetta's death scene in the last act when I, as the good doctor, come onto the scene. With all the staging and restaging we'd gone through, I was given nothing in the way of specifics other than I was to take Violetta's pulse and, in an aside, to the others say, 'She's got about an hour left.' When my cue came, I walked on the stage and over to the bed where Sills, eyes closed, was languishing. I knelt down, took her wrist in my hand, then looked over to the others, and sang my line. After that, I didn't know what to do. I just stayed there with my head bowed. Beverly started singing and then opened her eyes. They really widened when she saw me. She shot me a look that said, 'Why the hell are you still here?' I got up sheepishly, slouched my way across the stage, and out the door. The funny thing is that my exit never was staged so I did the same thing at all the performances, but quicker. There were two presentations of *Traviata* for which I was paid a total of $500. My hotel room cost a lot more than that and I had to pay for it myself. I really went in the hole for that engagement. To be honest, I don't think I could have afforded another appearance with the Opera Company of Boston.

But a few years later I did appear in another Caldwell production. The New York City Opera borrowed her *Barber of Seville,* maybe I should say 'imported,' it sounds better. The production was well received. When Caldwell was good she was very, very, good, indeed.

"In January of 1973, out of the blue, I got a call one morning while I was at work. It was City Opera asking me to come down that afternoon to do a stage audition. I had a number of arias prepared 'just in case,' as we singers say, and among them was the *Diamond Aria* from *Hoffman.* I'd made up my mind that the next time I was called, that was what I would sing. I wanted to do it that afternoon but I hadn't sung it for a while. I really needed to go home and work on it. I went to Mr. Vance and told him the story. He let me off just like that. What a great guy. I dashed home, got out the aria, and restudied like crazy. That afternoon I arrived at the State Theatre, walked out on the stage, and sang for John White. He was second in command to Julius Rudel who was then head of the City Opera. Mr. White spoke to me when I finished singing.

"Yes, that was very good. But you'll have to come back tomorrow to sing for Maestro Rudel."

"Sure, fine," I said unhesitatingly. I realized that I'd have to rely on the kindness of John Vance once again. No problem there. He was his usual generous self and gave me another day off. I returned the next afternoon and sang the *Diamond Aria,* the *Serenade* from *Faust,* and the *se voul ballare* from *Figaro.* I was a bit nervous but I didn't take anything to relieve my jitters. I never used beta-blockers or stuff like that because I believe a little 'nerves' is good, it kind of gets you up in a funny way. When I finished singing, I was complimented on my performance and told that the company definitely wanted to add me to their roster. I raced back to Academic Press. "Mr. Vance," I announced to my boss, "I'm going to make my New York City Opera debut and I want you to be there!"

"Okay, I had reached the goal I set for myself back at Wichita State, but one detail remained, I really had to have someone to represent me. When I auditioned for City Opera it was obvious that I didn't have an agent, if I'd had one he'd have been with me. Now I had to sign a contract and I was not about to do it on my own. I asked Bob Lombardo, who did stuff for opera singer friends of mine, to come with me to the meeting. My first contract was for the spring season of 1973. City Opera has a fall and spring season and in those days at the end of the fall season the company went to Los Angeles to perform at the Dorothy Chandler Pavilion for a month. Following the spring season, they went to the Kennedy Center in Washington for two weeks. Today, both cities have their own resident opera companies so, except for an occasional foray, City Opera pretty much sticks to New York. And the same goes for the Met. My contract called for two performances of Zuniga in *Carmen* and one performance of Don Alfonso in *Cosi fan Tutti* with an option for the next two and a half seasons. I had to assume that City Opera would pick up my option. Still, I had no real assurance of financial security and my singing career had reached the point where I could no longer keep a day job. I would earn some money singing, and with Carrie at RCA, we weren't going to starve. Once I signed the City Opera contract I gave my notice to Academic Press. Part of me was sad about leaving; I really liked working there. Then again I really liked singing in those church choirs. You just come to the place where you give up some things you sort of like to do in order to do what you're meant to do. My pals at Academic Press threw a big going away party. I said my goodbyes and thanked everyone for their support, especially my boss. I'll always be grateful to John Vance for allowing me to take all that time off."

SAMUEL RAMEY: American Bass

# Sam's Song

Sarah Caldwell's Opera Company of Boston production of *La Traviata*, notwithstanding, Samuel Ramey regards his appearance in *Carmen* with the New York City Opera on March 11, 1973, as his professional operatic debut. Julius Rudel well remembers that performance. "Sam put himself into the role of Zuniga and went at it as though Escamillo didn't exist, as though the opera was called *Zuniga* not *Carmen*. The intensity of his performance was unbelievable." *The New York Times* critic also was impressed. In a review, which proved to be a portent of critiques to come, he singled out the "very good bass-baritone who should fit well into the mold of the Norman Treigle repertoire." In one fell swoop, Sam got his debut, his accolades, and something else he was looking for, an agent. And not just any agent, but the very man he wanted, Matthew Epstein.

Matthew Epstein entered the music field somewhat circuitously. After receiving his undergraduate degree from the University of Pennsylvania, Epstein was slated to go on to law school. He, however, was far more interested in opera than in torts. Over the course of his undergraduate years, Epstein was a standee regular at the Metropolitan Opera House. He became an ardent fan of Marilyn Horne and, in time, a real friendship developed between the diva and the student. Epstein often sought Horne's counsel. He confided to her that he had no interest in becoming a lawyer. He was going into the law to please his parents. He planned to specialize in entertainment law in order to do something with music. "Why go through law school?" was the diva's terse response. "Go to business school and get into music management." Horne's advice gave Epstein the spur. He dropped the law, went to business school, and after receiving his degree, went to work for Harold Shaw. In due time, and with the support of friends and backers including Evelyn Lear and Thomas Stewart, he thought about opening his own agency, a logical step for a young man on the fast track. Rather than chancing it on his own, however, Epstein joined Columbia Artists Management (CAMI). After a long and fruitful tenure there, he went into a diverse slew of opera-oriented positions at home and abroad. He was general director of the Welsh National Opera, the first American to head an opera company in Great Britain; he was artistic director of BAM Opera at the Brooklyn Academy of Music; he was Artistic Director of the Lyric Opera of Chicago and he has served as an artistic consultant to a number of other musical organizations. In 1987, in one of his proudest moments, Epstein initiated Music for Life, a music industry-wide collaboration and benefit concert, which raised funds for AIDS. In 1992, he oversaw the Rossini 200$^{th}$ Birthday Celebration Gala at Lincoln Center, an internationally televised event starring, among others, Samuel Ramey. As a manager, Epstein was instrumental in building and guiding the careers of stellar American singers such as Kathleen Battle, Renee Fleming, Susan Graham, Catherine Malifitano, James Morris, Neil Shicoff, Tatiana Troyanos, and Frederica von Stade. At the present time, he is back with CAMI and along with managing, he is giving singing lessons. In his early managerial years, no one was more dedicated to his clients, no one ever worked harder for them, and the same holds true today. By his own admission, Matthew Epstein may not be everyone's cup of tea but he always has been a force with whom to be reckoned. In his chosen profession he has touched upon practically every venue except performing himself. Epstein was with the Shaw Agency when he and Sam connected but his memory of the events leading up to their association differs slightly from Sam's.

"Brent Ellis had told me about his friend, a bass who could sing high A flats, but I really was concerned about coping with the basses and baritones I already had, like Brent, Richard Stillwell, Alan Titus, and Ben Luxor, who were doing the same stuff as Sam. I was sort of controversial because of all the young 'domestic' talent I represented. Harold Shaw, my boss, was after me for taking so many of them on. He told me to cool it because 'these people don't make any money.' Sam wrote me two letters while I was at the Shaw Agency and no matter what *he* says, I wrote back to say that I was full up. I heard Sam at the Metropolitan Opera auditions and while I thought he was okay I didn't think he was that wonderful. He sounded to me like a baritone. I remember thinking 'interesting color and I should watch this guy' but nothing more, kind of a 'put him on the back burner' thing.

"The next time I saw Sam was at his debut in *Carmen*. I was there because Gwendolyn Killebrew, whom I represented, was the *Carmen*. Sam sang a small role but wow, what he did with it. It didn't take more than a few bars to know he had it. Some artists are great auditioners and not such great performers and others are great performers and not good auditioners. Sam definitely was the latter. Because Sam never was great at them, a lot of people who auditioned him were kind of equivocal; but once you saw him in performance, you knew! Hearing him in the State Theatre that afternoon, I was instantly convinced of his potential. I went backstage during the first intermission and, after I saw Gwen, I dropped into Sam's dressing room to congratulate him. Another man from the City Opera administration was in the room with him. 'We should talk,' I told Sam. Whereupon, the other man laughed, pointed his finger at me, and said to Sam, 'Stay away from that guy.' In those days, I was all over the place and I had a reputation for being a crazy boy. A lot of people were put off by me. Sam wasn't. Apparently, Gwen urged him to call me, which he did the next day, and we began working together that fall.

"One of the first occasions I heard him outside City Opera was in New Jersey. I went to Newark to see him in *La Gioconda*; he was singing Alvise, a heavy Italian bass part. It was funny, even though Alvise was a bigger role than Zuniga, Sam didn't make the same impression as he had in *Carmen*. That's because he was made up to play a much older man and wore a long, gray beard. I let him have it. 'When you really have a gray beard then you can do those parts. But until you do, DON'T. Right now, you should use your youth, your sex appeal, and your slim physique to your advantage instead of powdering your hair white and padding your body. You should only do parts where you can be young and fresh.' Well, Sam kind of liked that—he enjoyed being himself. Later, he got the reputation of always taking his shirt off and showing his physique. Listen, he did it because he could. Once he got rid of the graybeards I knew he'd be a wonderful Figaro and Colline and Basilio and Escamillo and I also knew that *Faust* was going to be great for him, but there was something else, something unique to Sam. His voice could really move."

What Matthew Epstein recognized, and what became a distinguishing characteristic of Sam's singing, was his incredible vocal flexibility, a result of his natural gift and his painstaking work with Armen Boyajian; not to mention all that he had done with Arthur Newman. Opportunely, Sam's astonishing vocal agility was in tune with the times. *Bel canto* was back! Following generations of neglect, the Italian vocal technique was revivified thanks, in great measure, to Maria Callas, who found an affinity for the abandoned system of song, and her heir apparent, Joan Sutherland. Save for a handful of masterpieces, eg. *The Barber of Seville*, *Lucia di Lammermoor*, and *Norma*, many works of Rossini,

Donizetti, and Bellini, demanding bel canto, had been overthrown by the dramatic and verismo operas of the nineteenth and twentieth centuries. Callas revived the tradition in the late forties, and soon after, opera houses regularly resurrected long neglected works. As seminal a figure as Callas was, in the opinion of one major bel canto scholar, she was not as proficient with every composer. According to Rossini expert Philip Gossett, "Callas's Rossini interpretations were awful but her interpretations of Donizetti were very special. Under Luchino Visconti's direction, she made it possible to hear the music in a way we hadn't heard before. My attitude about who really brought back the bel canto is very definite. It was Marilyn Horne, nobody else."

Audiences of the day came to expect the *bel canto* style but specifically from female voices. The reason? The ladies were the ones who could do it. Some theorists believe it has to do with the fact that female vocal cords are thinner and more flexible than the male's and thus are able to vibrate at the accelerated rate required by rapid, ornamental singing. Conversely, the lower a man's voice, the thicker and less supple are his vocal cords. According to Matthew Epstein, "It was granted that the women's parts would be sung sensationally and the men's would be cut as much as possible. By 1980, tenor, baritone, and bass parts were abbreviated because no one could sing the music. Then Sam came along and decided he could do it. He fit into slots no one else could." Apropos of the thickness/agility paradigm, at the height of his career, Sam got an infection and went to see his throat specialist, Dr. Eugen Grabsheid. Grabsheid examined him and then called over his assistant, Scott Kessler.

"Here, take at look at this," said the doctor pointing into Sam's open mouth.

Kessler peered in, and cried, "Oh my God!"

"What's the matter?" asked Sam, nervously.

"Oh, don't worry," said Dr. Grabsheid, "he's just never seen such a large set of vocal cords."

Sam Ramey, the taciturn Midwesterner, and Matthew Epstein, the quintessential New Yorker, became good friends as well as business associates. And their all-encompassing personal and professional relationship extended to Sam's wife. From the beginning, Carrie Ramey proved to be an integral part of *teamSam*, which included his teacher and managers. She was in on the infrastructural planning and many associates who met with Sam and Carrie agree that while he was pleasant and polite, she dominated conversations. Of course the Rameys may have been playing their version of the "good cop/bad cop" game. As accommodating as he is by nature, Sam always knew what he wanted and how best to get it. He just did not feel comfortable exerting the kind of necessary pressure that Carrie Ramey had no qualms about exerting for him.

When he became Sam's agent, Epstein was about to leave Shaw and start with Columbia Artists. He asked Sam if he wanted to go along with him. Sam was more than agreeable. Epstein joined CAMI but it would take a year for Sam to get there. During that interim, Epstein's crusade never slackened. "Matthew arranged stuff for me on the side before I actually signed with Columbia Artists. It was difficult to get releases from City Opera but Matthew managed to get me a few things. I remember doing a *Pique Dame* up in Canada with Richard Bonynge conducting. Things like that." In the fall of 1973, Sam formally signed with Matthew Epstein and Columbia Artists Management but not before a final hurdle. CAMI required prospective clients to do a formal audition. Despite Epstein's dour take on his client's auditioning skills, Sam passed the test.

In the relatively short time since his arrival in New York, Sam had forged important and enduring relationships with his wife, his teacher, and his agent. Soon, he would establish another major alliance. After Sam signed with the City Opera Dan Rule, the casting director, called the young bass into the theatre to discuss future repertoire. Naturally, Sam's agent went along. The three of them were in Rule's office when a knock came at the door. In walked Julius Rudel, then the head of City Opera. The courtly conductor took one look at Sam, then looked over at Epstein, then looked back at Sam and cried, "Oh my God, are you with *him*, too!" Disregarding Rudel's gibe, Epstein credits the conductor and John White with discovering Samuel Ramey. Julius Rudel not only discovered Sam, but also proved to be one of the singer's staunchest supporters.

A prominent figure on the New York musical scene both as a conductor of international renown and later as director of the City Opera, Julius Rudel arrived in New York City in 1938. The seventeen-year old émigré from Nazi infested Vienna immediately enrolled in the Mannes School of Music on New York's Upper West Side. There, he continued studies that had been interrupted by the rise of the National Socialist Worker's Party. His first professional job was as a rehearsal pianist with the brand new City Opera Company. His title was Musical Assistant, and his salary was $50 a week. That was in 1943. A year later, he made his conducting debut and went on to become the company's principal conductor. In 1957, he was appointed City Opera's Music Director, a position that evolved into General Director. In 1980, Beverly Sills retired from singing and became joint director of the City Opera. When Rudel left, the former diva took over.

Julius Rudel was General Director when he met the young bass destined to become one of the outstanding artists of his tenure. "Sam's audition was like so many others; he had a good voice and good looks and even though he seemed to be kind of a hick, there was something about him, something special. We took him on believing that the special quality would emerge. We had a policy that when we found performers we thought were ready, we would try them out in particular roles. Tenors we usually put into Pinkerton, baritones into Schaunaud, and for basses it was

Zuniga. The thought behind this casting was simple. These roles were not that pivotal, and if the performer laid an egg, the audience would not be cheated. On the other hand the roles were volatile and exciting enough to show what the person could do. And that's what happened with Sam at his debut in *Carmen*. Zuniga is only in the first two acts; I watched Sam at the rehearsal and after the first act, I was floored. Sam was taut as an arrow bow and moved and sang with an authority you'd never expect to see in a 'hayseed.' I ran to the phone and called my wife, Rita. 'You better come down here right away,' I told her, 'something extraordinary is happening.' She rushed over for the second act and, like me, was overwhelmed."

Julius Rudel immediately recognized that the City Opera had come up with someone special, and it could not have happened at a more opportune time. The company recently had lost its premier bass, Norman Treigle, who, if not the most tragic figure in American opera, is a strong contender for that sad title. Born in New Orleans in 1927, Treigle joined the New York City Opera in 1953, in the prescribed-for-young-bass role of Colline, and remained with the company for twenty years. Although he successfully essayed Figaro, Escamillo, Don Giovanni, and Boris Godunov, Treigle rose to the top of the City Opera's roster on the wings of his brilliantly sung and unflinching depictions of opera's standard bass villains. From Mephistopheles to Mefistofele, to the four Hoffman fiends, Treigle seared his vivid singing/acting imprimatur onto the satanic roles. In fact, company members referred to the Offenbach work as, "The Tales of Treigle." In the opinion of critic Peter G. Davis, Treigle was "a singer who often sacrificed musical fidelity to a broad theatrical effect, but that total effect was what distinguished his performances." Although he was acknowledged as one of the outstanding basses of his era, Norman Treigle never sang at the Metropolitan Opera. His only brush with the big house was as a cover for Justino Diaz in a run of *Fausts*. Denied the imprimatur of America's premier opera house, Treigle suffered the consequences. Major recording labels looked to the "stars" for their albums, thus, when it came to casting, the Metropolitan Opera House played Metro Goldwyn Mayer to City Opera's Monogram Pictures. As a result, Treigle is barely represented on disks. Furthermore, because a Met appearance offered an international recognition that City Opera could not hope to match, Treigle received a mere handful of overseas engagements. It was a lot for him to bear.

The coup de grace came in 1966 when City Opera mounted a new production of Handel's *Julius Caesar* specifically for its star bass. While this may not sound that daring today when Handel is staged as frequently as Mozart, it should be remembered that Handel was not performed at the Metropolitan Opera until Marilyn Horne brought *Rinaldo* there in 1984. According to Rudel, he heard Treigle sing some Handel and that "started the whole business. I thought I should take a chance and so we put on the *Caesar* just for him." Although Treigle sang well and received critical acclaim, the evening belonged to the Cleopatra. Indeed, had Gaius Julius Caesar himself showed up that night, no one would have noticed. All eyes and all ears were on Beverly Sills. This was her breakthrough performance, the one that caught the attention of the public and the press, put her on the cover of Newsweek, and catapulted her into super stardom. All this from a production intended to showcase Norman Treigle. Sills's emergence, in what was meant to be Treigle's vehicle, precipitated his "falling apart." Because he had a very close, almost sibling relationship with Sills, Treigle could not take it out on his beloved 'Bubbles.' Everything was internalized. He smoked constantly which seemed not to affect his singing one whit. He drank to excess and yet Sills is on record as saying she never saw him in any way impaired by his drinking. In the spring of 1973, he left the City Opera. Two years later, he was dead at the age of forty-seven, leaving behind an indelible mark on roles that eventually fell to Samuel Ramey. The heritage was a mixed blessing. Treigle's reputation ran deep and Julius Rudel, among others, knew that Sam would be up against it. For his part, Sam was thrilled to follow in Treigle's footsteps.

"I was a big fan of Norman Treigle and had been ever since my days in the Central City Opera chorus. I watched from the wings every time he sang Don Giovanni and when I moved to New York, I subscribed to the City Opera. I went to see him as much as I could. I thought he was fantastic. I went backstage a couple of times to tell him that Arthur Newman said hello, but I never had any real contact with him. He was gone by the time I was singing at City Opera. I never knew why he left although there were rumors that he and Rudel had a little rift. Supposedly Norman got mad because Rudel started taking solo curtain bows. That's sounds pretty ridiculous to me, but I heard it. Anyway, when I joined the company I jokingly went around telling everybody I was hired to 'replace' Norman Treigle. Right. Robert Hale was the first bass and doing all the roles I thought I should have been doing because I "replaced" Treigle. The truth is, especially in the beginning, I wasn't even in the first casts. It didn't bother me; I wasn't a tenor. What I mean is, it's usually decided from the beginning whether a tenor is going to be a major voice or a comprimario, that is, a secondary singer. Promising tenors start at the top. It's much more common for basses and baritones to begin with smaller roles and move up. They say it's because the lower voices take longer to mature and I guess that's as good a reason as any. Basses are late starters but there's a plus. We kind of stay around longer because we can go back into comprimario roles at the tail end of our careers, whereas tenors usually call it quits when they can't do the premium parts anymore. As a bass, you accept the little roles at the beginning because you expect to get to the big ones later.

"Two days after my City Opera debut I got a call from the Metropolitan Opera. They were looking for someone to do a particular role in *The Trojans* and asked me audition on the stage. I figured, gee, they must have heard how good I was in *Carmen*. I went racing over to the Met at the appointed time and found the place covered in wall-to-wall basses. Every bass in town had been called for the audition. And I thought I'd been asked because of my brilliant Zuniga. We didn't know who'd gotten the part until a while later. One night, a bunch of us were sitting around in the City Opera lounge talking about the *Trojans'* call, when someone said 'does anyone know who got it?' Richard Gill, the number two guy in our company after Bob Hale, piped up, 'I did.' Son of a gun, he never said anything till that moment.

"I got in a little bit of trouble with the City Opera in my first season. I'd done some auditioning for opera companies in Ohio and New Jersey and was offered a few things that I took. When City Opera said they were picking up my option, I had to tell them that I'd signed for *Manon* in Dayton and Toledo. John White was furious. 'How could you do that, how could your agent let you do that!' he practically screamed. I played dumb. 'I did it myself,' I explained. 'I didn't realize that I couldn't accept anything.' That was stretching it a bit but I had to protect myself. It didn't seem quite right to me that I didn't have the freedom to work while they were making up their minds. What if they didn't pick up the option? I would have been left high and dry. White calmed down and somehow they managed to work around my Ohio dates. Thinking about it, that was probably the only hitch in my long association with the New York City Opera. After that minor incident City Opera became my wellspring. I loved the place, I still do. It was like a big family and the perfect setting in which to develop my skills. Not just in singing, either. I played on the company's softball team.

"My contract was for one season with two and a half years of options and repertoire to be decided. Before the season started, I got a letter stating, 'Your assignments are this, your roles are that.' It was very cut and dry. For a while, I did nothing but small parts, Zuniga, Baron Duphol in *Traviata*, Trufaldino in *Ariadne auf Naxos* and the small bass roles in Donizetti's, *Anna Bolena*, and Bellini's *I Puritani*. In my apprentice years I did a lot of operas with Beverly Sills. Beverly used to say, 'When people look at my annotated scores, they're going to see.... *I walk to Sam, I turn to Sam, I grab Sam, I go out with Sam....* and they're going to wonder, who's Sam?'

"In my second season, I began getting more roles, Creon in *Medea,* Crespel in *The Tales of Hoffman*, Gualtiero in *I Puritani*, Angelotti in *Tosca*, the first Nazarean in *Salome*, Raimondo in *Lucia* and Timor in *Turandot.* I was doing four and five performances a week plus rehearsing every day and I was covering more and more. Covering simply means learning a role and being available to go on for an indisposed singer. It's like understudying in the theatre. If a scheduled singer doesn't go on then the first cover takes over, and if for some crazy reason the first cover can't do it, then the second cover is called. As you might imagine, second covers usually can count on NOT being called, but even if you're not, it's good experience in that you get to learn different roles. In that second season, I covered the role of Baron Douphol in *Traviata* and was supposed to sing a few performances. My luck, that particular season the orchestra went on strike, and the strike wiped out my performances. Consequently, I never really studied the part that much because I wasn't going to do it. The strike finally was settled and I was covering the last *Traviata* performance, a Saturday matinee. Friday afternoon I was sitting in the little canteen at the State Theatre having a cup of coffee. All of sudden, Felix Popper, a conductor and administrator, walked in and called out, 'Mr. Ramey! Mr. Ramey!' I got up and walked over to him. Popper looked very concerned. 'Mr. Ramey,' he said, 'Mr. David Rae Smith has cancelled tomorrow's performance of *Traviata*. You will sing it.' Well, ordinarily I'd have been delighted but like I said, I never studied it. I mean I knew it musically but I certainly hadn't gone into it. Anyway, they threw me into a rehearsal that afternoon. Patricia Brooks was the Violetta, and Raymond Gibbs was the Alfredo. Douphol is only in the gambling scene and that's what I rehearsed with them. I got the staging and knew where to go but not much more. When I got home that evening, I did something I'd never done, I put on a recording. I listened to the gambling scene over and over until I was totally familiar with the music. I can't remember whose interpretation I was following but the next day the performance went just fine.

"As far as being assigned more roles, I learned pretty fast that getting into a company is only half the battle. Once you're in you have to start scrambling to get more parts. I'd see John White in the halls and I'd go right up to him and say things like, 'You know, I sang Henry VIII in Paterson, I could cover for it, really I could.' And I'd follow that with, 'Oh, and I've done the Hoffman guys too, and I'm ready to cover for them, etc. etc.' I pestered that poor man to death. As far as landing any big parts, my badgering didn't seem to make a difference but I couldn't really complain. I was gradually expanding my repertoire and then it happened. Unbelievably, being a second cover turned out to be my big break.

"In the fall season of 1973 I was the second cover for Basilio in the *Barber*. It looked good on paper but I expected nothing, especially since the first cover was scheduled to sing the last performance on November 11, 1973. God knows why but he cancelled at the last minute and I was thrown into the production. Basilio is a special role, fun to act, and to sing. His big aria, *La Calunia*, has got to be among the greatest comic solos ever. I had a ball doing it and I had a really good success that night. A reviewer from *Opera News* wrote that mine was the 'best bass singing since Norman Treigle left the company.' You see, I was right; I did replace Norman Treigle, it just took a while. The night I sang Basilio, I reached another momentous milestone: Lois Kirschenbaum came to my dressing room after the performance. Okay, this may not sound like much but let me explain.

"Lois was known as 'the world's most famous opera fan,' as well as 'queen of all the autograph seekers.' Whether it was the New York City Opera, or the Metropolitan, or concert performances at Carnegie Hall, or Avery Fisher, whatever the venue, Lois was there. She was an avid autograph collector and had to be in the right place to get the signatures she wanted. Because of that she often knew the artists' schedules better than they did themselves. Singers used to joke about phoning Lois to check on their upcoming performance dates. She is the only "fan" ever featured in an OPERA NEWS profile and you can still find her waiting around stage doors to this day. The only difference is her hair is now snow white.

Lois Kirschenbaum was the celebrity yardstick. That's why, when Armen Boyajian spotted her in my dressing room after the *Barber* performance, he leaned over and whispered, 'Sam, look who's here! You've made it!'"

SAMUEL RAMEY: American Bass

# The Song Continues

Sam certainly did make it, in a well-paced ascendancy from his debut at the New York City Opera in March 1973, to his last performance at the State Theatre as Massenet's, *Don Quichotte,* in 1986. By that time he had become a guest artist and only returned to the company for productions mounted especially for him. Patience is a virtue, especially for singers, and exercising restraint helped secure and insure Samuel Ramey's career. He never rushed, he watched, he listened, and he studied. He had to overcome the hurdles, low pay and lots of little roles, which, with rare exception, are built into the making of any career, great or not so great. Fortunately, he was helped by others whose numbers increased as his career moved along. In the beginning there was his wife, his teacher, and his agent; later came Julius Rudel, Beverly Sills, Edgar Vincent, Marilyn Horne, Warren Jones, Philip Gossett, et al. Still, no matter how many others became involved, Samuel Ramey's own talent, and his tenacious, intelligent pursuit of ways to refine that talent, are responsible for his success. While he always appears nonchalant and laid back, his underling drive manifests itself in lip chewing and fingernail snapping that are as much a part of him as his ready and warm smile.

At the time that Sam was preparing for his City Opera debut, Edgar Vincent, a highly respected manager/publicist whose client list included Beverly Sills and Placido Domingo, bumped into Julius Rudel on Columbus Avenue near Lincoln Center.

"Where are you rushing?" asked the publicist.

"I have to get to the opera house. There's a new bass and I want to hear him," explained Rudel.

"What's he singing?"

"Zuniga."

"Zuniga?" thought Edgar Vincent. "Julius can judge a performer from a Zuniga?"

His curiosity piqued, Vincent went to a *Carmen* performance where he discovered that Rudel could, and did, correctly judge Samuel Ramey based on a Zuniga. Edgar Vincent made note of the young bass's name for future reference. That future was not far off.

In those days, if a singer gave a great performance who, other than the comparatively small audience in the opera house and perhaps a small listening audience, would know? Enter the publicist, whose task, admittedly, became easier with the advent of televised broadcasts. A good publicist can give a healthy boost to an artist's career by making noise in the media. This was not a concept that Sam Ramey readily embraced. "Matthew kept telling me I had to hire a publicist, which I kind of fought. I mean, to pay someone to make me famous sounded awfully self-serving. But I trusted Matthew's judgment, so I interviewed a couple of P.R. guys. I wasn't that impressed, and then I met Edgar Vincent. Right away, I knew he was the one. The question was when should we start working together? Edgar asked me what I had coming up on my schedule. I told him I was singing Basilio in a new production of the *Barber* starring Beverly Sills as Rosina. 'Well,' he said, 'you don't need me for that because it's going to be all about Beverly. Why don't we wait until you have something of your own? We can start then.' Edgar's way of doing business impressed me. He didn't want to start charging me money while he was putting all his energy into another client. He was definitely my kind of guy."

SAMUEL RAMEY: American Bass

Edgar Vincent, like Julius Rudel, was a European émigré. Half Dutch-half Italian and born in Hamburg, Germany, Edgar Vincent Julius Rafaelle Simone Pos grew up in an Amsterdam household where, because his Italian opera singer mother did not speak Dutch and his father, a Harvard-educated dentist, did not speak Italian, many alternate languages were spoken. "Although my mother finally learned Dutch, my father never learned Italian and, until the end of their days, a sentence could start in one language and five languages later was finished. My mother's family was Treviso where my granduncle was the bishop of the Assisi church. My father, one of eleven children, was born in Paramaribo, and my paternal grandfather was the governor of Dutch Guiana. Truly, my background was like something out of grand opera. Growing up I had two goals. First, I wanted to be a concert pianist and second, because my father adored America, I wanted to go to the States. It was my dream. My mother began giving me piano lessons when I was seven and by the age of thirteen, I knew I would never hit the top. I decided to stop. My mother asked me what else I might like to consider, and I answered, 'how about acting?' A few years later, while I was still in my teens, she used some contacts to get me a contract at Warner Bros. I arrived in Los Angeles with an accent you could have sliced with a knife, had a screen test, did some extra work, including a non-credited role in *Juarez*, a Paul Muni/Bette Davis epic, and then was dropped. 'Come back to us when you're thirty-five,' the Warner's people advised, 'then you can play some of those suave Europeans.' Age-wise, I had a ways to go. While waiting to 'mature,' I joined a small L.A. theatre group where my accent didn't seem to matter that much."

During Edgar Vincent's theatrical venture his acting caught the attention of the theatre company's publicist, Muriel Francis. Impressed by the suave, young man, she arranged a few press interviews for him. For a while, his career continued, but in less than a spectacular manner. In search of greater challenges and more work, he took off for New York where he hoped to find greener pastures in radio and early television. By chance, he bumped into Muriel Francis in the NBC Studio at Rockefeller Center. Since their last meeting, Francis had opened her own public relations office specializing in classical music and was conducting business out of her town house in the East 60s. Her clients were top of the line and included Eleanor Steber, Rise Stevens, Dorothy Kirsten, Lily Pons, Andre Kostelanetz and Samuel Ramey's future idol, Ezio Pinza. The problem, Muriel Francis confided to Edgar Vincent as they chatted in the NBC studio, was finding someone to work with her who had a knowledge of music, a command of languages, and a knack for publicity. After a quick stocktaking, Vincent made an on-the-spot decision. Believing that it might be wiser for him to represent performers rather than be one, he proposed himself for the position. Muriel Francis took him on. Soon thereafter, he began his new career as a publicist not, however, as Edgar Vincent. To keep his stage name, just in case, he resumed his acting career. He rechristened himself 'Charles Becker.' As it happened, Charles Becker's first client was Ezio Pinza.

Ezio Pinza was at a turning point in his career. He had left the operatic stage and was currently in New Haven with the Broadway bound Rodgers and Hammerstein musical, *South Pacific*. Pinza was a very unhappy man, primarily because the director, Joshua Logan, never directed him. Apparently, Logan worked under the assumption that Pinza was a star and therefore should know what to do. Every night the disgruntled singer was given a rewrite to learn which he interpreted to mean that he was not good enough. His confidence badly shattered, Pinza telephoned Muriel Francis to say he wanted out. She, in turn, called her new assistant into her office and explained the situation.

"You're an actor. You speak Italian. Go to New Haven and work with Pinza," she ordered. Vincent took the train to New Haven, where he remained for eight days bolstering the beleaguered Pinza. Upon his return to New York, he reported to Francis.

"When this man opens on Broadway we have two choices. We simply say it's the greatest voice Broadway has ever heard or we publicize him as a new matinee idol."

"You're crazy," answered Muriel Francis. "He's fifty-seven years old, he can't be a matinee idol!"

"Just wait."

*South Pacific* opened on Broadway on April 11, 1949 and the rest is history. Ezio Pinza became a matinee idol, winning a Tony Award for his performance, and launching his new career and his young publicist's as well. Convinced that he had found his métier, Edgar Vincent reclaimed his real name, and retired Charles Becker. In time Vincent became Muriel Francis's partner. After her retirement, he took over the agency, which was renamed Edgar Vincent Associates. Edgar Vincent remained at the helm of his firm and was actively involved in the business of music until his death in 2008 at the age of 90.

*South Pacific* opened and Edgar Vincent soon discovered that being Ezio Pinza's publicist was no walk in the park. Pinza's agent, the brother-in-law of Dore Schary, head of MGM, had negotiated a deal for the charismatic bass to appear opposite Lana Turner in *Mr. Imperium,* which was about to go into production. Vincent had been coaching Pinza for radio and television appearances, and the opera singer-cum-matinee idol asked him to take a look at the *Mr. Imperium* script. Vincent read it and advised his client that it was a worthless piece of junk.

"It's a terrible script," he told the singer. It's just one long kiss.

"No," protested Pinza, "it's love eternal!"

"Look," admonished the publicist, "if you want to kiss Lana Turner in private, okay. But don't do it on the screen."

"You don't understand my career anymore," responded

Pinza.

"That's possible," answered Vincent.

Despite the fact that he had a run of the play contract, in April of 1950, Pinza opted out of *South Pacific* and left for California. That was that, thought his publicist.

"*Mr. Imperium* came out and, while it was not a big success, Ezio liked Los Angeles and took up residence there. I didn't hear from him. One Sunday, I was visiting Efrem Zimbalist, Jr. in Connecticut, and Pinza called from California. He was all excited. 'Oh Edgar, I'm starting a new picture called *Strictly Dishonorable* with Janet Leigh and I thought you might like to spend your vacation with me in Hollywood. We could work on my part a bit.' I was so mad, but I knew how to handle him.

'Ezio,' I told him, 'if I give up my vacation it will cost you money.' That ended that episode.

"He learned his lesson, though, and I did work with him again. Truthfully, you couldn't resist Ezio. He was a quite a man and there was never a dull moment with him. Over the next few years he did a sitcom called *Bonino* and various musical specials for television. I was with him for his television work and for the filming of his third movie, *Tonight We Sing*, the story of the impresario, Sol Hurok. It was Ezio's best work on the screen. He gave a very convincing portrayal of Feodor Chaliapin and sang an aria from *Boris Godunov*. The movie did nothing at the box office. I later heard that the Hollywood crowd referred to it either as *Tonight We Sink* or *Tonight We Stink*. Frankly, either title summed it up."

Ezio Pinza no longer was singing opera at the time Edgar Vincent met him but the young publicist's association with the hot-blooded Italian gave him unique insights into the nature of the bass. Consequently, when he heard Samuel Ramey sing he recognized a quality, which, although different from Pinza's, was special in its own way. After Sam became his client, Vincent often was asked to compare the two singers. "I cannot really do that," was his standard response. "Musically, I could not judge Ezio that well because I was with him at the end of his opera career. I never heard him sing opera in person. I heard his records and, while he was a real basso cantante, he may have lacked the *fioratura*. Both of them were phenomenal singers but completely different. Ezio was an extrovert and Sam is only an extrovert on stage, not in daily life. He's a Gary Cooper, a Jimmy Stewart. When I think about the two of them, what really stands out is the fact that Ezio was Sam's idol and ninety percent of the young basses today, idolize Sam. It's a full circle.

"As far as the Treigle business, I look back and am amazed at the way Sam rose so quickly to the top at City Opera. He had a tough time convincing certain people that he had a right to Norman's repertory. When he got the parts, he worked at them, and developed his own characterization. He became better and better, and took over roles that Treigle didn't really like that much, such as Figaro. Still, I wouldn't compare Sam to Norman anymore than I would compare him to Ezio. Sam's his own man."

Following Sam's City Opera debut, Julius Rudel continued to watch over the young bass knowing that in the long run, Sam would have to confront the ghost of Treigle Past. Similarities existed between the two basses, as did obvious differences. In Rudel's opinion, others in the company were just as happy to accentuate the former and forget the latter. For his part, Rudel wanted to ease rather than push Sam into a repertoire indelibly stamped by his predecessor. "Although Sam had a Treigle-like intensity, I knew it would be a mistake to force him into becoming a Treigle clone. He had to develop his own style. The difference between Sam and Norman was Colby vs. New Orleans. Norman was suave; he had a continental touch and therefore was a more identifiable Ladies Man type. Sam is a lot sexier on stage than in person. In person, Sam generates affability. Norman, on the other hand, was sexy on and off the stage. He would look at a woman and there was something there." Treigle's colleagues and friends were aware of this something. In the late sixties, Treigle and Beverly Sills appeared with the Boston Symphony at Tanglewood in the Berkshires. A girlfriend of Sills came up from Boston for the weekend and joined the soprano, her husband, Peter Greenough, Treigle, and a few others for dinner. Treigle sat opposite the young woman. From her vantage point at her end of the table, Sills watched closely as Treigle animatedly engaged her friend in conversation. Before dessert was served, the two women went to the Ladies Room together.

"What's a singer's mask, Bev?" asked her friend as they stood in front of the washbasins.

"Why do you want to know?" queried Sills.

"Well, Norman Treigle keeps patting my cheeks and telling me I have a 'singer's mask.'"

"Mask, shmask," laughed Sills, "he's coming on to you, dear."

Treigle definitely had an eye for the ladies, yet Julius Rudel observed an ironic twist to those flirtations. "Norman seemed sophisticated to American women and to American audiences, but on the Continent it was exactly the opposite. We took him to Europe once and he was very uncomfortable. He sang Olin Blitch in *Susanna*, a signature role for him, at the World's Fair in Brussels and he was unhappy the whole time. He didn't speak any foreign languages and he felt cut off. It's hard to be charming, which he was, when you can't communicate. Basically, Norman was at home only in America, whereas Sam felt at home wherever he sang. Even if he didn't speak the language, Sam was comfortable, which I think was attributable to his mid-Western roots. One big difference between them was I guess what you'd call ego. Norman was full of his own persona and had a particularly strong feeling about himself as a performer. And he was quite a performer. He had the ability to stand still on a stage and have all eyes be on him. Sam always had a good stage physique and over the years developed a sort of personal stance of his own, although never to the extent that Treigle did. I think Sam's eventual mastery of stage presence was a conscious effort whereas Norman's was innate. When Norman did not get the encomiums he thought he was entitled to, it triggered something and that something eventually led to his downfall. Norman and Sam definitely were equals on one score. Each of them had a good sense of humor and neither was afraid to show it on stage.

"At first, Sam was a bit of a rube, a square, but still exciting. He was guileless and Norman was, to say the least, complex. In performance, Norman was more like a snake while Sam was a lion. With such obvious differences in their styles, for the company to ask that Sam simply copy what Norman did was unfair. The roles had to be re-tailored to Sam's strengths, but there was a catch. Tito Capobianco, who staged quite a few operas for Treigle, did not welcome alterations to his productions. He had a vision, and customized his concept to fit a Treigle or a Sills or whomever. No matter who eventually took over the roles, he got very upset if singers didn't do exactly what he'd originally staged. Look, Broadway musicals live on that principle. Once a show is set, the stage manager has to make sure it goes exactly that way, but opera is different. It really wasn't fair to the singers, and Sam wasn't the only one affected. Patricia Brooks stepped in for Beverly Sills several times and was very unhappy because she was made to do stuff that was superimposed Sills, not Brooks. It was the same for Sam. When he began appearing in roles associated with Treigle, instead of assessing *his* interpretations, the reviews kept comparing the two of them. As a result, Sam got a few unwarranted raps in the newspapers. He never complained. He was disciplined and humble, and did what he was asked to do. But *I* complained because I thought all that Treigle/Ramey nonsense would stifle Sam's personal style. I didn't want to lose a good talent for stupid reasons."

Matthew Epstein shared Rudel's fears that comparisons with Treigle were counterproductive. He reasoned that the best way to block them was to go directly to his client's strengths. "As Sam's manager, I wanted to find a different way for him, a way that was interesting, one that would show his flexibility and ease in the high register. I worked on his repertoire with City Opera, but I always worried about the Treigle business. Although Sam definitely was the successor to Treigle and would fit into many of the productions created for Norman, he had to find his own approach. In the beginning, Sam really wasn't a low bass. The upper part of his voice was stunning but the lower was a little not so stunning. In fact, from 1973 to 1974, we seriously considered baritone parts for him. There even was talk of his doing Count Almaviva in *Figaro* for a Juilliard production. Ultimately, we decided against it. Sam's strength lay in that 'altitude,' but he also had this demonic thing, the *Faust*, the *Hoffman*, that he did so well."

Epstein demanded a lot from himself and was no less demanding with his singers. He insisted that they thoroughly prepare their roles. Eager to explore all aspects of his art, Sam went along with his manager's thinking. In the mid-Seventies, at Epstein's prodding, Sam went to Europe for two summers to study with two outstanding pedagogues, Luigi Ricci and Janine Reiss. The former, an Italian coach who had worked with Puccini, was teaching the Italian style in Rome; the latter, an expert in the French style, had her studio in Paris. Sam told Epstein that he particularly wanted to study Verdi arias and roles with Ricci. Using the first person plural, a phenomenon that occasionally crops up in manager/client speak, Epstein cautioned his client. "It's okay to work a bit on the Verdi, but we're not going to be singing those roles until later. Right now, we'll do the Rossini stuff and the French repertoire. Remember, we're aiming for the bel canto."

In the summer of 1974, Sam went to Rome to see Ricci and, eschewing Verdi for the moment, asked first to work on the role of Henry VIII in *Anna Bolena*. The old man shook his head and replied, "I'm sorry. I really don't know that opera very well." For whatever reason, Donizetti and Verdi took a backseat throughout the lessons. Sam and Ricci concentrated almost exclusively on Mozart, not arias or ensembles just recitatives, which proved to be extremely beneficial. "Recitatives are where the drama takes place," explains Sam. "You could leave out the arias and ensembles in a Mozart or Rossini opera, sing the recitatives, and have the whole story. Because of my work with Ricci those recitatives are so firmly fixed in my mind, to this day I could get up and sing them at the drop of a hat." According to conductor Donald Runnicles, that aptitude for Mozart was a key to Sam's sonorous, seamless singing. In an interview with the San Francisco Chronicle, Runnicles said of Sam, "I hear a voice that knows no break in it. I think the fact that he is always in a position to return to Mozart is crucial. I wish more singers would have that as one of their Ten Commandments, posted above the bed: 'Thou shalt always sing Mozart.'[3] From Rome Sam went on to Paris and Janine Reiss. "I knew I was going to be doing Mephistopheles and I wanted to nail the French style which is much more subtle than the Italian. Janine was amazing and really set me up beautifully. I'll still go and do some brushing up with her whenever I'm singing in Paris. Working with Ricci and Reiss I got a better understanding of the different styles. I also got a good enough working knowledge of the languages themselves so that I'm comfortable in French and Italian. Most important, I know what I'm singing."

During his first season at City Opera, Sam often saw Beverly Sills around the opera house yet despite the Arthur Newman connection and their brief Boston encounter, he

---

[3] Steven Winn, San Francisco Chronicle, 15 Oct. 2003.

felt it was not his place to say hello. "When you're doing small roles you don't hang around with the 'biggies.' And, nobody was more of a biggie than Bev. I was in awe of her. But when I was given the minor role of Lord Rochefort in *Anna Bolena* and she was singing the title role, I figured that since we were appearing together, I could say something. At the first *Bolena* rehearsal, I casually, in my mind casually, walked over and reminded her of our backstage meeting in San Antonio as well as our brief stage appearance together in Boston. She immediately said of course she remembered and then we just began gabbing. As huge a star as she was Bev was very down to earth, easy to talk to, and had no airs. We hit it off." Sam never knew that, after that first *Bolena* rehearsal, Sills went home and telephoned her friend, Joel Carr. "Beverly was all excited," says Carr, and I remember her exact words. 'Joel, wait till you hear this kid who's singing Rochefort. He blew my mind.'" Sills recognized Sam had something special. Later, after he had taken his place in the bass pantheon, she proclaimed, "Every time Sam opens his mouth, he gives a vocal lesson to every singer;" high praise from a very high roller.

Sills formed a special friendship with the young bass, not the same as she had with her contemporary, Treigle, but quite wonderful in its own way. She, too, was asked many times to compare the two men and her response was as resolute as Edgar Vincent's. "I'm never going to compare Sam with Norman. You can't compare two singers in the same repertoire. Would you compare Callas and Sutherland? It's apples and oranges. There was a youthful quality about everything Sam did, even when he was Mephistopheles. His Don Giovanni was an extremely likeable roué and his Olin Blitch had John Travolta-like vulnerability. Sam could be sweet and soft, but he had to fight to be evil. Sweet and soft didn't come easily to Norman. When he did those bad guy roles, he *was* evil. As far as singing, Sam's voice is a healthy, dark, marvelous instrument with flexibility to boot. Norman had a deep, sonorous voice, but he didn't have the flexibility. He fell short in the arias, because he didn't have it. That really was what hurt his Julius Caesar. But, his recitatives were masterful. No one can do them the way Norman did; he was like John Gielgud in those recitatives. Another thing that worked for Sam was his adaptability. Sam will adjust; Norman never would. He came in with *his* Mefistofele, *his* Don Giovanni, *his* Figaro, whereas Sam is adaptable as well as adorable."

Sam and Sills frequently appeared together as he moved steadily up into her starry territory. They shared many laughs off and on stage. "We'd pal around together especially on the road. I remember one time in Tulsa when we spent an entire afternoon antiquing. Bev was a shopper. She never met an antique she didn't buy and that afternoon she bought a truckload of what she called *tchotchkes*." Sam delights in telling tales of Sills especially in recalling performance slip-ups where he had to fight to keep from breaking character. "While we were appearing together in an *Anna Bolena*, I had gone from singing Rochefort to Henry VIII, Bev was having dental work. She was wearing temporaries, and in the middle of the big finale, a couple of them popped out of her mouth. She got down on her hands and knees and groped around the floor in front of me, trying to find them. I'm sure the audience thought she was pleading for her life, or something like that but she was just looking for her teeth.

"Bev and I were almost instantaneous buddies but my relationship with Julius Rudel was a slower take. Julius wasn't so easy to get to know or to get friendly with. He's European, formal, kind of intimidating, and at first I found him a bit standoffish. He was the boss, and I was in awe of him. Gradually, we got to be friends, and I realized that, among other things, he had a great sense of humor. One time, the City Opera softball team was playing in Central Park against a team of Broadway actors and Julius rode over on his bicycle to watch. He did this quite often. I think it was because he got a kick out of seeing his singers chasing around the diamond. That afternoon, he stood on the sidelines calling out encouragement. I was all over the place, playing practically every position except catcher. I came up to bat for the second time when Julius began yelling at me. 'Sam," he shouted, 'you have a *Mefistofele* tonight! If you get beaned, I'll consider it your fault!' I wish I could remember if I got a hit, all I can recall is standing in the batter's box laughing my head off. At work, Julius was always very solicitous and encouraging. I was about to do Henry VIII for the first time and he generously offered to coach me privately. I went to his studio and we went over the score note by note. That was the beginning of many sessions with him. I had a really good working relationship with Julius Rudel but as friendly as we became I could never call him anything but 'Maestro.' No joke, it took ten years for me to be able to say 'Julius.'"

Sam had good relationships with just about everyone at the City Opera. Because it was a repertory company, the members were like one big family, and the camaraderie continued from season to season. Unlike the Metropolitan and other international houses where casts might bond during a production only to disconnect once the opera ends its run, long-term friendships were forged in City Opera's cozy company. The Metropolitan came closest to being a united company during World War II when European artists, unable to return to their homelands, stayed put and became part of the Met family. City Opera was, and is, a cohesive collection of artists. Occasionally, less complimentary opinions about the company were expressed. Sam remembers one incident of City Opera bashing. "Edgar Vincent arranged for me to audition for Erich Leinsdorf. At the start of the audition, Leinsdorf asked me where I was singing. 'City Opera,' I answered. 'Oh,' said Leinsdorf, 'you have to get out of that place, it's a bordello!' It was a strange thing for him to say especially since he'd been the head of City Opera for a while. I never figured out what he meant, but I got to do a Mahler Eighth Symphony with him and the National Symphony in Washington."

In the fall of 1974, Sam took that giant step up from the minor role of Lord Rochefort to the role of Henry VIII in *Anna Bolena*. At the first performance Marisa Galvany, who bore a striking resemblance to the soprano, Clara Zamboni, sang the role of Anna. Later Beverly Sills would return to the part, and Sam would sing opposite her. The upward spiral continued with Sam going into productions, such as *Faust* and *Tales of Hoffman*, that had been specifically created for Treigle. The former was a Frank Corsaro production; the latter was the work of Tito Capobianco. "I have to admit," remembers Sam, "as happy as I was to get those parts, the Treigle thing kept hanging over me."

Hanging over, indeed. For a while Samuel Ramey literally lived in the shadow of his predecessor. He stepped into the Treigle repertoire (*Don Giovanni*, *Faust*, *Marriage of Figaro*, *Mefistofele*, *Susanna,* and the *Tales of Hoffman*) and walked into a wailing wall of comparisons. As complimentary as Sam's reviews were, Treigle's name invariably was invoked. Considering that Sam was an up-and-coming young singer and Treigle had been a polished veteran, the constant evaluations were unnecessary and unjust but not unprecedented. When Enrico Caruso first appeared at the Metropolitan Opera House, he was compared to the elegant Jean de Reszke and often found wanting. More recently, Placido Domingo became the Othello of his day but when he began singing the role, people still were talking about Mario del Monaco.

The point being, as Ms. Sills aptly commented, "It's apples and oranges."

Jane Scovell

# Star Turns

On September 20, 1974, Samuel Ramey made his first City Opera appearance as Mephistopheles, a role that many consider his greatest. In fact, after dodging the question for years, Sam recently took a stand and acknowledged that, "If someone put a gun to my head and said, 'What's your favorite role of your life?' I'd probably say Mephistopheles." By mid-September, *Faust* rehearsals were well along when a break was called during an extended session on set. Grateful for the chance to relax, Sam walked off the stage and into the orchestra, where he slumped in a front row seat. Ordinarily, he would have taken the opportunity to grab a quick nap but before he had a chance to close his eyes, Julius Rudel came over and sat down next to him. They chatted a bit about the *Faust* then Rudel paused, smiled, and said, "You've done some big parts this season, Sam, and you've done them well, so well that we have something special in mind for you. We're very eager to bring back *Mefistofele* and wonder if you would be interested in doing it. Of course, it's a few years down the road, but we want to make sure it's something you'd consider before we go ahead."

Sam thought he was hearing things. He truly believed that particular role never would be a possibility for him, and with good reason. Although a favorite vehicle for European artists such as Nazzareno De Angelis, Tancredi Pesaro, and Chaliapin, whose first appearance outside of Russia was as Mefistofele (La Scala, 1901), Boito's opera rarely was seen outside the Continent. Ezio Pinza and Cesare

Sicpi each appeared in the opera, but only Siepi recorded it. The New York City Opera brought *Mefistofele* into the American repertoire in a 1968 production, showcasing Norman Treigle. From the moment Treigle slithered, Nosferatu-like, onto the proscenium, his thin wiry form encased in a nude body stocking, his face painted pasty white, his eyes kohl-rimmed, and his head crowned by an unruly mop of platinum hair, he *was* the Devil. Other City Opera bassos, including Michael Devlin and William Chaplin, sang the part but Norman Treigle inhabited it. Little wonder that, following his last appearance in the spring of 1973, the opera was performed a couple of times, and then removed from the repertoire. Without Treigle, the spark was gone. Everyone, including Sam, believed that *Mefistofele* had been buried in the opera graveyard.

"Armen Boyajian said all along that they should bring it back for me but when Julius told me that they actually were going to revive it, I was dumbstruck. I'd been crazy about that opera ever since my LP collecting days. Cesare Siepi's recording was one of my earliest acquisitions. I bought it 'cold' and the first time I listened, I was stunned. I couldn't get over what a great part it was. I got a hold of the score and sang along with Siepi, over and over again, never dreaming I'd ever get to do it myself. Well, maybe *dreaming*, but never thinking the dream would come true. And now it was a reality. I felt good that City Opera wanted to bring it back for me, I also felt the pressure. I had seen Treigle in the opera at the State Theatre a few times, and his performance was mind-blowing. He had a huge black voice, the loudest voice I ever heard. This small, skinny guy opened his mouth to sing and it knocked you to the back wall. Adding it to my repertoire, however, presented a built-in problem. The *Fausts* and the *Hoffmans* were hard enough, but *Mefistofele*? Treigle *owned* it. It's different if you go into an opera house where a role is up for grabs and a hundred different people have sung it; you've got plenty of room to move around in.

Thanks to Norman Treigle, I wouldn't have that luxury. But nothing could stop me from doing it!"

From Sam's Zuniga days on, Julius Rudel realized that the young bass was Treigle's logical successor. As Sam assumed one role after another, the casting wheel turned in Rudel's brain until, confident that Sam was ready to take on Treigle's most recognized portrayal, Rudel began pushing for a revival. It took some doing but he was able to convince his colleagues that the time was ripe. At the same time, Rudel wanted to make sure that the production catered to Sam and that any Treigle traces were removed. "Most of the operas that had been done for Norman were directed by Tito Capobianco who, as I've mentioned, was absolutely immovable in terms of changing anything for anyone. This created a problem. Norman was a sneaky sidestepper with certain sinuous, snake-like, movements. What he did was marvelous but for him, not for Sam. When the time came to revive the *Mefistofele*, although I was a bit apprehensive, I contacted Tito. We talked and, as I feared, he made it clear that he wanted Sam to do everything exactly as Norman had done it. 'Look,' I told him, 'you're putting this kid into things he can't physically do. It's wrong. He's different and the action has to be modified to suit him. I don't want the reviews saying he doesn't do a good enough imitation of Norman. And, for sure, he's got to have a new costume not that body stocking.' Capobianco wouldn't budge. I had no choice. I decided not to use him. Instead, I hired David Hicks, the assistant director on the original production, and we worked together tailoring the staging to suit Sam. As far as I'm concerned, that *Mefistofele* was the moment in time when Ramey became Ramey."

Ramey, however, would have to wait to become Ramey. *Mefistofele* would not return to the repertoire until the spring of 1977. It was 1974, and Sam had to concentrate on Mephistopheles, the beginning of his legendary line of satanic portrayals.

## SAMUEL RAMEY: American Bass

"My first appearance in *Faust* was a big hit and for me it's still the best production of *Faust* I've ever appeared in. I've been in a lot of terrific ones and I can't tell you exactly why it's my favorite but I think lot has to do with concept of the director, Frank Corsaro. For example, he saw Mephistopheles as a different character in every act. That approach fit in with the theory that the devil appears in many guises so you never know how he's going to show up. In that production I showed up in a lot of different costumes, and each outfit kind of represented my changing personality. *Faust* was a touchstone and it had a domino effect on my career. About a month later I got to sing another top bass role, Don Giovanni. I was told that I was going to sing the Don and I had some rehearsals, but none of them took place on the actual set. The day of the performance, November 2, 1974, I walked onto that set for the very first time. Trust me, that's not something you want to do. When you're singing a new role, especially a big one like the Don, you want to have a pretty damn good idea where you're going, and what's surrounding you. Musically, I did okay, but action-wise, I did not get through that evening unscathed. Hell, I didn't even get past my first entrance without a mishap. Right after the overture, the curtains parted and Donna Anna, whom I've just seduced, and I made our entrance on a landing at the top of a high staircase. During our duet we were supposed to work our way down the stairs where we would run into Donna Anna's father, the Commendatore. And, after a brief musical exchange, I would kill him in a duel. Fine. I stormed out on stage and as I did I heard this r-r-r-ripping noise. I took a quick look and saw that my cape had caught on something. I figured it was no big deal and kept going. Donna Anna and I rushed down to the bottom of the stairs and met up with the Commendatore. He called me every name in the book and challenged me to a duel. I was supposed to sing *misero attendi*, draw my sword, and duel him to his death. That's what was supposed to happen. I grasped the hilt of my sword and pulled. Nothing. I pulled again and still, I couldn't draw it out. What I didn't realize was that when my cape got caught, it had split into two long strips. During the duet with Donna Anna, one of those strips had wrapped itself around my sword. The damn thing was stuck. Julius Rudel was conducting and when he saw that I was having trouble he had the orchestra hold the note as I sang "*se vuoi mo............rrrrrr....ir,*" dragging it out so I could arm myself. The sword wouldn't budge. Meanwhile, Julius simply had to move on to the dueling music. He gave the signal and in desperation I yanked with all my might. Out came the sword barely in time for me to kill the Commendatore. Irwin Denson was singing the role that evening and he told me afterwards that as he stood there watching me struggle, he was trying to figure out how he was going to kill himself. A flimsy cape and it caused a major screw-up."

Screw-up yes, but minor, not major. The review in *The New York Times* did not mention the dueling farce per se, but the reviewer might have been alluding to it when he wrote:

"*... a few rough edges aside, his was a most impressive performance. With his lean figure and athletic agility, Mr. Ramey suggests Norman Treigle in this and other roles. But actually Mr. Ramey's voice is rather different from Mr. Treigle's stentorian bass. Mr. Ramey has a large basso cantante, mellow in sound. Yesterday, neither his stage deportment nor his phrasing offered the utmost in elegance but one imagines that he didn't have much preparation before being inserted into the patchwork production.*"[4]

One might have imagined, indeed. Sam's interpretation of Don Giovanni would grow, both in "phrasing" and "stage deportment," and, by the spring season of 1981, he was comfortable enough as the Don, to step away and take on the role of Leporello. In her autobiography, *Beverly*, Sills

---

[4] The New York Times, 3 Nov. 1974.

wrote, "The company's performances of *Don Giovanni* were a smashing success, primarily because Sam Ramey and Justino Diaz agreed to alternate with each other in the roles of the Don and his sidekick, Leporello. Ramey and Diaz played off each other so flawlessly they drove audiences wild."

Sam continued to expand his repertoire at City Opera and elsewhere. Elsewhere, it should be noted, did not include the house across the way. Ironically, even before he sang *Mefistofele* at the City Opera, and long before he sang *anything* at the Metropolitan Opera House, the quintessentially American Samuel Ramey found lasting fame in Europe.

A century-and-a-half ago, Gioacchino Rossini opined that the newfangled passenger trains signaled the end of singing excellence. He meant, of course, that because singers could travel from place to place with relative speed they would take on too many engagements and not give their vocal cords sufficient rest. One can imagine what Rossini might have to say about present day artists jetting back and forth from continent to continent, from country to country, and from city to city. In the early 1970s, however, flying around to far-flung opera houses had not reached its present peak of recurrence. Although planes were flying, American artists appeared in Europe far less frequently than today. This was due both to some singers' reluctance to spend huge blocks of time away from home, and the red tape involved in setting up foreign engagements. Communication between artistic managers and presenters was snail-paced compared to today's laser-like Internet action. Thus, American agents relied on their European counterparts, men and women who worked with artists anywhere other than in the States. One such agent was Tom Graham, an expatriate CAMI employee who settled permanently in London in 1973. From this vantage point Graham often worked in concert with Matthew Epstein. In the summer of 1975, Epstein, eager for his client to get exposure in a variety of venues, arranged for Sam to stop on his way to Janine Reiss in Paris to meet with Graham in London. The two men immediately hit it off and have remained good friends. Graham is delighted to reminisce about his role in the care and feeding of performing artists.

"I grew up in Detroit Michigan, the ugliest most horrible city in America. If you start in a place like Detroit you have to go somewhere. I left as soon as I could. As a kid I played the trumpet and I had a passion for music but my passion was an inchoate block. I had no idea if a way of working in music existed, or if there was such a thing as a 'music business.' But that's what I wanted and I knew I would not find it in Detroit. I came to New York and applied for a job as an usher at Avery Fischer Hall where the New York Philharmonic played. They turned me down. I was told it was because I wouldn't know where to buy sandwiches for the summer park concerts. As good a reason as any for not hiring me, I guess. I think the real reason was because I wasn't a New Yorker. I began submitting applications here, there, and everywhere, and getting nowhere. One day I was standing in front of Carnegie Hall, just looking at it. I wanted to take a peek inside so I went around to the back and slipped in through the Stage Door. It's hard to believe but in those pre-security days you could walk in any place. I got through the Stage Door but the door to the actual stage was closed. A man was standing at the door, listening. I went up and listened, too. Someone was singing. The man looked at me and said, 'What are you doing here?' I later discovered that in the music business everyone is suspicious of anyone listening to anything. If you go to a performance it's 'why are you here?' Of course it couldn't be because you like music.

"'I'm just standing in Carnegie Hall and looking for a job,' I told him.

'What kind of a job?'

## SAMUEL RAMEY: American Bass

'Any job in the music business.'

"The guy stared at me for a minute or so then he took out piece of paper, wrote something on it, and handed the paper to me. It was the address of a building down the street. He told me to go there and to ask for 'Arthur Judson.' 'Tell him Tony Russo sent you.' So I went down the street, walked into the building, and asked for Arthur Judson. They sent me up to an office. I walked in and saw this old man standing at an old-fashioned roll top desk.

'Who are you?' he asked.

'I'm Tom Graham and I just met Tony Russo at Carnegie Hall. He told me to come here and ask for you.'

'Why?'

'I'm looking for a job in music.'

"Judson questioned me about myself and I answered truthfully, that is to say I made no bones about knowing absolutely nothing about the music business. I guess he liked my forthrightness.

'Well, Tom,' he said, 'here's what you should do. Go down the street to Columbia Artists Management and tell them you want an interview. They'll give it to you. One thing, though, don't mention my name.'

"I went down the street and into the Columbia Artists building. I filled out an application and was interviewed. I was told I was too young, didn't have enough experience, and so on and so forth. I didn't know what it was that I didn't have enough experience in, but I didn't expect anything to come of it, anyway. Even so, I left my application and went home. Eventually, I had to take a job, any job, in order to stay in New York, so I entered an executive training program at the Chemical Bank. I wasn't there long when I got a call from CAMI to come over for an interview. I went and kind of talked my way into a position by saying I'd do whatever I had to do. I came home and told my wife that I was leaving the bank and going to work at Columbia Artists Management.

'What's that?' she inquired.

'I'm not sure,' I replied.

'How much are they paying you?'

'I was afraid to ask.'

"On my first day at CAMI I picked up people at the airport, shuffled papers around, and, in general, made a nuisance of myself. This pattern continued for a while until I started getting a few somewhat more challenging assignments. I knew absolutely nothing about music management but I learned and worked my way up to a managerial position. I also found out about my benefactors, Tony Russo and Arthur Judson. Judson was a founder of the company that eventually became Columbia Artists Management. He was part of a purge in the early sixties and he and a few cohorts went on to create their own management firm, Judson, O'Neill, Beal and Steinway. Tony Russo was a manager who worked for CAMI, then for Judson, O'Neill, et al, then back to CAMI and finally to ICM. Arthur Judson was a big name in the music business. You almost could say he put the 'business' into the music business. And to think I simply lucked into meeting him because I sneaked into Carnegie Hall.

"In 1973, I moved to London and became CAMI's European connection. London was then the capitol of the classical music-recording world and for a very good reason, money. Although recordings were made in America, it was expensive and the choice of singers was limited. In London you had your choice of major orchestras and singers from the Continent. Generally speaking the big opportunities were overseas. That's where I came into the picture regarding Samuel Ramey. Matthew Epstein sent word that Sam would be in Europe and asked if I could arrange auditions for him. I was glad to do it. I liked working with Matthew. He was helpful, supportive, and cooperative, a really good colleague, which was more the norm then than it is now—at least in my opinion. So, Sam arrived, or I should say, Sam and Carrie arrived. In those days, it was 'SamandCarrie,' never just Sam. Whenever we got together, he was pleasant and polite but Carrie did most of the talking. Carrie was okay, though, and I don't think anyone had anything negative to say about her. I set up an audition for Sam at Glyndebourne and also arranged for another in the Crush Bar at Covent Garden. Glyndebourne immediately hired him for the next season. He didn't get any opera engagements out of the Crush Bar audition but Erik Smith, head of Artists and Repertoire at Phillips Records, was there and liked what he heard. It was through Erik that Sam got his first recording contracts."

Sam credits Erik Smith, "the producer of choice" in the glory days of classical recordings, with giving his career a jumpstart. In the 1950s, Smith was one of those men behind the scenes who transformed the recording industry. The son of composer/conductor Hans Schmidt-Isserstedt, Smith was born in Rostock, Germany in 1931. Five years later, his Jewish mother fled Nazi Germany with Erik and his brother in tow. They settled in England, where Erik's father later joined them. Smith became a naturalized citizen. He had graduated from Cambridge and, fluent in German, French, and Italian, Smith took a job with an avant-garde music publisher in postwar Vienna. He then switched careers and joined Decca where he began producing stereo recordings. His first effort was the complete *Peter Grimes* with Peter Pears recreating his stage role and with the composer, Benjamin Britten, conducting. Smith's career took him to Europe where he made a *Boheme* with Tebaldi and Bergonzi, which, like the *Peter Grimes*, became a classic. Later, he was one of the principal forces behind the acclaimed Solti recording of *The Ring Cycle*. In 1966, in an unprecedented move, Smith and his entire Decca team were "borrowed" by CBS to record *Falstaff* with Leonard Bernstein conducting the Vienna Philharmonic. And, in 1968, Smith went to Philips where he was artistic director of its classical division for over two decades. Erik Smith died in 2004 by which time the industry he had helped to create was moribund. But in the days when classical music was big business, his was one of the biggest names.

While Sam did establish a strong beachhead the summer of 1974, a year would pass before he actually appeared on a European stage. In the interim, City Opera remained his artistic home. During the 1975 spring season, Sam was covering Richard Gill in *Boheme* while Gill was covering Robert Hale in *Puritani* and *Anna Bolena*. Hale became ill and Gill was put into the *Puritanis* and *Bolenas*. Meanwhile, rehearsals were going on for *Boheme*. With Gill occupied, Sam took over the role of Colline but just for the rehearsals. The upshot? When the conductor, Giuseppe Morelli, discovered that the young bass with whom he was rehearsing, would not be singing the performances, he immediately went to the front office. "It's not right," Morelli protested. "That young man is doing all the rehearsals and he's terrific. He should be given the performances." Morelli presented Sam's case well enough for the powers-that-be to decide that Gill was perhaps too busy with his other roles. Sam sang the Colline. "I honestly didn't know why I was put into the *Boheme* but I was grateful for the opportunity. I found out later that Maestro Morelli got me that chance." That summer, Sam went to see an opera production at the Caramoor Festival in Westchester, New York. A smiling young woman came over and introduced herself. Her name was Joyce Arbib and she was Matthew Epstein's new assistant. Later, when Epstein left CAMI, Arbib became Sam's manager and represented him until her retirement in May of 1998. Arbib, as ardent a supporter of her clients as her predecessor, holds a special place in the chronicles of Columbia Artists Management. In May 1998, she resigned from her position of manager and entered a convent.

In the summer of 1976, Sam made his European stage debut as Figaro in the Glyndebourne production of Mozart's *Marriage of Figaro*. Since 1934, Glyndebourne, in East Sussex, England, has been home to a renowned summer opera festival. The manor house dates back to pre-Elizabethan times and from the mid-nineteenth century was the home of the Christie family. In 1920 John Christie came into full possession of the estate. He added a music room, which housed one of the largest pipe organs in the British Isles. Amateur opera evenings frequently were held in the "organ" room. After Christie married Audrey Mildmay, a singer, the little opera soirees went professional, and a modern 300-seat theatre, complete with an orchestra pit, was built onto the existing music room. Three exiles from Nazi Germany were hired to run the place, Fritz Busch, as conductor, Carl Ebert, as artistic director, and, as general manager, Rudolf Bing. Bing remained there until he went to the Metropolitan Opera in 1949.[5] The original idea was to mimic the Wagner festival in Bayreuth, but Glyndebourne opted for Mozart operas, which were more suited to the theatre's intimate scale. Gradually, the theatre was enlarged and improved and, by the late 1970s, the seating capacity had grown to 850. During World War II, productions ceased when the house became an evacuation center for London children; after the War, the Festival resumed. In 1952, the Glyndebourne Festival Society was formed to handle the company's financial management and when John Christie died in 1962, his son, George, took over. In 1994, a completely new 1,200-seat theatre was inaugurated with a production of Mozart's *Marriage of Figaro*, the same opera that had opened Glyndebourne's first season sixty years before to the very day. Part of Glyndebourne's draw is its unique schedule as well as its charming setting. Performances begin in the afternoon and, after a long interval, during which attendees eat in restaurants or dine al fresco on the extensive and beautiful grounds, resume in the early evening. Once

---

[5] In 1983, in a conversation with the author, Carl Ebert's daughter confirmed a long-circulated rumor that when Bing was being considered for the position of General Manager, he put his name at the top of Ebert's curriculum vitae and sent it to the Metropolitan Opera

most famous for its Mozart presentations, the festival's repertoire has burgeoned to include a wide range of operatic works from Janacek's *Cunning Little Vixen* to Gershwin's *Porgy and Bess*, and from a variety of Handelian opuses to Stravinsky's *Rake's Progress*. In the last named, Sam sang his first Nick Shadow, which became one of his most distinctive roles. Over the years, Samuel Ramey became a familiar presence at Glyndebourne.

"I sang Figaro at my Glyndebourne debut and I'll never forget it. On opening night, at the end of the first act, I started the aria *non pui andrai* completely unaware that I was singing in English. I'd always sung Figaro in English at City Opera but Glyndebourne's production was in Italian. It was my first time doing it in the original language and I guess my concentration went south for a moment. I was able to switch after a couple of phrases but it was a close call. Despite my gaffe I did okay and I began a happy association with the festival. Glyndebourne was a fabulous place to work; it was like something out of a picture book of stately English homes, while combining aspects of Central City and Santa Fe, in a bit more sophisticated way. The place has been completely redone since I first appeared there. Back then, part of the theatre had been the old stables and there were still bats in the rafters. No matter what the opera they'd fly out and at any given moment you could have three or four of them circling above you. They kind of fit in with the graveyard scene in *The Rake's Progress* but were very out of place in Count Almaviva's gracious home. The funny thing is no matter how many bats were soaring, you had to keep performing. Eventually, you got used to them. I did, anyway. Other singers were less stoical. During one *Figaro* performance, Michael Devlin was singing Almaviva. He had just started the big dramatic recitative at the end of the third act when a bat did a nosedive right into him. Devlin froze. He just stood there with his mouth open. Bats and all, I sang at Glyndebourne for three straight summers, the

*Figaro* in 1976, then the wonderful Hockney production of *The Rake's Progress* in 1977 and in 1978. In the same year, I also sang in Hamburg and in Amsterdam. I was making a name for myself, for sure, but on the other side of the Atlantic. At home, I still hadn't been able to cross the Lincoln Center quadrangle to the Met. Somewhere in the back of my mind, I'm sure I was pinning my hopes on City Opera's *Mefistofele* to bring me to the Met's attention, another reason for me to score big in the role. I really wanted to pull it off so in the fall of 1976 when Matthew called to say that he had found an opportunity for me to do it before New York, I jumped at the chance. *Mefistofele* was such a performance rarity, I immediately asked Matthew where and when it was going to be done.

'Bob Jones University,' he replied, 'in March.'

'Bob Jones University?'

'Right.'

"I didn't know that much about Bob Jones University except that it was a Fundamentalist Christian school in Greenville, South Carolina. I was amazed to discover that every year the university brought in professional singers and used their own chorus and orchestra to put on an opera. The truth is I would have gone anywhere for a chance to try out *Mefistofele*. I went to Greenville and really wasn't prepared for what I found at Bob Jones U. It was like stepping into another world, really bizarre. The security was awesome; going onto the campus was like entering a fort. The place was totally self-sustained, an entity unto itself. They had their own farms where they raised cattle and produce. And even though it was 1976, they still had 'dating parlors' and 'chaperones.' Somehow Bob Jones University managed to avoid the 1960s. I was well treated but, most important, it gave me an opportunity to get into the role. It was a great help to perform *Mefistofele* before an audience. I was primed for opening night in New York on August 31, 1977."

Samuel Ramey was now a breath away from being

crowned the New York State Theatre's leading bass. Each of the Treigle-stamped roles he took on, Mephistopheles, Don Giovanni, Figaro, and the four Hoffman baddies, pushed him onward, and when he assumed the role of Mefistofele, his name would lead all the rest. Strangely, considering Sam's eventual success in *Mefistofele*, Edgar Vincent cautioned him against it. He told Sam that Pinza regretted doing the part. "It's a voice killer, Edgar," complained the redoubtable Italian bass, "and I wish I never had sung it." Vincent never forgot Ezio Pinza's statement and was wary about everything, until Sam actually sang the part. At that point, the publicist was happy to capitulate. "I was concerned because of what Pinza had said but I didn't need to worry. Sam has two different kinds of techniques and voices, one is the coloratura bass, and the other is the heldenbass or whatever you want to call it. He has this incredible high and yet never lost the low so he was able to gobble up roles that stymied others, even Pinza. Sam knew exactly where to put the notes and *Mefistofele* became his calling card." In Edgar Vincent's opinion Sam found the key to Mefistofele and the key was in not letting it kill him.

"I have to say I had a pretty good success with *Mefistofele*. I was fortunate that the director didn't insist that I copy what Norman Treigle had done, which allowed me to fit the role to my strengths rather than his. I found out later that I had Julius Rudel to thank. He was behind the scenes making sure that I got out from under Norman's shadow. Much as I admired Treigle's performance, I wanted to work out pieces of my own 'business' that would put my Mefistofele in a league with his. At the end of the opera, when Mefistofele exits, Treigle would flail about wildly as he went into the wings, and it was very effective. I wanted to come up with something as good but different. I experimented a bit and then decided to lie down on the floor and roll off. That was pretty damn effective, too. I do think I put my mark on the role but I have to admit that I also put my foot in my mouth, big time.

"In those days, *The New York Times* ran a little column that featured stories about up-and-coming stars from the theatre and the concert stage. If someone made a big splash and was not well known, they'd do a piece. Well, I splashed in *Mefistofele* and I wasn't that well known so they decided to do a story on me. In the article, Robert Berkvist wrote that I sang the part 'beautifully,' had measured 'up to the memory of the Treigle characterization,' and made my 'own light shine through Mr. Treigle's shadow.' So far, so good, right? I was further quoted as saying that I knew comparisons would be made but that I was going to approach the role in my own way, which would be far less acrobatic than Mr. Treigle's famous physical contortions. *My* overall concept emphasized the elegance of the devil and I was more concerned about the vocal and musical aspects. So far, I was still okay. I came a cropper when my quote concluded with, 'Without, I hope, sounding egotistical, I do feel I sing it better than Mr. Treigle did, although he, of course, was famous for his acting in the role.' So help me, I wasn't trying to detract from Norman Treigle. I was just being honest. And, I wasn't the only one who believed that his interpretation was performance rather than musically driven. I didn't realize that my quote could be interpreted as a put down. It certainly wasn't meant that way. On the other hand I have to say there was only *one* way to interpret the extrapolated quote printed in the caption below a large photo of me in devil make-up. It read: *"I do feel I sing it better than Norman Treigle did."* Oh boy, did I hear about this. I became the anti-Christ for real! I got letters and phone calls from strangers as well as from my colleagues at the City Opera. Patricia Brooks let me have it, and Suzanne Marsee told me I should never have said what I said. My only excuse is, and I don't even know if I need to make an excuse, I was brought up to say what I felt, not what I felt other people wanted to hear. Like everything else, the Treigle/

Ramey thing finally died down and I just continued to do what I did best, sing.

"After the *Mefistofele,* I was sailing along at the City Opera and doing my stuff in Europe where, I have to say, I was beginning to be kind of a big deal. The European opera fans were much more hardcore, and very knowledgeable. They made a fuss about opera singers. Really, we were treated like rock stars. I liked it. Because I was so well known internationally, everyone assumed that I was a star of the Metropolitan Opera. People were shocked when I told them that I was a member of the New York City Opera and had never sung at the Met. A lot of them just didn't believe me. It was around this time that I'd also started my recording career, thanks to Erik Smith who heard me in the Crush Bar. In the summer of 1976, I recorded *I Due Foscari* with Jose Carreras and Katia Ricciarelli for Philips. A little later that summer, I did Angelotti on a *Tosca* recording with Carreras and Montserrat Caballe. And, at the end of the summer, I did a *Lucia* also with Caballe and Carreras. (I really enjoyed working with Jose. Not only did I do my first recordings with him, we also sang together at City Opera. He was, perhaps, my favorite tenor.) Three recordings in three months, but that wasn't unusual in those days. One recording that I did *was* unusual, and it happened in London in the late seventies. I was contracted to do Sparafucile in *Rigoletto* with Sills, Sherrill Milnes, and Alfredo Kraus for EMI. Well the guy singing Monterone, a smallish role, fell ill so they asked me to do it. And I did, and I got two credits on the cast list. The industry was in high gear then, and I loved making records. It's a bit of a different feeling when you know you're singing for 'posterity' rather than the moment. I especially remember one recording "for the ages," a *Don Giovanni* for DeutscheGrammaphon. It was memorable because the conductor was Herbert von Karajan for whom I later sang the Don in Salzburg. I got to Karajan through his assistant, Uli Merkle. Merkle attended a concert version of *Semiramide* that I did in Hamburg with Horne and Caballe. Karajan was in the market for a Don Giovanni and I impressed Merkle enough for him to tell the maestro about me. I was asked to send Karajan a tape. I sent it and then got word he wanted me to audition. I was on my way from New York to London for another recording session when I got the call, so I went right on to Salzburg to meet with Karajan. I didn't even have the whole score of *Don Giovanni* with me, just some arias, and I was about as jet lagged as you could get. Karajan made me sing the entire first scene of the opera and then asked me to do the *Serenade*, which is a killer! I didn't think I sang that well, and was really astounded when Herbert von Karajan told me that I was his *ideal* Don Giovanni.

"That DG *Giovanni* was memorable for many reasons. Before the recording even began the entire cast was flown to Salzburg for *piano* rehearsals with the Maestro. Just sitting there working with him was one of the greatest experiences I've ever had. As a conductor he was unique. It sort of happened with him. He didn't stop and tell you what he wanted, he did it all with his hands, you could tell what he was after just by the way he moved them. I can only describe what he elicited from his fingers as a kind of poetry. He had a tough reputation but I loved working with Karajan and found him to be a delightful gentleman. While he holds a special place for me, Karajan wasn't the only maestro who impressed me; there were lots of them. Georg Solti, for instance, was extremely important in my career. I was a comparative unknown when he hired me to sing Figaro for his Decca recording in the early Eighties. I know that a lot of people, including the record producers themselves, were asking, 'Ramey? Figaro? Who's this Ramey?' Even when I showed up on von Karajan's *Don Giovanni* most people still didn't know who the hell I was. Soon enough I 'caught on.' I began doing stuff with important conductors like Muti, Patane, Scimone, Pretre, Chailly, Maazel, Mariner, Ozawa,

Bonynge, Colin Davis, Sinopoli, Previn, Abbado, and, of course, Rudel. Every one of them was great to work with, no kidding. I really didn't do a lot of opera with Abbado, just one, but that one was quite some thing. Although Musicologists knew about Rossini's *Il viaggio a Reims*, it had been lost for the longest time. Philip Gossett found it in the most extraordinary way. Phil goes to Rome every summer to do research and the people in the library know that he's always on the lookout for anything pertaining to Rossini. One summer, he was working away when a librarian came over. "We found this and we thought it might be of interest to you," she said, and she dropped a pile of yellowed papers on the table in front of him. In looking through them, Phil discovered that it was all this material that Rossini had done for *Viaggio*. What a moment. *Viaggio a Reims* is a strange work. It's really not an opera. I mean it doesn't have a story line. It's a series of arias patched together. Phil believes that it was something that Rossini assembled to show off his favorite singers. Our *Viaggio* premiered at Pesaro and from there we took it to La Scala and Vienna where we did a semi staged concert version with the Berlin Philharmonic. For a quirky piece, *Viaggio* turned out to be a very popular work.

"I worked a lot with Ricardo Muti. He's quite a guy and a terrific conductor. He's so intimidating it was difficult to get comfortable with him. He gets this air of extreme confidence and everybody thinks of him as being pompous and arrogant. Well, there is a bit of arrogance and he has a right to it because he's fantastic. At La Scala, musical rehearsals were held in the Yellow Room, which contains a big conference table. During rehearsals everybody sat around the table with Muti at one end. There were hours and hours of musical preparation and I loved every minute of it. I'd like to say that Muti and I became friends over the years and I hope he feels the same. I knew Lenny Bernstein pretty well; we saw each other a lot in Salzburg but only socially, at parties. I worked with him just once, at a Carnegie Hall AIDS Benefit. Later, I got to work with Jimmy Levine, another genius. What I most enjoy about working with Jimmy is the manner in which he puts everything together. After a rehearsal he always has a note session where he gathers the artists around the piano. He goes through the score and gives each of us particulars on our individual parts. It's illuminating because of his insights into the music.

"In more recent times I've had the opportunity to work with Valery Gergiev. I did *Boris* with him at the Met in the 1997/98 season and while his technique is a little strange, he brings out a special something, especially in the Russian repertoire. Right after the *Boris,* he invited me to St. Petersburg where the Maryinsky Theatre was honoring Chaliapin. I'm not sure what the actual event was but I have a feeling it might have been the hundredth anniversary of Chaliapin's first appearance on the Maryinsky stage. It was an all-bass concert; there must have been sixteen of us and I was the only non-Russian. I swear those Russians can go so low it makes the rest of us sound like mezzos. They must have vocal cords the size of fingers. After the concert, we had a reception upstairs in the theatre. Except for Paata Burcheladze, most of the singers didn't speak much English, but with all the vodka that was flowing we seemed to understand each other pretty well.

"In the early years of my career I was dubbed 'the darling of conductors' and it kind of stuck. I'm pretty sure it was because I didn't make waves, not because I was the greatest singer in the world. I have to say, whatever the reason, looking back at that list of conductors impresses even me. I'm always struck by how different things were then, especially in the recording industry. I was privileged to be a part of that industry for a good long time. It was especially thrilling at the beginning of my career because I got the opportunity to work with a number of great singers before I got to actually appear opposite them on stage. I wasn't a novice when I recorded *Norma* with Joan Sutherland, Montserrat Caballe and Luciano Pavarotti; still, to be in the presence of those giants was something else. I also had a chance to sing the role of Oroveso, an opportunity I never had in the theatre. I only appeared on stage with Sutherland once, in *Puritani,* so it was a real pleasure to be able to record with her. Caballe and I worked together a few times. We did that famous *Semiramide* in Aix en Provence and we also were in a few concert versions of it. I have to tell you about Caballe, she's a great singer, and a real character. During a rehearsal break in Hamburg where we were doing one of those *Semiramide* concerts, Montserrat and I were chatting. I knew the Aix production that we'd done together had been taken to Avignon and that she sang with a bunch of other singers. I said, 'Montserrat, how did the Aix production in Avignon go?' You have to understand that Caballe never felt that she really was good in *Semiramid*e, which of course she was. And when I asked the question she beamed and cried, 'Oh Sam, can you imagine, I was the best one!'

"I appeared with Luciano a few times and he, too, was amazing. But I have to say something; great as he was I always had the impression that he was not that concerned with what was going on around him. He seemed to be more concerned about his voice and his performance and wasn't really into camaraderie. Again, that was my impression. I may have read it the wrong way and, let's face it, however I felt about him, nothing can take anything away from his glorious singing. On the other hand, Placido Domingo is great to work with, both as a singer on stage and as a conductor in the pit. I sang under his baton early in his conducting career when he came to City Opera for a *Tosca*. I was Angelotti, not Scarpia. Placido had been singing with the Met for a while but he made a deal with City Opera that he would come and sing one or two performances *if* they would let him conduct. So he wound up being one of the few, if not the only artist, who had a foot in each house.

Okay, back to that *Norma* recording, which I think was the first time Sutherland and Caballe had recorded together.

"At the first session, I arrived early, and then Joan arrived. A bit later, Montsie walked in carrying a big bouquet, which she brought over and presented to Joan, complete with a curtsy. Joan took the bouquet and said, 'Oh, flowers for the prima donna." Montsie stepped back, flashed a big smile, and said, 'Ah no. Flowers FROM the prima donna.' You can't beat moments like that. As far as 'unbeatable' moments, here's another. In the mid-Eighties I got a call from Simon Estes. 'Sam,' he said, 'I was supposed to do a recording of *Porgy and Bess* with the Cleveland Orchestra but I can't. I suggested that you do the title role.' I really liked the idea and for a while it looked as though it might happen. Then, the record company decided that it wouldn't be quite right for me to be the only White singer. I remember thinking that it would be nice if someday it could work both ways and not matter at all.

"It took a while for my records to catch on in the States and for a time it was easier to get them in Europe. Vicki Secrest, whom I knew from Colby, was in Paris in the late 70s and dropped in to Fernac's, an enormous music store, where every genre had its own room. Vicki went to the classical section and asked for anything with Samuel Ramey. The clerk's face lit up. 'Ah oui, Samuel Rameeee.' He took her to a section with stacks of my recordings. Vicki bought a whole bunch and lugged them home. Quite a contrast to what was happening here. If you went to a record store in the States around that time and mentioned my name, you'd have gotten a blank stare. I'm happy to say things changed. Pretty soon, you didn't have to go to such lengths. My recordings began selling in America. That was then. Now, things really have changed. It's mind boggling to think what happened to the recording industry. It was such a vibrant and vital part of the music world; it's hard to believe it dried up. I feel damn lucky to have been around when it was in full swing.

"As far as stage appearances I continued to do very well in Europe. Tom Graham told me that he could tell how big I'd gotten just by the way the opera houses contacted him. Instead of saying: 'We're doing *Faust*, is Sam free,' it became, 'when can we have Sam Ramey and what would he like to do?' Yep, in Europe my career was moving along nicely but I was still no closer to the Metropolitan Opera than that old *Trojans* cattle call. And that was kind of a thorn in my side. The Met ignored me, but I was riding high at City Opera, high enough for my counsel to be sought on a very important company issue. One evening I was invited to dinner at the home of David Lloyd Jacobs, a prominent board member. At the end of the evening we were sitting around talking when, out of the blue, John Samuels, another board member, asked me a question. 'Sam, what do you think would be the reaction if Beverly Sills were to become the General Director of the City Opera?' I said I thought it would be a great idea to have a singer running an opera company. Now I'm not saying it's because of me that Beverly Sills was offered the job; I'm just saying I was glad I could give my friend and colleague a 'recommendation.' Bev took over the general directorship in 1980 and she did a helluva job running the company. When you think about it, I was a lucky guy to work under the leadership of two wonderful people, Julius Rudel and Beverly Sills. One of my great regrets was not being able to participate in the gala they had when Bev retired from singing. I had a prior engagement and that was that. Being a performer herself, Bev understood that we can't always be where our hearts want us to be. I know she'd have smiled and said, 'It's okay, Sam.' The same damn thing happened at her memorial, in July 2007. I couldn't get to the Met because I was singing somewhere else. Again, I could see Bev smiling and saying, 'Don't worry, kid, I know you wanted to be here. It's fine, really it is.' I miss that lady a lot. She was absolutely one of a kind.

"My goal when I came to New York was the City Opera. My teacher had been there and it became my designated destination. I'd achieved my goal. I loved the place especially the philosophy, a repertory company doing a lot of different repertoire. But I'd be a liar if I didn't say that once I became aware of the big picture, I kept looking out of the corner of my eye at the Met. Let's face it, the Metropolitan Opera was (is) *the* goal. As the saying goes "a cat may look at the king." In my case I could stare as much as I wanted, but the Met's gaze was fixed elsewhere. I'd heard things about the Met's policy that seemed to verify my feelings of being shunned. I was a big star at City Opera so why should the Met hire me if people could see me next door? In other words, who would pay to see the kid around the block when they could see him around the block? In my dumb way, I figured that because I'd achieved success at the City Opera and in Europe, there should be a place for me at the Met. It was naïve thinking, I guess, but that's the way I saw it. No matter how I saw it, though, for a very long time it was a cat and mouse game between the Metropolitan and me.

"That's not to say there weren't some overtures. Periodically, Matthew would call and say 'Jimmy Levine wants to hear you on the stage of the Met.' So, I'd go over and audition. I remember at least two such occasions. I also auditioned for Jimmy at Carnegie Hall. Nothing happened. Then, when I was in Glyndebourne in 1977, Matthew called to say that the Met had made me an offer. They wanted me to sing Escamillo in *Carmen*. Sounds great, but it wasn't. For one thing, I already was signed up for a bunch of *Bohemes* in San Francisco not to mention the fact that, at the time, Escamillo wasn't a part I'd had much success in. To top it off, it was in a second cast of *Carmen*, hardly an auspicious setting for a debut. Matthew and I talked it over. We both felt I'd eventually get to the Met but we wanted it to be in the right vehicle. I was tempted but we turned it down. Believe me, there were so many times afterward, especially when nothing much was happening, when I'd think, 'Aw, I should've done that Escamillo. If I had, I'd have been a regular at the Met and singing all the time.' Doublethink, hindsight, I went through it all. The truth is, I was damn lucky I didn't do it, and I have Matthew to thank. I relied on his judgment and he was right to urge me to decline. Those are the times when a manager can make the difference between a good career and a great career. Marilyn Horne wasn't far off the mark when she said that as far as my career, "Matthew was the one!' Eventually, I did sing Escamillo at the Met and because I waited till I really got into the role, it was the success that it never would have been the first time around.

"After the second cast *Carmen* episode, the Met did get back to me with an offer to debut as Sparafucile in *Rigoletto*. It's a fun part, he's an assassin for hire, but he's a secondary character and I already had been doing lead roles. Why would I want to come in as a comprimario? What's more the *Rigoletto* was one of those matinee student performances when busloads of kids are brought in to see what opera's about. It was a wonderful opportunity for the kids but not such a wonderful debut opportunity for me. We turned it down.

"My relationship with the Metropolitan Opera House remained status quo for an awfully long time. Who knows how long the stalemate might have gone on? In fact, if it hadn't been for Marilyn Horne I might have suffered the same fate as Norman Treigle.

SAMUEL RAMEY: American Bass

# Well Met

However chafed he felt by the Metropolitan Opera's indifference, the repeated rebuffs put Samuel Ramey in illustrious company. Sam was slighted for a mere decade but for its one hundred year existence the Metropolitan had spurned the operatic works of George Frideric Handel, the musical genius Beethoven called "the greatest composer who ever lived." To be fair, in Handel's case there were mitigating circumstances. His elaborate *opera seria* were out of favor at the time the Metropolitan opened its doors. Nevertheless, after baroque opera made an astounding comeback nearly a century later, the Met continued to dawdle. The New York City Opera presented *Julius Caesar* in 1968. It was not until the Met's centennial season of 1983/84 that the august company would right an old wrong to a great composer and embrace, at last, a great contemporary singer.

On January 19, 1984, G. F. Handel and Samuel Ramey made their Metropolitan operatic debuts together. The catalyst for this momentous occasion was Marilyn Horne who, like Sam, long had suffered the Met's apathy. For years she had been offered a succession of less than stellar debut opportunities, none of which would she accept. Enter Joan Sutherland. The Australian superstar was scheduled to appear during the 1970 season in the role of Bellini's Norma, and requested Horne as her co-star. Despite General Manager Rudolf Bing's initial refusal, he famously cracked, "To my knowledge Miss Sutherland is not in charge of casting," Dame Joan's 'request' carried the necessary wallop. Marilyn

Horne debuted in the role of Adalgisa and for the next two decades reigned as the acknowledged queen of the baroque and bel canto repertoire. From that exalted position she was able to do for Sam Ramey what Joan Sutherland had done for her, with an initial assist from Matthew Epstein. In the fall of 1979, Epstein, aware that Horne was seeking a bass capable of handling the tricky coloratura part of Mustafa for an upcoming recording of Rossini's *L'Italianna in Algeri*, brought her to a City Opera performance of Rossini's *Le Comte d'Ory* in which Sam was appearing. Everything went according to plan. Marilyn Horne found her bass, as well as a future colleague and life-long friend, and, thanks to his manager, Sam made the all-important Horne/Ramey connection. Matthew Epstein engineered that serendipitous mezzo/bass match-up, even as he fought to get his client into the Metropolitan Opera House.

"I was quite an aggressive salesman when I was a managing agent and really pushing Sam. Because of the Treigle situation there was a glut of roles for him to do at the City Opera and that kept him busy. Meanwhile, I was on the lookout for people who could influence his career, and I found them. I brought Gerard Mortier to the City Opera to hear Sam and out of that came Sam's first contracts in Hamburg. I introduced Sam to Bernard Lefort who was running the Aix-en-Provence festival, and that resulted in a memorable *Semiramide*. And, of course, there was Glyndebourne where he made his first European appearances. We developed relationships in San Francisco, Chicago, and Houston. His recording career started and he was busy, busy, busy. He took to everything like a duck to water especially the European work, which he really loved. He even did some "crazy stuff" like learning *Hoffman* in German for a production in Amsterdam. But he was willing to do it and, in a funny way, glad to do it. By the late 1970s, he was very well known internationally and still, the Met wouldn't budge.

"Basically, they had enough basses. They had James

Morris, an exceedingly talented young American who was moving up in the same repertoire as Sam, and Paul Plishka, who was moving up in the heavier, darker, repertoire. Plus, the Met was bringing in world singers like Ghiaurov and Raimondi, not to mention the fact that Siepi and Jose van Dam were still active. So, if you think about it, they didn't need Sam. To tell the truth, had I been in the Met's position I probably wouldn't have hired Sam, either. However, since they were enough aware of him to offer him secondary roles, I found it surprising that someone didn't come forward and say, he's got real potential, so let's bring him in on an appropriate level. Joan Ingpen, the Met's Artistic Administrator, knew Sam from the Paris Opera where she'd been director of planning in the mid-1970s. She'd engaged him to sing Colline in Paris and was pleased with his work. Colline was an important role for Sam in those days. He sang it in San Francisco and Chicago and during one season he did 56 performances of *Boheme*. It got to the point where if you woke him up he'd start singing *vecchia zimarra*. There are those who think Joan Ingpen blocked American singers from the Met but I think the prejudice lay more with Ingpen's predecessor. I know she thought well of Sam and my guess is she just couldn't find enough wiggle room at the Met."

Epstein exonerates Joan Ingpen yet others, close to the situation, remain convinced that she disdained the young American bass, and was not shy about expressing her scorn. One of those others was at the opening of *Attila* at the State Theatre. Standing in the lobby during the intermission, he overheard the following exchange as an enthusiastic member of the audience rushed over to Joan Ingpen, crying,

"Oh, isn't Sam Ramey wonderful!"

"He's okay for this house," smiled Ingpen, ".... not the Met."

It was further alleged that when one of Sam's inner circle tried to connect the singer with the big house, Ingpen cut him off saying, "Listen, I'm busy trying to get Raimondi, I don't have time for this." Once in a while, the Met was called to account for its anti-Sam stance. On one of those occasions, Beverly Sills ran interference. She was hosting a Lincoln Center gala of stars for an AIDS benefit. In looking over the program, she noticed that while the Met had a number of artists on the program no one from City Opera was scheduled. Sills called the planning committee and insisted that Sam Ramey and Diana Soviero be included. When her request was denied Sills announced that they had better start looking for another host. It was a pure and simple case of blackmail. Beverly Sills was a major draw, no one could bring in the people and the money the way she could. Ramey and Soviero sang.

Continuing its policy of offering roles that were not up to snuff, the Met tendered Sparafucile in some first cast performances of *Rigoletto*. Again, Epstein refused. "Why would Sam go into a part that didn't even have a big aria when he was very busy starring in major roles at City Opera and overseas? Obviously, the Met corporate ego couldn't believe that anyone could be important without them. Anyway, we said a polite 'no, thank you' and we didn't hear another word, nothing. It grew into a bit of an unpleasantness. I became very strong on the subject and was outspoken in my criticism. In my opinion, the Met was missing the boat; no matter how many basses were on the roster, none of them had Sam's special talent. We were at loggerheads, and then came the magical moment in 1984, when Marilyn Horne brought *Rinaldo* to the Met."

Handel's *Rinaldo*, the first Italian opera composed for the London stage, premiered at the Haymarket Theatre on February 24, 1711. Legend has it that during the performance, as recorders in the orchestra busily imitated chirping birds, real birds were released and flew above the audience leaving "their mark not only on the opera and the press, in the persons of Addison and Steele, but on the heads of the audience."⁶ The production featured two prominent castrati, Nicolo Grimaldi and Valentino Urbani, and was very well received, which did not prevent the opera from passing into baroque/bel canto limbo for over two centuries. In 1975, with Frank Corsaro directing and Marilyn Horne in the title role, the Houston Grand Opera presented the American premiere of *Rinaldo*. In 1982, the production went to the National Arts Centre in Ottawa, Canada as part of Festival Ottawa. Horne had it in mind, all along, to bring this production to the Metropolitan Opera as a *fait accompli*, trusting that the Met would grab the opportunity to present a handsomely crafted Handel work. By the mid-1980s, Marilyn Horne and Samuel Ramey had formed a formidable musical alliance. Among other accomplishments they participated, in that seminal production of Rossini's *Semiramide* at Aix-en-Provence (1980). Matthew Epstein had engineered that production because, according to Tom Graham, "he was the only one in the world who knew that opera," an exaggeration that contains a grain of truth. Others may have known the opera but it took a Matthew Epstein to get it produced. The staging, as well as the score, turned the music world on its ear and catapulted Samuel Ramey, in the role of Assur, into the operatic stratosphere. "Assur's mad scene is among my favorites," Sam admits. "I learned something invaluable during that Semiramide run, too. Jackie Horne and I had a conversation about repertoire and I asked her how she figured out whether a role was interesting to do. She said the key for her was to look at the last ten minutes of the opera to see what was happening to her character. After she told me that, I always took the character's final moments into consideration when I looked at new roles. That's the singer's ego thing, 'where's my character at the end of the opera?'"

On many fronts, Aix's *Semiramide* was groundbreaking, and Sam was one of its most important elements.

⁶ E.A. Lovitt, Internet review, 22 Dec. 2007.

At long last, here was a genuine coloratura bass whose technique matched the ornate virtuosity exhibited by Sutherland, Horne, and Caballe. In the early 1980s, Philip Gossett, now on the faculty of the University of Chicago and the University of Rome, became aware of Sam's technical prowess. It was a revelation.

"I'd heard *of* Sam, of course, but I actually heard him for the first time when he did *L'Italiana in Algeri* in Pesaro. It was startling. Suddenly, instead of Mustafa's aria being something you want to get over with as fast as you can, it became the hit of the show. From that moment, we knew that, finally, a Rossini bass had appeared. Up to then, there hadn't been one, period. Some buffo singers did parts Rossini wrote in the bass register, but no one could do what Sam could do. If you listen to recordings of Rossini's serious operas from the 1960s you'll see that the bass parts are all simplified beyond belief. The basses barely sing the notes not to mention feel comfortable in them. For every three notes that Rossini writes they sing maybe one. Sam was the first in the modern era to say, 'It is possible to sing these parts; you just have to develop a certain technique.' That technique was similar to the one that the ladies hadn't quite lost. Actually they had lost it, that is, the very particular way Rossini wanted it sung had been lost. I've never pretended to be an expert in singing per se; I'm just someone who knows a lot about Rossini and historical performance practice. I don't necessarily think that the thickness of the vocal cords is the answer as to why the men lost the ability. Look, it's clear that in Rossini's time there were plenty of singers who could do it. I think the real point is that no one *asked* for the singers to do it. By the time you get to Donizetti and Bellini, the basses aren't singing that kind of thing anymore. And, of course, in Verdi and Puccini, there's nothing like it. You get generations of singers in which all the most up-to-date composers aren't asking them to sing florid music, so they don't train themselves to do it. If the ability had

Grace Irene Mallory and Robert Guy Ramey. Wedding Day, 1918.

The Mallorys. Grandfather John is seated center with Grandmother Fannie Rebecca on his left. Sam's mother, Grace, is standing second from the right. Sam cannot identify the others because, he says, "they were so much older when I knew them."

The Rameys. Grandfather Henry Milton Ramey seated left; Grandmother Rebecca Jane Ramey seated opposite him. Sam's father, Guy, stands far right. Sam met three of his paternal uncles but can identify only Tony, the youngest, held in Rebecca's lap.

Brothers Joe and Leonard, sister Darlene, and proud father Guy stand by as Grace cradles baby Sam. A cast, put on to correct Sam's clubfoot, can be seen on his left leg.

Leonard and his pal Sam Lunsway. Samuel Ramey was named after his brother's close friend and Lunsway remained a positive presence for his namesake.

Leonard holds their baby brother as he, Darlene, and Joe smile at the camera. The age disparity between Sam and his siblings is evident.

Leonard and his wife Idalu.

Darlene and her husband Joe Alcott.

Joe Ramey and his wife Flora.

Rub-a-dub-dub, a future bass in a tub.

Sam got his sea legs early. Years later he would portray a less amiable sailor, the harsh John Claggart in Britten's *Billy Budd*.

Happy School Days in Kansas.

Still smiling. Notice the name "Gene Autry," America's popular Singing Cowboy, on Sam's collar.

Father and son hang out on the back porch in Quinter.

The Rameys of Colby. Sam, Joe, and Leonard standing behind Darlene, Guy, and Grace.

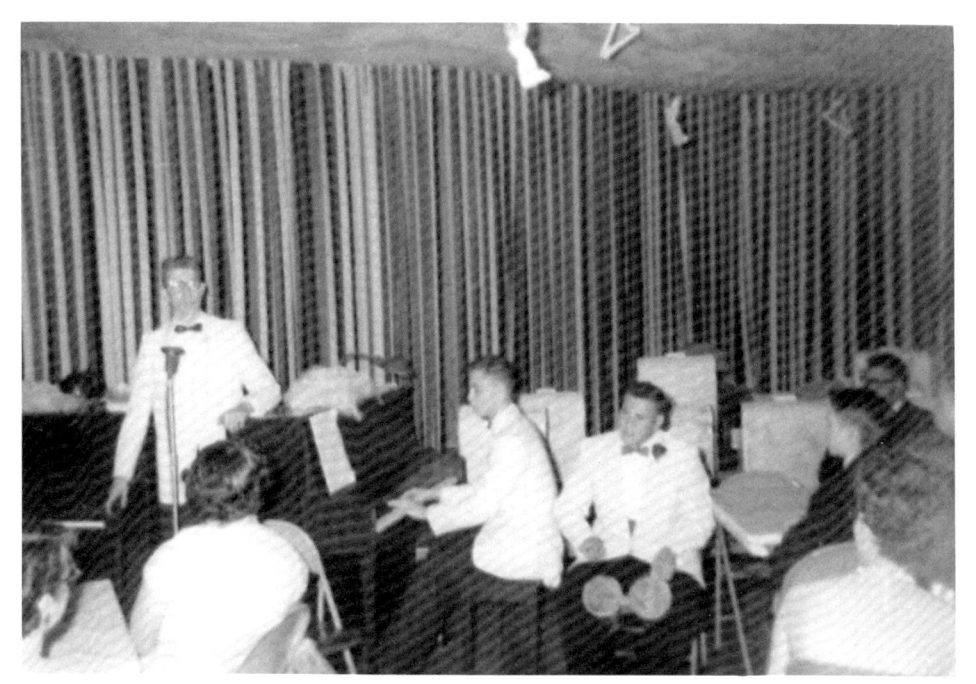

Colby Community High School. Sam, Paul Ackerman, and Phil Harrison formed a trio seen here at their junior prom.

Paul Ackerman and Sam in front of a blackboard at Colby Community High. According to Paul, he was giving Sam some singing tips.

The Colby Community High School Basketball Team. Sam, number 12, is seated second from the right.

Sam in action on the court. His number also jumped, from 12 to 13.

Yearbook graduation photo. Sam sports a popular hairstyle of the day known as the *buzz*, *whiffle*, or *crew*, cut

Sam and his father, Guy, 1944.

Sam and Lindsey Larsen were married on June 29, 2002 at the First Lutheran Church in Sioux Falls, SD. "The happiest day of my life," says Sam. "The second happiest day was May 27, 2003, when my son Samuel Guy was born."

Guy and his father, Sam, 2008.

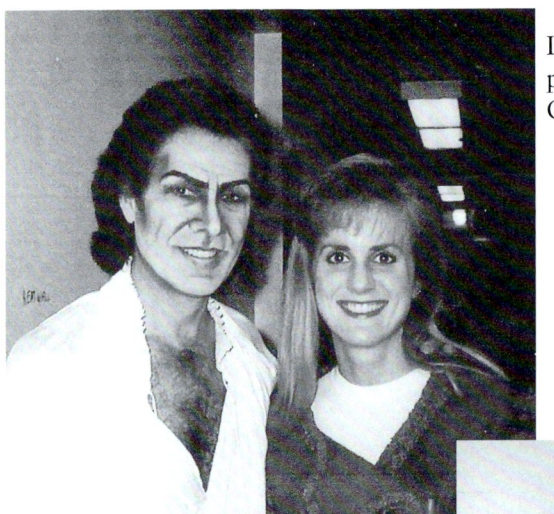

Lindsey and Sam backstage at a performance of *Boris Godunov*. Chicago Lyric Opera, 1994.

Lindsey Ramey and her two devils.

According to Lindsey, "Wherever we were—Chicago, New York, Paris, Barcelona, Rome—Sam commandeered the stroller and pushed Guy around."

A boy and his dog. Guy and Rikke. August 2009. [photo: Lindsey Ramey]

In Verdi's *Falstaff* at Wichita State University. Sir John is the one role Sam regrets not having sung professionally. [photo: the collection of Samuel Ramey]

Wichita State's staging of Britten's *A Midsummer Night's Dream*. Sam, sans donkey head, is Bottom. [photo: the collection of Samuel Ramey]

Mozart's *Don Giovanni* at the Central City Opera. A bewigged Sam stands next to Herbert Beattie (Leporello). Norman Treigle, as the Don, surveys the scene from the balcony. 1963. [photo: Louise Pote/Central City Opera]

Sam had to join the American Guild of Musical Artists when The Little Orchestra Society hired him to sing in the American premiere of Britten's *The Prodigal Son*. The 1968 production marked Sam's first professional appearance in New York City. [photo: the collection of Samuel Ramey]

Sam cannot remember the occasion for this photograph—a rarity for someone with almost total recall of his appearances.

Vicki Bolen, Sam's first wife. The marriage was brief but they remained friends.

March 11, 1973. Sam's New York City Opera (NYCO) debut as Zuniga in *Carmen*. Herman Malamud is Don Jose. According to conductor Julius Rudel, "The intensity of Sam's performance was unbelievable. He sang the role as though Escamillo, the lead bass part, didn't exist, as though the opera was called *Zuniga*, not *Carmen*."
[photo: ©Beth Bergman]

Sam assumed the role of Escamillo at the NYCO in 1976 and sang as though the opera was called *Escamillo*, not *Carmen*. [photo: ©Beth Bergman]

Don Alfonso in Mozart's *Cosi fan Tutte*. NYCO. 1973. [photo: ©Beth Bergman]

Creon in the NYCO production of Cherubini's *Medea*. 1974. [photo: ©Beth Bergman]

In search of a true bel canto, Marilyn Horne went to a performance of Rossini's comic opera *Count Ory*, heard Sam sing the Tutor, and knew immediately that she had found one. NYCO. September 23, 1979. [photo: ©Beth Bergman]

Colline sings goodbye to his overcoat in Puccini's *La Boheme*. Sam appeared so often in the role his manager quipped, "If you woke him from a deep sleep, he'd start singing *vecchio zimara*." NYCO 1977. [photo: ©Beth Bergman]

A scene from Donizetti's *Anna Bolena*. Henry VIII (Sam) in a domestic squabble with Anne Boleyn (Marissa Galvany). Smeton (Hilda Harris), the court musician, looks on. NYCO. 1974. [photo: © Beth Bergman.]

Sam (Basilio), with a clock in his hat, surrounded by Beverly Sills, William Harness, Alan Titus, and Donald Gramm in Rossini's *Barber of Seville*. The NYCO production was borrowed from Sarah Caldwell's Opera Company of Boston. NYCO. 1976. [photo: © Beth Bergman.]

Sam, as Basilio, looms over Beverly Sills, as Rosina, in the Sarah Caldwell/NYCO production of the *Barber*. [photo: the collection of Beverly Sills]

Basilio again, this time with a "Cyranose" twist. NYCO. 1978. [photo: © Beth Bergman.]

Mephistopheles pouring on the charm in Gounod's *Faust*, directed by Frank Corsaro. NYCO. 1974. [photo: © Beth Bergman]

Another view of the Devil in the same *Faust*. Corsaro's version remains Sam's favorite. "I like it because the Devil appeared in a different guise in each act and gave me the chance to do a variety of interpretations." [photo: ©Beth Bergman]

Two views of Sam as the Devil in the 1977 NYCO revival of Boito's *Mefistofele*. Previously, Norman Treigle had owned the role. He, in fact, was so identified with Mefistofele that the opera was dropped from the repertoire after Treigle left the company. Julius Rudel was instrumental in bringing it back for Sam who triumphed in the part. [photos: ©Beth Bergman]

Two more views from *Mefistofele*. The Devil entices Faust (Ermanno Maura) and Margherita (Johanna Meier). NYCO. 1977. [photos:©Beth Bergman]

Sam's first complete role on stage was Doctor Miracle in Offenbach's *Tales of Hoffman* at Wichita State University. He went on to perform all four *Hoffman* villains. In this photograph, the "bad" doctor is exhorting Antonia (June Anderson) to sing. NYCO. 1980. [photo: ©Beth Bergman]

The "four faces of evil:" Lindorf, Coppelius, Dapertutto, and Dr. Miracle. NYCO. 1980. [photo: ©Beth Bergman]

Figaro (Sam) and Susanna (Catherine Malfitano) get together in Mozart's *Marriage of Figaro*. NYCO. 1977. [photo: ©Beth Bergman]

Figaro takes a bow. [photo: Elaine Klein, the collection of Samuel Ramey]

NYCO General Manager Beverly Sills came up with the idea of Sam and Justino Diaz alternating the roles of master and servant in Mozart's *Don Giovanni*. Sam is pictured here as the wily Leporello. NYCO. 1980. [photo: ©Beth Bergman]

Dragged off to Hell by the statue of the Commendatore, the libertine Don (Sam) gets his just desserts. NYCO. 1980. [photo: ©Beth Bergman]

Sam as the blind, old Timor in Puccini's *Turandot*, with Fay Robinson playing the faithful Liu. NYCO. 1975. [photo: ©Beth Bergman]

Sam as another blind, old man, King Archibaldo, in the 1982 NYCO production of Montemezzi's *L'Amore dei Tre Re*. [photo: ©Beth Bergman]

Attila the Hun(k). [photo: the collection of Samuel Ramey]

When Sam became a star of the NYCO, General Manager Beverly Sills gave him the choice of doing whatever opera he wanted. Sam picked Verdi's then obscure *Attila*. For the next decade, Sam performed the role more times than any bass since the original Attila, Ignazio Marini. NYCO. 1981. [photo: ©Beth Bergman]

*Attila* premiered at the Teatro La Fenice in Venice in 1846. The Fenice production in which Sam appeared was based upon sketches from the original sets and costume designs. Linda Roarke-Strummer played the heroine, Odabella. [photo: the collection of Samuel Ramey]

Olin Blitch, the tormented preacher in Carlisle Floyd's *Susanna*. NYCO. 1980. [photo: ©Beth Bergman]

*Susanna* in Geneva, Switzerland. 2000. [photo: Inge Klepitsch]

Sills and Sam in a NYCO production of Bellini's *I Puritani* in Tulsa, OK. The photograph was taken during one of the company's annual tours. [photo: the collection of Beverly Sills]

*I Puritani* again, this time at the Metropolitan Opera House. Joan Sutherland is the beleaguered heroine. 1986. [© photo: Beth Bergman]

Two of Samuel Ramey's staunchest champions, director Frank Corsaro and conductor Julius Rudel. [photo: ©Beth Bergman]

The legendary manager/publicist Edgar Vincent, another of Sam's champions, speaks at Birgit Nilsson's memorial service. Alice Tully Hall. 2006. [photo: ©Beth Bergman]

Sam pouring forth at his dazzling Metropolitan Opera debut in *Rinaldo*. The other debutante that evening was the composer, G. F. Handel. 1984. [photo: ©Beth Bergman]

*Rinaldo* opened in Houston and went to Ottawa, Canada before arriving at the Met. This Ottawa photograph shows Sam's dramatic entrance on a chariot. (That entrance produced an unexpected glitch at the Met opening.) 1982. [photo: Fernand R. Leclair, Ottawa]

Sam, his teacher Armen Boyajian, and Marilyn Horne at the *Rinaldo* premiere in New York City. Horne's dogged determination brought Sam *and* Handel to the Metropolitan Opera House. Boyajian's pedagogic efforts were amply rewarded by his pupil's phenomenal success. [photo: the collection of Samuel Ramey]

Sam's first teacher, Arthur Newman. His studies with Newman at Wichita State formed the basis of Sam's vocal technique

Getting made up as Mephistopheles for a London appearance in *Faust*. 1986. [photo: Donald Southern/Royal Opera House]

A candid shot from his first season with the Rossini Festival in Pesaro, Italy. 1982. [photo: Inge Klepitsch]

In matadorial splendor as Escamillo in *Carmen*. Vienna. 1981. [photo: Inge Klepitsch]

The ebullient Figaro. An early *Marriage of Figaro* appearance in Hamburg, Germany. [photo: the collection of Samuel Ramey]

Marilyn Horne as Arsace and Sam as Assur in Rossini's *Semiramide*. Another bel canto triumph for the mezzo and basso superstars. Metropolitan Opera. 1990. [photo: ©Beth Bergman]

Assur's mad scene, nearly twenty-five minutes of arduous singing and acting. Whenever they performed together in *Semiramide*, Marilyn Horne stood in the wings to watch and listen to this scene. [photo: ©Beth Bergman]

Sam as Rossini's Maometto II, the "most difficult" of all his roles. Pesaro. 1985.
[photo: Tornasole Comunicazione]

*Maometto II*. Standing on the shoulders of two extras and holding on to the hand of another, Sam made a spectacular entrance which still can be seen on YouTube. Pesaro. 1985 [photo: the collection of Samuel Ramey]

Wearing a headache-producing turban as Selim in Rossini's *Il Turco in Italia*. Pesaro. 1983. [photo: the collection of Samuel Ramey]

Sam as Mustafa, Marilyn Horne as Isabella, and Domenico Trimarchi as Taddeo in Rossini's *L'Italiana in Algeri*. Venice. 1981. [photo: the collection of Samuel Ramey]

In 1980 Sam had to decline an offer to debut at the Rossini Festival in *La Gazza Ladra*. He was recording and did not have enough time to learn the role. Nearly a decade later he finally appeared in *La Gazza Ladra*. Pesaro. 1989. [photo: Amati-Bacciardi, the collection of Samuel Ramey]

A soulful portrait of Sam as Colline taken early in his career. [photo: the collection of Samuel Ramey]

Charlton Heston laughed when Sam told the actor that he, too, had played Moses—not for Cecil B. DeMille, but for a Paris Opera production of Rossini's *Moise*. [photo: Jacques Moatti]

While Sam did sing in a concert version of Meyerbeer's *Robert le Diable* for Eve Queler's Opera Orchestra of New York, his one and only stage performance as Bertram took place in Paris in 1985. [photo: Jacques Moatti]

As Lord Sidney in a Teatro alla Scala production of Rossini's opera pastiche, *Il viaggio a Reims*. [photo: Lelli & Magotti/Teatro alla Scala]

Sam appeared as "guest artist" in a new production of Massenet's *Don Quichotte* at the NYCO in 1986. He repeated the role at the Opera National de Paris in 2000. [photo: Inge Klepitsch]

"The Knight of the Sorrowful Countenance." Opera National de Paris, 2000. [photo: Eric Mahoudeau]

Prince Gremin in a German language version of Tchaikovsky's *Eugene Onegin*. Staatsoper, Hamburg. [photo: Hans-Joachim Lieske]

Banquo in Verdi's *Macbeth*. Metropolitan Opera. 1988. [photo: ©Beth Bergman]

Attila amidst a bevy of beauties, one of whom nestles in his lap. Grand Theatre de Geneve, 1992. [photo: Marc Van Appelghem]

Girls, Girls, Girls. Sam scrutinized by a pair of ladies in the Met's 1987 production of *Carmen*. [photo: ©Beth Bergman]

Still the ladies' man. Sam as Don Giovanni. Chicago. 1988. [photo: the collection of Samuel Ramey]

Mussorgsky's Boris Godunov, the role Sam was advised not to sing. [photo: the collection of Samuel Ramey]

The Coronation Scene from *Boris Godunov*. Sam wears a crown, a robe, and a three-piece suit. Salzburg. 1983. [photo: Inge Klepitsch] 1993

Time is running out for the tortured Tsar. Metropolitan Opera. 1997. [photo: ©Beth Bergman]

Bartok's *Duke Bluebeard's Castle*. The serial wifeslayer has a grim moment of retrospection. Metropolitan Opera. 1989. [photo: ©Beth Bergman]

Bluebeard and his wife Judith (Jessye Norman) trying to make their marriage work. Metropolitan Opera. 1989. [photo: ©Beth Bergman]

A bonanza of bel canto singers—Samuel Ramey, Lucianno Pavarotti, and Aprile Milo—in Verdi's *I Lombardi*. Metropolitan Opera. 1993. [photo: ©Beth Bergman

A 1993 concert version of *I Lombardi*. Lucianno Pavarotti, James Levine, Lauren Flanigan, and Sam. Frankfurt. 1993. [photo: Inge Klepitsch]

Offenbach's *Tales of Hoffman*. Placido Domingo (Hoffman), Suzanne Mentzer (Nicklausse), and Sa: as Coppelius. Metropolitan Opera. 1992. [photo:©Beth Bergman]

Two of Armen Boyajian's students. Sam as Basilio and Paul Plishka as Dr. Bartolo in *Il Barbieri di Siviglia*. (Sam's career jump-started when he stepped in for Plishka at the Paterson Lyric Opera Theatre's presentation of *Faust*.) Metropolitan Opera. 1997. [©Metropolitan Opera/Winnie Klotz]

*Il Barbieri* again. A quartet composed of Diane Damrau (Rosina), Peter Mattei (Figaro), Sam (Basilio) and, in disguise, Juan Diego Florez (Almaviva). Metropolitan Opera. 2006. [photo: ©Beth Bergman]

Sam as Figaro with Frederica von Stade as Cherubino in Mozart's *Le Nozze di Figaro*. Although they did not often appear together on the operatic stage, von Stade and Sam have been giving joint concerts for the past decade. Metropolitan Opera. 1991. [photo: © Beth Bergman]

Sam sings *non piu andrai* at the Met. He believes that Figaro is the character closest to his own personality. [photo: ©Beth Bergman]

Don Giovanni is closely watched by Zerlina (Dawn Upshaw) and Donna Anna (Karita Mattila). Metropolitan Opera. 1990. [photo: ©Beth Bergman]

*Don Giovanni* on TV. Sam's back is to the camera. [photo: Inge Klepitsch].

Displaying Don Giovanni's hauteur. San Francisco. 1995. [photo: Inge Klepitsch]

Disguised as Leporello, Sam maintains Don Giovanni's sang-froid. Vienna. 1996. [photo: Inge Klepitsch]

Sam serenades in *Faust* at La Scala, 1997. [photo: Inge Klepitsch]

Leporello delivers the redoubtable Catalogue Aria in which he enumerates and possibly exaggerates Don Giovanni's conquests. Metropolitan Opera. 2005. [photo: ©Beth Bergman]

Leporello gives an earful about his master to Donna Elivira (Adina Nitescu). Metropolitan Opera. 2005. [photo: © Beth Bergman]

Coppelius

Dapertutto

Dr. Miracle

Three out of four *Hoffman* villains: Coppelius in Vienna, 1999, Dapertutto in San Francisco, 1996, and Dr. Miracle in Paris, 2000. [photos: Inge Klepitsch]

Hakan Hagegard as Roderigo kneels before Sam as King Philip II in Verdi's *Don Carlo*. Geneva. 1988. [photo: the collection of Samuel Ramey]

The many faces of King Philip:
[photos: Inge Klepitsch]

Chicago, 1996.

Vienna, 1996.

Venice, 1997.

In this *Don Carlo* composite, Sam, as both King Philip and the Grand Inquisitor, confronts himself. [photo: ©Beth Bergman]

A classic Mephistopheles in Berlioz's *Damnation of Faust*. Paris. 2004. [photo: Inge Klepitsch]

An avant garde Mephistopheles in another version of the Berlioz work. Los Angeles. 2003. [photo: Inge Klepitsch]

Procida, in Verdi's *I Vespri Siciliani*, returns from exile and gets right back into the action. Metropolitan Opera. 2004. [photo: ©Beth Bergman]

Glyndebourne's 1977 presentation of Stravinsky's *The Rake's Progress* marked the beginning of Sam's spectacular European career. [photo: Philip Ingram, the collection of Samuel Ramey]

Nick Shadow bedazzles Tom Rakewell. Sam and Jerry Hadley as the sly villain and the hapless hero in the Lyric Opera of Chicago's production of *The Rake's Progress*. The two men became good friends. [photo: ©Beth Bergman]

The Art of the Deal. Nick Shadow cuts the cards. [photo: ©Beth Bergman]

Rambaldo (Sam), in Puccini's *La Rondine*, gives a bit of fatherly advice to his son Ruggero (Roberto Alagna). Metropolitan Opera. 2008. [photo: ©Beth Bergman]

More fatherly advice. The Count Des Grieux counsels his son the Chevalier des Grieux (Rolando Villazon). Metropolitan Opera Gala. 2007. [photo: ©Beth Bergman]

Would you buy a used car from this man? *Mefistofele*. [photo: ©Beth Bergman]

*Mefistofele*: the devil in armor. [photo: Inge Klepitsch]

From his triumphant stance, Mephistopheles appears to have snared a soul. *Faust*. Metropolitan Opera. 1997. [photo: © Beth Bergman]

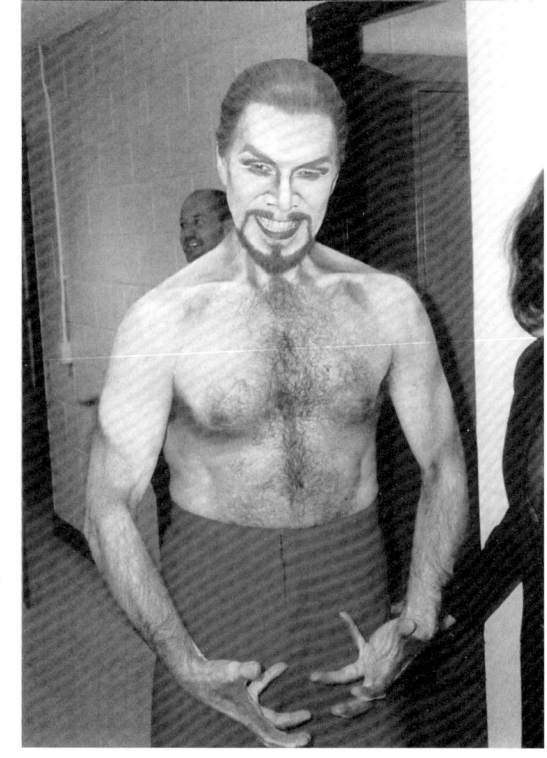

In this manifestation of Mefistofele, Sam's hair, beard, and trousers are a bright, cherry color. His son, Guy, called him "my Red Daddy".
[photo: the collection of Samuel Ramey]

The San Francisco Opera's 1999 production of Charpentier's *Louise* was Sam's only appearance in the role of The Father. The Louise is Renee Fleming. [photo: Inge Klepitsch]

Sam as Schicchi in an unconventional double bill of Puccini's comic *Gianni Schicchi* and Bartok's dark *Duke Bluebeard's Castle*. William Friedkin directed the Los Angeles Opera production in 2002. [photo: Inge Klepitsch]

Puccini's *Tosca*. (Hildegard Behrens) warily watches Scarpia as he offers her a glass of wine. She has good cause for apprehension. Royal Opera House. 1991. [photo: Clive Barda, the collection of Samuel Ramey]

Captain Claggart, the mean Master-at-Arms in Britten's *Billy Budd*. Chicago. 2001. [photo: Inge Klepitsch]

Mephistopheles fiddles in *Faust*. Chicago. 2003. [photo: Inge Klepitsch]

In 1847 the Paris Opera commissioned a new work from Giuseppe Verdi. The composer reworked the score of an earlier opera, *I Lombardi*, used a French libretto to simplify the plot, et voila! *Jerusalem*. Sam scored a huge hit in the Vienna Opera's production. [photo: Inge Klepitsch]

Verdi again. This time *La Forza del Destino*. Sam, as the Marquis of Calatrava, attempts to comfort his daughter Leonora (Deborah Voigt). Metropolitan Opera. 2006. [photo: ©Beth Bergman]

The role of Fiesco in Verdi's *Simon Boccanegra* provided the opportunity to sing *il lacerato spirito*, "the bass national anthem." San Francisco Opera. 2001. [photo: Inge Klepitsch]

The High Priest Zaccaria preaches to the crowd in Verdi's *Nabucco*. Metropolitan Opera. 2004. [photo: ©Beth Bergman]

*War and Peace.* [photos: ©Beth Bergman]

Two views of Field Marshall Kutusov from Prokofiev's epic *War and Peace*. In one, he urges his followers to battle (war), and in the other he welcomes victory (peace). Metropolitan Opera. 2002.

The singer and some of the managing agents who helped guide his career. Left to right: Jeff Vanderveen, Alex Treuhaft, Joyce Arbib, Tom Graham, Sam, and Matthew Epstein. [photo: the collection of Samuel Ramey]

A photograph taken in Hamburg, Germany in the early 1980s. Left to right; Sam's second wife, Carrie, singers Francisco Ariza and Carl Schultz, Sam, and Marilyn Horne. [photo: Jane Scovell]

A recent photo taken during a visit to Wichita.

In Wichita with high school classmates Betty and Paul Ackerman.

With Emily and Doc Severinsen. Doc wanted Sam to go on *The Tonight Show* but, through no fault of Sam's, it did not happen. Why? A reigning diva bombed on a broadcast and Johnny Carson closed the door to opera singers. Two memorable exceptions were veteran guests, Marilyn Horne and Beverly Sills. [photo: the collection of Samuel Ramey]

Receiving the coveted Rossini Medal. Pesaro. 1985. [photo: the collection of Samuel Ramey]

Sam being greeted by United States Senator Nancy Landon Kassebaum, the daughter of Alf Landon. Alf Landon had been a Governor of Kansas and a one-time Republican candidate for President. [photo: the collection of Samuel Ramey]

With Herbert von Karajan and Ferruccio Furlanetto at a recording session of *Don Giovanni*. Berlin. 1985. [photo: the collection of Samuel Ramey]

Samuel Ramey and William Warfield, two renowned American basses. [photo: the collection of Samuel Ramey]

Celebrating the Met's new production of *Don Giovanni* with its director Franco Zefferelli. 1990. [photo: Metropolitan Opera/Winnie Klotz]

Escamillo and a cast of Muppets. [photo: the collection of Samuel Ramey]

Taken at the Carnegie Hall concert launching the Marilyn Horne Foundation on January 16, 1994. Back row (left to right) Klaus Donath, Warren Jones, Sam, James Levine, and Manuel Bugueras. Standing in the middle row are Martin Katz, Renee Fleming, Horne, Ruth Ann Swenson and Olafur Bjarnason. Seated in front are Helen Donath, Frederica von Stade, and Montserrat Caballe. [photo: Henry Fair]

A book signing at the Met. Nora London, widow of George London and author of his biography, is seated between two big bassos, Sam and Rene Pape. [photo: ©Beth Bergman]

Sam, Montserrat Caballe, Marilyn Horne, and conductor Jesus Lopez-Cobos at a *Semiramide* concert in Berlin. [photo: the collection of Sam Ramey]

Enjoying a good laugh with Beverly Sills. [photo: Henry Grossman, from the collection of Beverly Sills]

Sam greeted by the Queen of Belgium. Gerard Mortier, then General Director of La Monnaie, The National Opera of Belgium, looks on. [photo: Guido Marcon, the collection of Samuel Ramey]

Sam and the late Senator from Massachusetts. The photo is inscribed: "To Sam Ramey, A tremendous musical artist. With my warm regards, Ted Kennedy." [photo: the collection of Samuel Ramey]

From the Playbill for the Met's *Don Giovanni*, Friday, April 24, 2009.

**Wolfgang Amadeus Mozart**

# Don Giovanni

CONDUCTOR
Louis Langrée

PRODUCTION
Marthe Keller

SET DESIGNER
Michael Yeargan

COSTUME DESIGNER
Christine Rabot-Pinson

LIGHTING DESIGNER
Jean Kalman

CHOREOGRAPHER
Blanca Li

STAGE DIRECTOR
Gina Lapinski

GENERAL MANAGER
Peter Gelb

MUSIC DIRECTOR
James Levine

Opera in two acts
Libretto by Lorenzo Da Ponte

Friday, April 24, 2009, 8:00–11:25pm

**Last time this season**

The production of *Don Giovanni* was made possible by a generous gift from Julian and Josie Robertson, Robertson Foundation and John Van Meter.

Additional funding was received from The Arthur F. and Alice E. Adams Supporting Foundation, Miami, Florida, The Annenberg Foundation, Karen and Kevin Kennedy, Mr. and Mrs. Paul M. Montrone, and the National Endowment for the Arts.

The revival of this production was made possible by a gift from The Dr. M. Lee Pearce Foundation.

Following the end of Act I, Samuel Ramey's 25th anniversary at the Met will be honored on stage.

Sam honored on stage at the 25th Anniversary of his Metropolitan Opera debut. General Manager Peter Gelb leads the applause as members of the cast look on. [photo: Metropolitan Opera/Ken Howard] anything to do with the thickness of the vocal cords Rossini certainly didn't know it. He was too busy writing for a lot of basses who could do it.

"When it comes to the Rossini style, as far as I'm concerned, Jackie Horne was the progenitor. She showed us how you could do it without slipping and sliding and swooping from one note to the other. My sense is she realized she wouldn't be able to sing the operas she wanted to sing unless she surrounded herself with singers who could do it in other registers. That's why she became such an extraordinary mentor to people like Sam, Rocky Blake, and Chris Merritt. A whole generation of singers really owes their sense of wanting to do this repertory to her. I can reel off a list of first-rate sopranos and mezzos who can do the repertory effectively well but they're not Jackie Horne. No one sings the way she did. I would say the same for Sam. There are basses who can do it, they're good musicians, they've learned how to bring their voices around, but they don't sound like Sam. There's something very special about him. I don't think that anyone would say that Sam sang this music in the 1990s as well as he sang it in the 1980s but that doesn't mean he didn't sing it well. By then his repertoire was changing and he was doing things like Philip in *Don Carlos* and Boris. And when you heard him in those roles you realized what a well-rounded and interesting performer he is in many different repertories. Sam is an intelligent singer, a real musician, and that's one of the reasons that so many of us are so fond of him as an artist. You just respect someone who tries to do so many different things and does them all so well. I heard Sam do an Attila in 2006 and he couldn't sing it the way he had. At some point, the body just can't do what it did, like breath control, etc. But I would rather hear a Sam Ramey sing something like that than hear a younger voice. It was a lesson in how you phrase, how you attack, how you pronounce the words, and the kind of rhythmic emphasis you give to every syllable. It's the kind of stuff only someone who has been a consummate master of operatic performance can do. Today there are fewer singers of the level of Jackie and Sam—singers that you can put on the stage and just turn loose and have them do it. (One big exception is Juan Diego Florez. I've heard terrific tenors, but he's is in a class by himself.) I guess the most important thing to say about Sam Ramey is that he reinvented a repertory. Suddenly, we got someone at the height of his artistic powers who could do it the way no one could before. And while everyone who's come since, and this includes some excellent singers, can do the repertory, none of them has Sam's characteristic presence and utter fluency. Nobody has it, or will have it, at least in my day."

The Aix-en-Provence *Semiramide* made Sam a super star in France and had a tsunami effect on his European career. During the *Semiramide* run, Sam received a phone call from an agent in Milan. He told Sam that La Scala was preparing a *Figaro* with Riccardo Muti conducting and asked if Sam would audition. Sam's answer was his generic "sure," and he flew off to Rome. The auditions took place at RAI (Radiotelevisione Italiana), Italy's public service broadcaster. Sam was ushered into an anteroom and kept waiting.

"There were a bunch of us sitting around but nobody was talking. Then these two men walked in. Everybody stood up and said, 'Maestro, Maestro.' I assumed that one of the guys was Muti. I found out neither of them was the conductor. I didn't know who they were but they took me to a small rehearsal room and I sang for them. They said it was fine but they wanted to hear me in the big hall. We had to wait until the hall was free so we sat around in the rehearsal room. I had my anthology of great bass arias on my lap. One of the men, a rather portly guy, asked what I was holding. I told him and gave it to him to take a look. He opened the book and started thumbing through the pages. 'Oh, how about this, can you sing a bit of this for me?' he asked, pointing to an aria. I said sure and went over with him to a piano. He sat and played, and I sang the aria, along with three or four others. Someone stuck his head in the door and announced that the rehearsal was over. We were let into the big hall where I sang a *Figaro* aria. They told me they liked me and would be contacting my agent. That was fine but who knew if they really meant it? I went back to Aix and told Marilyn Horne what happened. 'Muti didn't come,' I explained, 'it was two guys, one was youngish and the other was an older, sort of heavy guy, he's the one who asked me to sing.' She started laughing. 'Sam, that was Siciliani! He's the one who brought Callas to La Scala. He knows singers. Trust me, if Siciliani liked you, you're in.' He did, and I was. I made my La Scala debut the next year.

"I had a good success with the Scala *Figaro,* I was especially moved when the *loggionisti* gave me a present to commemorate my debut. It was a plaque with the comedy and drama masks on one side, and the program on the other. Loggionisti are the diehard fans who sit in the loggia way up at the top of the opera house. Years ago, they were called the 'claque.' Singers would pay claques to keep the applause going, or to start it, and even more important, not to boo. Let's face it; it was a kind of blackmail. Claques were once a way of life in Italian opera houses but by the time I made my debut, their importance had greatly diminished. Still, when the *capo del claque* came around to my dressing room before the La Scala opening, I gave him some money to distribute among his pals. I really wasn't buying anything, paying them off had become more of a *tradition* than anything else. And who was I to break with tradition?"

Sam was off and rolling on the Continent and soon became a regular on European stages and in the recording studios. "Everyone seemed to want Sam and in whatever he wanted to do," remarked Tom Graham. "But for me, the most amazing part of it was the way Sam, the American, was accepted, particularly in Italy. It's one thing to go to Italy and sing Wagner or French operas, they don't care because they don't consider that real opera. But to sing *L'Italiana* or *Don Carlo* or anything Italian and have the Italians accept it is amazing. You can't imagine what a coup it was when the Rossini festival at Pesaro, an Italian bastion, asked him to come there and sing. My God, they asked Sam before they asked Jackie Horne! He went there in the second year of the festival with *L'Italiana* and then he became a Pesaro fixture for six more summers. It was extraordinary for an American to be so embraced. That's why in the early part of his career, for ten years at least, he spent three quarters of the time in Europe. Look, we're not talking about huge fees, they were low but they were more than he could get in America. And I think Sam and Carrie kind of liked life on the Continent. Then came the *Rinaldo* at the Met, which changed everything. His career in America zoomed and his presence in Europe diminished. He didn't need to travel to sing."

Sam was a prominent part of the Marilyn Horne *Rinaldo* package. He had scored a huge success as Argante, the Saracen magician, in both Houston and Ottawa. Nonetheless, in her negotiations with the Metropolitan Opera for *Rinaldo*'s January 1984 premiere, Horne unexpectedly met with resistance to her carefully wrought ensemble. "I was sitting at a table discussing the casting with a group from the Met's upper management including Jimmy Levine," recalled Horne. "Everything was going smoothly until we got to the big bass part of Argante. I was flabbergasted when they started saying, 'well, we want this one, or that one.' I let them finish and then I put my elbows on the table, leaned forward, and said to Levine, 'Jimmy, you *want* Sam Ramey.' He looked at me and said, 'That's it!'" Soon thereafter the Metropolitan Opera announced that Samuel Ramey would be making his debut. Speculation varied as to why the Met dragged its heels about signing him. Many believed the received information that buzzed around the city, to wit, the Met was huffy because Sam had become a superstar with-

## SAMUEL RAMEY: American Bass

out them. It is one thing to bring in a great singer whose reputation has been made in Europe but quite another to overlook, and then tardily present the "boy next door." In effect, the Met would not be unearthing a genuine American talent but simply getting on the bandwagon of a City Opera discovery, perhaps too much humble pie for the senior opera house to digest. Others suggested that James Levine's loyalties lay with his resident bass, James Morris. And finally, there was that question of money. Who on earth would pay premium prices to see an artist who could be seen next door where the tickets cost a lot less. For all these reasons, and more, Samuel Ramey's debut became a cause celebre.

Sam may have smarted at his treatment by the Metropolitan muckety-mucks, but he had to have been gratified by the reaction of the opening night audience, and the critics. His first entrance drew gasps and not just for his singing. A large metal gate opened to reveal Sam standing in a chariot drawn by two sturdy extras. To the sound of trumpets from the orchestra and applause from the audience, the chariot was pulled swiftly around the stage in a wide circle and drawn to a sudden halt. To set the vehicle upright the extras dropped the rod they had been holding. Suddenly, the chariot lurched and at that moment Samuel Ramey came perilously close to being catapulted onto the floor. "I felt like an ass," grimaces Sam. "What happened was the front end of the rod hit a bump on the stage and the chariot was really jolted, like someone had slammed on the brakes. I held on for dear life and began my aria." The drama of that entrance fit in with the larger drama being played. Observed one pundit, "It was the right role at the right time and it hit like a thunderbolt. It was David versus Goliath and all New York was rooting for Sam Ramey." The reviews were excellent although at least one dissenter stood out. Martin Bernheimer, music critic of the Los Angeles Times and a fervent admirer and champion of Norman Treigle, never cottoned to Sam. In Bernheimer's opinion, Sam just "sang loud all the time." "Ramey, in my estimation, never had a *fraction* of the talent that Norman had," said Bernheimer. "[But] Ramey became that 'super-star' that Norman wanted to be."[7] Sam took the knocks in stride.

"Look, everyone's entitled to his opinion and as far as criticism goes, you can't please everybody. Most people thought that what I did in *Rinaldo* was a real tour de force. I mean I had to come out and sing a rousing aria with ten or eleven high F#s. Then, I left the stage and returned almost immediately to sing a soft, gentle aria. I had barely a minute to compose myself and I sang two completely different pieces of music. I thought I did a good job of it, so did most of the critics. The truth is, the critics usually did well by me. Not always, though. I still remember Andrew Porter's assessment of my Attila at City Opera. He said I sang fine but I couldn't act. Oh well, you can't expect praise all the time. Better yet, at one point I kind of gave up reading my reviews. The truth is looking back at the way the critics treated me, I can't complain." Although it had nothing to do with the critics at the time of his Metropolitan Opera debut, Sam *did* complain and to, arguably, the country's most influential newspaper, *The New York Times*.

In the opera world, it is a truth, universally acknowledged, that an artist in possession of a great talent is in want of a superlative showcase in which to exhibit his or her talent. Samuel Ramey achieved that objective. He had made it to the Met and had been greeted enthusiastically by both the critics and the public, so why not keep his mouth shut except to sing? Bucking conventional wisdom, Sam opened up to Bernard Holland, a *Times* music critic, and said things that few if any performers in his position would utter. The resulting article rocked the music world.

---

[7] Brian Morgan, <u>Strange Child of Chaos: Norman Treigle</u> (New York: iUniverse, Inc., 2006) p209.

## SAMUEL RAMEY: American Bass

*Samuel Ramey's current success at the Metropolitan Opera has brought him some short-term fulfillment but still hasn't resolved his longstanding dissatisfaction with the people who run the house.*

*A star at the New York City Opera since the mid-1970s, hugely successful as a performer and recording artist in Europe for the past four years and generally considered America's leading operatic bass, Mr. Ramey made his first-ever appearance at the Met last Thursday in Handel's "Rinaldo." According to Donal Henahan writing in this paper, he created a "tremendous impression with his powerful, pliable bass voice."*

*The satisfaction has come in the chance to sing at the Met, though Mr. Ramey's prior successes elsewhere have tempered the excitement. "It's always a goal for an American singer," he said over the weekend. "People kept asking, 'Aren't you excited?' But for me it was one more debut, though an important one." ——*

*The puzzlement and concern - which is shared by many in the music community – is why the Met, an American company, has shown so little interest in Mr. Ramey in the past and will not be exploiting his talents more thoroughly in the future. "The Met offered me a cast-change Escamillo in 'Carmen' in 1978, but I had to sing in San Francisco and it wasn't that interesting an offer to begin with," he said. "Later they asked if I'd do Sparafucile in 'Rigoletto' for some student performances, which I and my management thought ridiculous."*

*Even for his current stay at the Met, Mr. Ramey has found the attitude strange. He has yet to see James Levine, music director of the house, since he arrived for rehearsals, he says, nor has any other high echelon person in the house bothered to come and say hello. "That's unheard of in Europe," he said. "At Covent Garden, at the Paris Opera, at La Scala, the intendant has always stopped in on the first day of rehearsals. I only met Mr. Bliss after the first performance of 'Rinaldo' when Marilyn Horne brought him over and introduced me.' Anthony Bliss is the Met's general manager.*

*Mr. Ramey a quiet, shy man of 42 says he finds it all a little weird, but seems really more bemused than insulted.*

*In 1986-87, he is scheduled for "I Puritani" and "Carmen" at the Met, but is "disappointed," he said, "in not being offered the operas I'm known for – such as "The Marriage of Figaro,' 'Tales of Hoffmann' and 'Don Giovanni.' "He is under contract for the two operas at the Met but is "having second thoughts," he said.*[8]

To have an artist refer to his first appearance on the Met stage as "just another debut" could not have been music to the Met's ears. Nor could anyone have missed the insinuation buried in the statement, "having second thoughts." Samuel Ramey was nailing his protests on the door, both by

---

[8] The New York Times, 23 Jan. 1984.

inferring that his Met debut was simply another notch in his belt and suggesting that maybe, just maybe, he might pull out of the less than desirable future operas he had been offered. Bernard Holland found him more "bemused than insulted." In fact, Sam was both insulted and hurt but even at that point he might have kept quiet. However, he was not the only *Rinaldo* participant who got the cold shoulder.

During the first rehearsal session on stage, Frank Corsaro, the director, Mario Bernardi, the conductor, and Sam were standing together when a prominent member of the Metropolitan Opera hierarchy came out from the wings, walked right by them, and went over to greet Marilyn Horne, by then, a Met fixture. After talking with her for a few minutes, he turned and again walked past the three men, exiting into the wings without so much as a nod in their direction. Corsaro, Bernardi, and Sam were making their Met debuts and none was acknowledged that afternoon. The director, the conductor, and one of the leading singers had been snubbed. Frank Corsaro believed that this was the very moment when Sam decided to speak out. Of note, Marilyn Horne played guardian angel for Frank Corsaro as well as Sam Ramey. In a 1986 interview, Corsaro explained what had occurred. "It was my understanding that the Met didn't want me. At an early planning meeting, the Met people said that I was too much associated with City Opera. Horne stood up and cried, 'So is Beverly Sills!' That broke the ice and I got the job."

Corsaro was right about how deeply the triple brush-off affected Sam. He contacted Edgar Vincent and told him how shabbily he, Corsaro, and Bernardi had been treated. Vincent, the consummate publicist, slyly passed the item on to *The New York Times* knowing full well that it would provide a hot topic. The day the Holland article appeared Vincent received a phone call from his client and good friend, the legendary Metropolitan Opera mezzo, Rise Stevens.

"Edgar, how could you have let that be printed?" she

demanded. "That's the end of Samuel Ramey at the Met!"

"Forgive me, my dear Rise," he laughed, "but you are wrong."

Edgar Vincent was right. By going against his Kansas grain and speaking his mind in a public forum, Samuel Ramey, quietly but firmly, had thrown down a gauntlet, which had to be picked up. Sam's dander was raised and he was even more outspoken in private than he had been in the *Times*.

"In those days there definitely was an attitude around the Met, which I experienced nowhere else. Perhaps some of it had to do with the fact that I was an American singer, we were not as esteemed as the European artists by some members of the administration. I had heard that Marilyn Horne went to bat for me. She never told me so herself, but according to the grapevine they tried to cast somebody else as Argante and only accepted me when she said we were a "package deal." I was, and always will be, grateful to her but I was pissed off at the Met and that's why I let loose when Bernard Holland called me. Actually, the first time we spoke on the phone I really wasn't that forthcoming about my problem. I talked about other stuff. Apparently Holland then called Edgar and complained that I was being tight lipped. Edgar then told me that I simply had to discuss the issue. 'I'm going to tell Bernard Holland to call you back and this time, Sam, *talk*.' So, I opened up and let *The New York Times* in on how I felt.

"I was sensitive because I knew the Met didn't want me in the first place and also because once I was there, nobody seemed to do anything to make me feel comfortable. Maybe I was still naïve but this was my debut *and* I was an established singer. At the very least, I deserved a handshake and a 'Welcome to the Met, Sam.' I expected common courtesy from the Met honchos and I didn't receive it. During the *Rinaldo* rehearsals, not one person in the Met's top administration contacted me. Even at the gala party after the opening, none of the bigwigs congratulated me. I sat at Bliss's table and he never said a word, he never even looked in my direction. It was beyond weird. Then, Jackie Horne took over. Jackie doesn't stand on ceremony. She was seated near Anthony Bliss and at one point during the meal she got up, went over to where he was sitting, took him by the arm, pulled him to his feet, and steered him over to me.

'I'd like to introduce you to someone,' she said to the Executive Director of the Metropolitan Opera House, 'this is Samuel Ramey.'

"I stood up and shook his hand. He was cordial and polite and a bit flustered. The idea that the head of the company had to be introduced to me by my colleague was baffling. I heard later that Bliss was an extremely shy man but that really wasn't much of an excuse. I'm shy, too. After my *Rinaldo* success, the Met got on the phone with my management. They wanted me back ASAP, and here's the rub. I was certainly willing to return, but in their eagerness to get me, the Met overlooked the fact that I was an international player and was booked years in advance. When I signed on for *Rinaldo* I couldn't accept any future engagements until the 1986/87 season, in which *Puritani* and *Carmen* were scheduled. When your schedule is set in advance, you have to accept the fact that there will be consequences. I learned that way back when I took those extra engagements while I was waiting for the City Opera to pick up my option. That was a little different, though. I wasn't actually signed up for anything by City Opera and they still were upset that I'd made plans. The fact is I've lost out on a few things I'd like to have done over the course of my career because of scheduling conflicts. For instance, I never sang at the White House. I was asked a number of times during the Reagan years, but I was always committed, usually overseas. I guess I spent about 75% of my time working in Europe in those days. Bill Clinton's the only President I ever met, but I never sang for him. In fact, I missed out on meeting a lot of famous people in America whereas I really got around in Europe and met tons of celebrities. Lots of times it happened as a result of my doing what I guess would be classified as a 'good deed.' Wherever I am, whenever I can, I try to contribute my services to local causes. One time I was in London during Wimbledon, and was contacted by my friend, Vittorio Selmi, who works for the American Tennis Professionals Tournaments and is a big opera fan. Arthur Ashe had died not long before and they were doing a commemorative evening in his honor at a London hotel. Vittorio called and asked if I would come and sing a couple of numbers. So I went and I sang *Old Man River* and *The Impossible Dream*. I was introduced to a whole bunch of tennis players and a lot of entertainment celebrities. I remember standing at the bar with Peter Ustinov, and Charlton Heston came over to speak to me. We chatted and then I said, "Hey, you know I've played Moses, too." I explained that I sang the role of Moise at the Paris Opera House. Heston got a kick out of it. Another time, I was doing a *Tosca* at Covent Garden and was asked to appear at a benefit for a small London ballet school. As it happened, Princess Diana was a patron of the school and attended the concert. When I finished singing I was introduced to her. She said that she enjoyed my singing very much. She also said that she'd been at the *Tosca* and really liked that, too. I thought she was just wonderful, a really gorgeous woman and so very nice. I've been asked any number times to name the people who've most impressed me and Diana would be right up there. I'd also have to include Supreme Court Justice Harry Blackman. Justice Blackman was a real music lover and started a musical series that still takes place in the Supreme Court building. I had the privilege of singing for that series at a recital honoring his retirement on May 26, 1994. During the concert, the black-robed Justices took their accustomed seats on the bench and an invited audience sat in the pews. I sang the first performance of

*The Long Shadow of Lincoln*, a song cycle by Stephen Paulus and a group of American songs ranging from Charles Ives, Charlie Rutlage to Cole Porter's *The Tale of an Oyster*. It was quite an experience doing my thing in the highest court in the land.

"Come to think of it, I got around a lot in those days although I never really did the television talk show circuit and that was where it was at, which I guess still holds true. I came pretty close to making the scene a few times. Doc Severinsen, Johnny Carson's bandleader and sidekick, is a friend and he kind of laid the groundwork for me to appear on The Tonight Show. Sills and Horne had been on many times and done very well. I think Bev actually guest hosted! Anyway, Doc said my people should get in touch with the Tonight Show people to set things up but by the time that happened, a moratorium had been called. A well-known soprano had appeared and was such a disaster Carson said, "No more opera singers." After what he went through I couldn't blame him, but I thought I'd be okay on his show, after all, we were both Midwesterners. I could go on and on about the famous people I've met but let's just say in my wildest Kansas dreams I never thought I'd be hobnobbing with the likes of a Princess or a Supreme Court Justice. Okay, enough of that. Back to my Met debut."

"As I was saying, I didn't like the idea that some people at the Met thought they could snap their fingers and have me come running to get whatever scraps they were handing out. Matthew had helped negotiate a nice fee for the *Rinaldo* but beyond that he couldn't get them to come forward with suitable roles. Although Matthew left CAMI in 1981, he was never totally out of the picture when it came to my career. He kept close watch over me and kind of worked ad hoc with Joyce Arbib. Matthew told the Met that they should put me in the new production of *Hoffman*, or in *Figaro*, or in *Italiana*, all of which contained a defining role for me and all of which were on the Met's schedule during the season I was available. It didn't happen. Instead, I was offered Giorgio Walton in *Puritani* and Escamillo in *Carmen*. *Puritani* has beautiful music but Giorgio Walton is not a central character. In *Carmen*, Escamillo gets to sing a well-known aria and that's pretty much it. Matthew calls *Escamillo*, 'a famously difficult, ungrateful part with one aria, and if you don't sing it better than it's ever been heard before, people say, oh, he wasn't that good.' Although I think I eventually nailed it, Escamillo wasn't one of my better efforts at that time. In Matthew's opinion neither Walton nor Escamillo would capture the public or do anything to advance my career. And I knew he was right. There was something else, too, something I didn't mention to *The New York Times*. The truth is I'd avoided doing some of the roles in which I'd had great success overseas because I was kind of saving them for the right occasion. I'd been offered the chance to sing a few of them with other American companies but I held out in hopes of debuting them at the Met. I'd passed on some good offers so naturally I was distressed when I was offered anything *but* those roles. For a while there it was pretty much a stand off between the Met and me. Then, the whole business ended, not with a bang or a whimper but with a negotiated rapprochement."

In the case of Ramey vs. the Met, or vice versa, there was no dramatic confrontation or deus ex machina intervention. The truth is life isn't grand opera and Sam's getting together with the Met was not a drum-rolling event, it was simply a matter of both parties connecting on mutual ground. Granted, there was an administrative change at the Met and that probably helped clear the air. Sam suggests, "We both kind of wanted each other and eventually we got each other. I wanted them because they were the Met and they wanted me because the audiences wanted me. One day they picked up the phone, called my agent, and asked not only when I would next be available, but what roles I would *like* to do. From that point on, we moved forward together and, pretty soon, the Met became one of my treasured houses. Sure, there've been a few bumps over the years. At one point, Edgar Vincent became irritated with the Met because they promised to give me a new production of *Mefistofele* to make up for some other stuff. Then, when they couldn't raise the money, they borrowed the Robert Carsen production, which was created for me in Geneva and had already been televised from San Francisco. It was my 'traveling production' and a little shopworn by then. Edgar thought it was a scandal for them to reneg on the new production. In fact, it may not have been the nicest thing for them to do. Well, I could go on but all things considered the Met and I have enjoyed a reciprocally satisfactory association that extends to this very day. I had a good rapport with Joe Volpe and I'm as excited as everyone else about what Peter Gelb is doing. He's giving new life to the Metropolitan Opera House and I can't tell you how much it means to me to be a part of it. In the 2007/08 season, I was pleased to reprise my role as Kutuzov in Prokofiev's *War and Peace.* Like most people I read *War and Peace* but it was a long time ago and I didn't reread it, I just concentrated on Kutuzov. It's funny, I was working so hard on my part I didn't have any idea of the scope of that opera. It's staggering. Come to think of it, *War and Peace* is a title you could apply to my overall relationship with the Metropolitan Opera. We had our battle but it's ancient history now and peace reigns."

SAMUEL RAMEY: American Bass

# Ya Gotta Have a Gimmick

By the end of the 1980s, Sam was riding high; he was recognized on the stage as a virtuoso bass, and, more and more, he was being recognized outside the opera house. He reveled in it. "Some people don't like people coming up to them on the street and saying 'I loved your performance,' or stuff like that. Not I. I'm always flattered because I'm like that myself. When I see stars, I want to stop them and tell them how much I enjoy their work. Although I usually don't do it, it's the first thing I think of, and it was very much in my mind when I learned that Barbra Streisand lived in the penthouse in my building on Central Park West. I always hoped I'd get a chance to meet her and I felt I had a good shot when CBS Sunday Morning did a television piece on me. They sent a camera crew to follow me around, and I thought the crew would act as a magnet for Streisand. That crew went everywhere with me. They filmed a segment in San Francisco when I did the *Mefistofele* and they were scheduled to come to Colby to film a recital in my hometown. My recital happened to coincide with an earthquake in San Francisco and the crew had to rush there to cover the 'bigger' story. Later, CBS arranged for me to be interviewed at my apartment by Eugenia Zuckerman, a flautist and television personality. Eugenia came over and when I let her in, she said, 'I know this building. Barbra Streisand lives here.' Streisand was filming the *Prince of Tides* at the time and Eugenia helped her pick out music for the soundtrack. We finished the interview and the camera crew wanted me to go outside so they could film me walking down the street. Eugenia and I got into the elevator, and instead of going down, it went up. I laughed and said, 'Maybe we'll see Ms. Streisand.' The elevator stopped at the penthouse, the door opened, and in she walked. Eugenia introduced us and I said, 'How do you do, Ms. Streisand,' and because I couldn't think of anything else to say, I added, 'I'm a singer, too.' She looked at me and nodded like, 'of course you are.' I'm not so sure Ms. Streisand knew what I was talking about but I know Eugenia got a kick out of it. Another time, I did *Mefistofele* in Los Angeles and after the opening I was walking towards the exit when I saw Burt Lancaster approaching. He was a big opera fan and a board member of the L.A. Opera. He flashed that toothy smile and said through his tightly clenched teeth, 'I thought you were just fine.' I loved it. Another "recognition scene" I really appreciated, happened in New York. I was walking down the street and a very tall, very distinguished gentleman, who looked vaguely familiar, came over and praised my Mephistopheles. He had an English accent. All of a sudden, it dawned on me that I was receiving compliments from Christopher Lee, the man who played Dracula in all those Hammer horror movies. We stood there for a while, just two fiends chatting away. He's still making movies, and Queen Elizabeth knighted him in 2009. 'Sir Dracula' and I have stayed in contact all these years. Most recently, he called to congratulate me on the twenty-fifth anniversary of my Met debut.

Although Samuel Ramey became about as identifiable as any opera singer can hope to be, including those populating the Hertz and Avis crowd, his Q score was no where near that of a pop star. In high school days, Sam knew how passionately popular artists were idolized because he was an idolizer and might have gone for a popular career had not his sister said he needed a "gimmick." When he could not come up with one, he dropped any ideas of becoming another Elvis Presley or Pat Boone. Instead, he eased on down the road that eventually led him to opera. His sister's advice may have helped set him on his true classical course, but Darlene was only half-right. The truth is, whatever the discipline, popular or classical, a gimmick helps, and, over the span of his musical life, Samuel Ramey had *two* gimmicks.

At the start of his operatic career, the gimmick was his vocal dexterity. Within his low E to high G range, Sam was the only bass in town who could maneuver through the jam packed vocal line of the baroque/bel canto repertoire. And because he literally ruled the lowest Rossini roost, his services were much in demand as more and more productions of that composer's works were revived and staged. One of the first American artists contacted by the Pesaro Festival, he sang there in the summers of 1981, 1982, 1983, 1984, and then was offered the title role in *Maometto II* for the 1985 season. When that offer came he immediately got on the phone with Marilyn Horne to get her input. Horne was staggered. "*Maometto?*" she cried, "Oh Sam, there's nothing but black notes!" He was not fazed. He took on Maometto and made the role his own. Marilyn Horne was Rossini's girl and Sam Ramey *definitely* became his boy. Armen Boyajian claims, "The two of them probably sang more notes per person than any singer of their day." A bass has to do something extra, though, something really sensational in order to grab the public. Sam's virility on stage was palpable and the "hook" was his ability to sing fast and furiously through the lowest end of the scale. He was fearless and in his halcyon days would tackle anything; anything, that is, which was good for his voice. In this respect he and his advisors vigilantly sorted the good from the bad. Much of what Sam sang and, equally important, what he did not sing, resulted from careful planning in collaboration with those he trusted most, Armen Boyajian, Matthew Epstein, and Julius Rudel.

To keep Sam at the top of his game, Epstein looked high and low for the parts to which his client was particularly suited. "When you're dealing with artists, you don't do things by the cookie cutter. You don't force artists into a particular shape. You find something they're really good at and you put them into it. Sam shone in the area of the bel canto, the Handel, the Mozart and the French. This was where he could be special and not like everyone else. While it was clear to us all that at that time in his career he didn't need to do the *graybeards,* one knew that eventually, he would do some of the standard parts like Philip II in *Don Carlo* and other 'older' Verdi guys. I remember one occasion when he sang Zaccaria, the aged Hebrew prophet, in a Paris production of Nabucco. Sam called me over and stuck his chin in my face. 'Look at this, Matthew,' he said pointing to a white hair on his unshaven chin. 'I'm a real graybeard!' On the whole, Epstein's master career plan suited Sam, but while Sam liked the idea of a graduated palate of roles, he also wanted variety. He himself said, "I never wanted to be a specialist, I always wanted to be a G.P." In the general practitioner vein, he took on some of those graybeard roles despite Matthew's caveat. "I covered the bass part in Monteverdi's *The Coronation of Poppea,* and they gave me some performances. It's beautiful music and I really loved doing it. The funny thing is, even though Seneca is not a very interesting character, he can steal the show if it's sung well. I remember that Speight Jenkins gave me an incredible review but even so, Seneca was one of those roles I did fairly early and never again."

Although Sam's initial repertoire was heavily tipped toward Rossini, Mozart, Handel, and early Verdi, his eye was on future prospects not all of which did his "board of advisors" sanction. Boyajian and Epstein were troubled by Sam's desire to do one particular role. They agonized over whether or not Sam should take on *Boris Godunov,* a benchmark for basses, but not necessarily all basses. The matter came to a head in 1986, when the Los Angeles Opera Company offered Sam the title role in a production of the Moussorgsky opera, scheduled for the fall of 1990. Neither Sam's teacher nor his quasi manager was happy with the prospect. Boris was on a list of roles which Boyajian already had discouraged Sam from accepting. The list also included an Iago in *Otello*, and a Jochanaan in *Salome* both with Georg Solti conducting. Boyajian felt that neither of those role suited Sam's voice. He was even charier of Boris.

"In the first half of the twentieth century there were perhaps a half dozen good bass roles," reflected Armen Boyajian. "You'd get them under your belt and if you were good enough you'd eventually go for Boris. Boris was the aim of every bass. It was considered the pinnacle, the best that you could get. But things changed in the 1960s when the Handel/Rossini thing started. Virtuoso bass roles were dusted off and *Boris* wasn't the be-all and end-all anymore. I was thrilled. I consider *Boris* a throat killer for a variety of reasons. You can't sing Boris without an F, which is right away a strain on a lot of basses. You've got to have a lot of meat and bite in the voice and you have support in order to yell without hurting yourself. Still, the role does occupy a special place, and a lot of that has to do with Chaliapin and Pinza. The thing is, people don't want to hear it sung the way it's written on the page, and you can trace that right back to Chaliapin. He used 'parlando' for dramatic effect, that is, he shouted and screamed words rather than 'singing' them. It's very effective from a theatrical standpoint, but disaster for the vocal line. Boris has great, great moments for singing but unfortunately there are more moments for shrieking. And if you don't do it the way Chaliapin did, you're not going to be favorably compared with him." Matthew Epstein concurred. "No matter how you slice it, singing that role is harmful to the lyrical line of the voice. It calls for someone who can declaim as opposed to someone who has a beautiful voice. With Boris, fine acting is more necessary than beautiful singing." To do Boris or not to do Boris was an ongoing conundrum. Both Boyajian and Epstein were in agreement that Sam might do better to stay away from it, at least until he was over fifty. Considering what goes into the preparation of such a part, *not* doing it would be a far easier path.

Learning a new role can be an arduous process, one that involves character analysis as well as musical preparation. Some singers go at it with a vengeance and do extensive research in order to create a complete personality for the stage, especially if that character is based on an historical personage. In this respect, Sam had an outstanding role model to observe during his early years at the New York City Opera. Beverly Sills approached her roles in a dynamic fashion. In preparing them, she virtually stalked her characters and wound up knowing them perhaps better than they knew themselves. When she was researching Elizabeth I, she read dozens of books on the subject, not just about the Queen, but also about that entire era of English history. She went to London for recording sessions and stepped up her research. She visited museums and galleries and stood for long periods of time in front of paintings and portraits of Elizabeth. She went to the Victoria and Albert Museum to see Elizabeth's death mask, and she visited actual historical sites which the Queen was known to have frequented in her lifetime. Sills wanted to form a complete picture in her own mind before she presented her Elizabeth to the public. The result was impressive. She looked and acted just like the Queen. Beverly Sills brought the same intensity of preparation to all her roles but that was her way of doing things. Sam Ramey was more laissez-faire.

"In order to learn new roles I would usually start with the piano score and mark it, just like an actor marks his script, you know, highlighting all my lines. Also, I'd look over the part to check the range and the vocal demands just to make sure it was possible for me to do it. I was offered

Iago in *Otello* and it was really tempting, it's such a great part but it was too high. It's a real baritone role and the tessitura doesn't lie comfortably for me. Look, I could have done it, but I thought it would damage my voice. My situation fit the old joke about how many bass-baritones it takes to screw in a light bulb? The answer is three: one to climb the ladder and screw in the bulb and the other two to stand there and ask, 'Isn't that a little high for you?'

"I could learn smaller, comprimario, roles quickly, Zuniga in couple of weeks, and Basilio in about three. Colline I did in six days but I prefer not to learn things that fast. I like to take the time. But some roles, including leading ones, naturally came fast. I first did *Don Quichotte* with a small company in Rouen, France and even though it's a lead, it still only took me about three weeks. But when City Opera mounted *Don Quichotte* specifically for me, I went back to the score and prepared it as though it were for the first time.

"Whenever I took on a new role, I read the libretto and did a little something with the history of the opera. But I never tried to formulate a rigid interpretation before going into a production, and that holds true to this day. I'll do some research, of course. I read Beaumarchais's *Figaro* and *Barber*, and when I sang Henry VIII, in *Anna Bolena*, I got some books and read up on him. However, I never burrowed into the books. I read *Don Quixote* when I was in school but when I sang *Don Quichotte*, I didn't go back to the book because I wasn't sure how much of Cervantes was in the libretto. It was the same with Mephistopheles. Gounod's *Faust* was hardly a direct retelling of Goethe's monumental work. Put it this way, it's valuable to bone up on your characters but for the most part, I didn't religiously research them. Partly it's because I would never think of walking into an opera production saying, "This is the way I do it." I've found if you go into rehearsals with too much of a preconceived idea of what you're going to do, it can often clash with what the producers want. I always try to let things evolve during the staging rehearsals. You have to work with your director and no two of them are going to have the same approach. Take Franco Zeffirelli, he was very interesting to work with. He didn't go into great detail with anybody; he was interested in the big picture. He just gave you a general idea and left you to create your own character within his basic blocking. Lots of times he'd walk around with his hands held up in front of his face framing scenes like a movie director. Other directors are far pickier and say things like, 'take three steps, turn, look left, turn, take four steps, turn.' When I made my La Scala debut, the director was Giorgio Strehler, a fabulous theatre director, who was absolutely exact about what he wanted. During the rehearsal time when the costumes became ready, he wanted a 'parade of costumes' to see everyone in them on the set. I walked on stage in my Figaro suit and Strehler called out, 'Troppo magro, troppo magro,' (too skinny, too skinny). All through the rehearsals he kept complaining. 'My problem is I have a count who's like a peasant and a Figaro who's very elegant. It should be the other way around.' The next thing I knew he made me wear a belly pad to fill me out and make me look bigger. I told Strehler, "You want a fat Figaro? You should have hired a fat Figaro!'

"Let's face it, every production has its problems whether it has to do with a costume, a specific character, or some general difficulty, and these problems become evident during the rehearsals. It's been my experience that if there's something not quite kosher going on somebody will point it out. I prefer not to be that person. You have to know your customers and most are better at expressing dissatisfaction than I am. One morning, I was rehearsing *L'Italiana* on stage at the Fenice Theatre in Venice with most of the cast. Marilyn Horne was singing the lead role and was to join us later that day. We finished going over some of the action, and during the break, a bunch of chorus members came over to talk to me. They were upset about the stage floor covering; it was slick and they were afraid of slipping on it. Because I was a featured artist, they asked me to speak to the management. While I agreed with them that it was potentially dangerous, I begged off being the spokesman. 'You don't have to worry,' I reassured them, 'just wait till Marilyn Horne gets here.' Sure enough, the minute Jackie stepped foot on the stage she demanded that the flooring be changed. And it was."

Sam Ramey's unautocratic attitude made him a director's joy as well as a much-esteemed colleague. He was a star, yet he never threw his weight around and, in many ways, became a role model himself. "I really admired the way Sam stayed on course no matter what," says Tom Graham. "He was a major player but he was never a prima donna; he never wasted energy. I used to tell some of my more excitable clients to watch how Sam Ramey handled things. Whenever there was any kind of kerfluffle during rehearsals, whether it involved action or costumes, Sam would step away and go out and sit in the auditorium. He'd wait until the air was cleared and then go back up on stage. He just wouldn't get into it. He didn't get on the phone and ring his agent and moan and groan. He concentrated on his work and believe me he had to. That Rolodex of roles in his head included not only words and music but languages and stage action as well. For example, he did umpteen productions of the *Barber of Seville* in umpteen cities and each one was different. How many times did he have to remember, oh this is the Hamburg *Barber*, I have to go left, or, this is the London *Barber* and I have to go right, or, this is Berlin, I don't do anything, and this is New York, ah, I jump up and down. And because he was so obliging, he'd do anything they wanted. If they wanted him to run across the stage, he'd run across the stage, if they wanted him to jump up and down, he'd jump up and down, and if they wanted him to wear a blonde wig, he'd wear a blond wig. If that sounds far-fetched, consider that, a few years back, the Met issued a blond wig to a prima donna singing Micaela in *Carmen*. She refused to wear it and she was fired. Not Sam, he would have worn it. He was very professional, never controversial. He did what the director wanted done and went along with everybody. If the conductor was Abbado or Muti or Joe Schmoe, it didn't matter to him, he just did his work. So many artists get all tangled up over issues that just rolled off Sam's back. The only time I ever saw him act up was during a production of *Faust* at Covent Garden. I forget who the director was but he wanted Sam to do something. Sam said, 'No, I'm not going to do that.' And since Sam had never raised an objection before, the director said, 'Okay, I guess you won't do it.'"

Sam himself says that in the early years he would do what he was asked, but as time went on and he became surer of himself, he no longer felt that he had to be one hundred percent accommodating. "I'm a very practical person but I got to the point where I actually would have walked out rather than do something dumb." While many a superstar remains convinced that his or hers is the one and only way of doing things, both on and off the stage, Sam Ramey does not act up professionally or privately. His humility is real and always in evidence. If you want to know what he is like, you can ask New York hair stylist Louis Schumaci who has been cutting Sam's hair for decades. That is no mean feat since Sam Ramey's lion's mane has received almost as much publicity as his bare-chested Rambo roles. "I do a lot of styling on performing artists, female and male," says Schumaci, "and the majority of them tell me exactly what they want down to the last strand. They can't give up control, not even in a salon chair. Sam's the opposite. When I ask how he wants his hair cut, he doesn't say do it this way or do it that way. He leans back in the chair and says, 'You're the professional, do it the way you see it.' So I do it the way I see it, and, ten times out of ten, he loves it. And here's something else that's really important: his attitude makes me feel good because it shows that he respects my knowledge and my skill." Sam's relaxed approach impresses his colleagues, too, especially high-strung performers such as the American tenor, Neil Shicoff. On one occasion the two of them were appearing together and, knowing Shicoff's off-the-deep-end nature, Sam dropped by the tenor's dressing room before the curtain went up. Shicoff, a mass of nerves, literally quivered in his boots and figuratively climbed the walls as Sam stood by calmly.

"Sam, Sam!" cried the tenor, "don't you ever get nervous?"

"Well, maybe just a little nervous," drawled Sam.

"A little nervous? Sam, don't you feel like you're going to DIE!!"

Sam never felt as though he was going to die and, with rare exceptions, remained unruffled at curtain time. His current manager, Jeffrey Vanderveen, can recall a few such exceptions. At present, the Managing Director of Universal Music Classical Management and Productions, Vanderveen most recently was with IMG after working at CAMI for many years. At CAMI, he was Joyce Arbib's assistant and became Sam's manager when she resigned. "People say that you need a break to get into any business," laughs Vanderveen, "and my break was working for a nice Jewish girl from New York who became a cloistered Catholic nun in Connecticut. You don't find too many breaks like that." Just as Arbib had taken over Epstein's client list, Vanderveen inherited hers, which included Samuel Ramey. The two men became close and when Vanderveen left CAMI for IMG, Sam went with him. Vanderveen is Sam's general manager in Europe.

"Sam could have been called a bass-baritone but it was more interesting to call him a bass because of his repertoire. It's good marketing to call him a bass because the truth is, he's got better high notes than any bass out there. Early on, he defined himself outside the traditional bass path by not taking on the big Verdi roles, even though there are so many fantastic ones. He went with the Rossini, and the devil, and did amazingly in both repertoires. Later in his career, he moved into the Verdi works. If he had done them earlier, I think he would have compromised who he was vocally, and not made the huge success he did. One role he did do earlier, Fillipo II, was a great one for him, but a lot of the other Verdi didn't suit him. By saving them for when he 'came of age,' he was able to do them well. I admire the way Sam has handled his career; he managed it beautifully. I just don't see any misses, which is really rare. Even Flicka von Stade, whom I also manage and greatly admire, will tell you that she had one real disaster. Against her better judgment, she sang Adalgisa at the Met. She said it was an absolute mess. She learned her lesson, though, and applied what she'd learned. Everyone wanted her to do Carmen but she never did because she knew that role, like Adalgisa, wasn't for her. I know that Matthew Epstein didn't want Sam to do Boris, but Sam was great in the role. The first time he sang it at the Met was the one and only time I ever saw Sam nervous before a performance. I'd seen the small nerves, which you turn into adrenalin, which in turn makes for a better performance but this was really nerves with a capital N. I was his principle manager at the time and before the performance, I went backstage to check things out. Gergiev was conducting and Sam was the only non-Russian in the cast. When I got to his dressing room, I was shocked to see that the door was closed. That's something I'd never seen before; he always left the door open. I knocked, and after a bit, I knocked again. The door opened and there was Sam. He looked terrible. He was visibly nervous, really a mess, like nothing I'd ever seen before. I asked what was up and he said, 'I don't know, Jeffrey. I don't know. Can I deliver this role in this house with nothing but Russians surrounding me?' He got himself together and went out and gave a fantastic performance. But I'll never forget seeing him so distraught. I guess I'll never forget because I never saw it again. Well, I saw him get nervous another time but it was a different kind of situation. He sang Olin Blitch in Houston and after the performance we went to a donor's home for dinner. I was standing around when Sam came running over. He was a bit agitated.

'Oh my God,' he said, 'some woman just asked me to sing grace before dinner. What am I going to do?' 'Quick,' I answered, 'get a glass of wine in your hand.' While he ran off to get it, I went over to the host and said, 'Gee, Sam would love to sing grace but he's had a couple of glasses of wine and he can't sing anymore tonight.' The host looked over, saw Sam holding the wine glass, and said, 'Of course, I understand.' I'm blowing Sam's cover now but it was a while ago and I'm sure the folks in Houston will forgive him. Strictly speaking, those situations were out of the ordinary, Sam's one of the calmest people I've known. He's really laid back."

In terms of laid back, Sam Ramey may have met his match in the person of pianist, Warren Jones. They met when Sam made his New York *Rinaldo* debut. Jones, a lanky, Southerner raised in North Carolina and an honors graduate of the New England Conservatory of Music, was an assistant conductor at the Met. "I had prepared the *Rinaldo* and was playing the harpsichord in the pit," recalls Jones. "Of course, I'd heard of Sam, everybody had heard of him, and I was looking forward to seeing him in person. His entrance aria was electrifying. No one had heard it sung that way before and you won't hear it sung that way today. Even then, there wasn't a bass voice around that combined the sound, size, and agility. The fact is, to have heard voices like Sam's, like Marilyn's and like Eda Moser's, or any of those voices that were so large yet so agile, was unforgettable. Today, voices go ninety miles an hour but they're teeny voices." While on tour with the Met, Sam and Warren Jones were assigned to the same hotel in Atlanta, Georgia, and decided to have lunch together. Jones well remembers that occasion. "We were sitting across from each other at the table and I asked, 'So Sam, what do you do when you're not singing?' He looked at me, kind of sheepishly, shrugged his shoulders and said, 'To tell you the truth, nothing.' And I said, 'Well, Sam we're going to get along fine because I can do nothing really well.' If I got it right, and I'm pretty sure I did, I think Sam meant that he wasn't obsessed with what he was doing. He's been that way since I've known him."

In the mid-1980s, Samuel Ramey and Warren Jones began giving 'vocal concerts' together, another way of saying Sam Ramey sang and Warren Jones played the piano. Jones, like many of today's artists, disdains the traditional word, accompanist. "I'm a musician," he avers, "and when I play the piano, either as a soloist or along with a singer, I am making music." Because of his strong feelings about his role, Warren Jones was in the forefront of those who played with the piano lid at its fullest height, an innovative act that broke with recital custom. While the top is fully raised for solo or concert performances, accompanists of the mid-Twentieth century, including Gerald Moore and Geoffrey Parsons, traditionally played with the lid barely cracked. Like Moore and Parsons before him, Martin Katz, long associated with Marilyn Horne, also favors the "half-stick." Explains Craig Rutenberg, a virtuoso pianist and currently the Metropolitan Opera's Director of Music Administration, "Things changed in the 1970s, when solo pianists, like Sviatislov Richter and Alicia de Larrocha, started to play for singers and used the full stick. I started doing it around 1992 with Thomas Hampson and never looked back. One simply has more control over the sonorities and dynamics. It's easier to play softly and more transparently with the lid up." Warren Jones's stick position is pretty inflexible, although in the past he did defer to at least one artist. "Warren tyrannized singers, but I wouldn't let him get away with it," laughs Marilyn Horne who, in her classical recital days, insisted that the lid had to be down. Down or up was all the same to Sam, which was all the more reason for him and Jones to get along.

"Sam and I began collaborating around 1983/84. I'm not sure of the exact date that we started working together but I do know that he and I gave the first vocal concert when Carnegie Hall reopened in 1986. It was my Carnegie debut, and though Sam had done some orchestral concerts, this was his first solo appearance. It was quite an evening; stage seats were set up because the auditorium was sold out. When we finished the first half of the program with a big aria from Rossini's *Maometto II*, Sam got hold of an unbelievably good high note at the end and held it forever, right through the piano playout. There was a nano second of silence and then the entire audience, like one person, YELLED at us. The noise was so loud, it almost knocked me off the piano bench. I am not exaggerating; it was that forceful. You know, I regard singing as incredibly sophisticated, but I don't derogate a singer who can control and manipulate what amounts to 'yelling.' I remember thinking to myself as we took our bows, 'Well, Sam yelled at them and they yelled back.' That's the way it worked. He got a visceral response from people unlike anyone else that I've played for. Kathleen Battle would get big ovations, Marilyn Horne got huge ovations, but it wasn't the kind of gut response Sam got. I think it has to do with the way he performs. Sam's an instinctive person on stage who has trained himself very carefully. He knows exactly what he's doing but then the instinct, the gut, takes over, and that's what grabs people. They got excited in an animal way listening to him sing. In rehearsals, Sam is very receptive and very reactive to what's going on around him but because he presents such an incredibly strong persona and projects his personality so forcefully when he's singing, it's hard to believe that receptive aspect exists. As amenable as he is, we've had our share of calamaties. The one I remember most happened years ago in Chicago. At the time, I was doing a string of concerts by memory. I felt that if I were performing, I should commit the music to memory just like the singer. The recital was in Orchestra Hall and that evening was the first time we put a group of Duparc songs into the program. It's kind of interesting because there used to be only fourteen known Duparc songs and then they found a couple of more and then they found the seventeenth, *The Gallop*, which was originally written for the bass voice. *The Gallop* is about a man on a horse going straight down a hill to Hell and it's like he can't get there fast enough. He's going full speed to his death. The song immediately appealed to Sam's satanic side. Now, this song has a lot of notes to play and a lot of notes to sing, it really is a gallop. As Sam and I walked on the stage of Orchestra Hall, I looked at him and said under my breath, "I'll see you at the end." I went to the piano, Sam took his place, and we began. Somewhere on the first page, which of course wasn't in front of me, I got off. The piece is in a circle of fifths and I went one too many and was wildly wrong, wildly. I kept on playing 'something' and Sam kept on singing. I figured in my head that I'd meet him at the G Minor section, and I did. We got together at the G minor, had a few bars together, and then Sam went off and began making things up, just as I had done a few moments early. Okay, I'm talking about a four-minute song and we're talking about minutes where I made things up and then he made things up. Poor Duparc. Towards the end we got together and somehow managed to finish at the same time. As this was the last song on the program, I got up from the piano, and the two of us stood there taking bows with huge smiles on our faces. When we walked off the stage, we collapsed with laughter. What I said to Sam before we started really made sense: I only did see him at the end. It's my opinion that the best way to learn your way around music is the same as learning your way around an unfamiliar city. Get lost. In either instance, once you find yourself, you won't get lost again. Well, that's exactly what happened with *The Gallop*. Neither of us ever tripped up again. Just for the record, the *Chicago Tribune* reviewer wrote that Sam and I were 'consummate musicians' and 'totally in command of Duparc's difficult *Gallop*.'

"Glitches aside, I regard the study and performance of music as 'truth seeking' and that's what Sam is about. When you're on stage with somebody you know what they are, you know if they're telling the truth and you also know if they're lying. It hasn't happened a lot but I've been on stage with people who, I knew, were lying about what they were doing. Singing is about communicating and that's what Sam does. He understands what he's saying and he says it and I think that's what people get onto. When he studies anything there's an implicit search for truth. He doesn't say much, there's not a lot of talking, but there doesn't need to be. It's a nonverbal thing. Fundamentally, Sam is one of the most honest people on stage I can imagine. He speaks with his voice directly, without any pretense, without any charade, without any kind of stuffing the front. There's no window dressing, it's just Sam singing. He understands what he's saying and he says it, clearly and simply. It's elemental. When he's onto a text, and that's a big 'when,' he says the words in the most open direct way and it kills people. Take Gershwin's *Embraceable You*. When Sam sang it, it was as though he reached out to every individual in the audience and said, 'Embrace me,' and they did! In all the years we've been doing concerts together, there's never ever been a time that he's ever done anything out of obligation. Nothing is sung out of duty, it's sung out of his desire to say something, to bring something to the audience. There's no artifice; it's straight on, honest, intuitive, singing. And you can't beat it."

While Warren Jones is high on Sam as a recitalist, others

believe that Sam's great strength was not as suited to the confines of the concert stage but lay in the broad strokes of opera where he was peerless. The late Robert Jacobson, editor of *Opera News* in the 1980s, whole-heartedly admired Sam's phenomenal flexibility and the brilliance, thrust, and color of his voice, but did express some criticism of his solo work. "Sam isn't a highly intellectual singer. He has an innate response to music and he's well studied but he doesn't go into deep analysis, which is a key to great lieder singing." Robert Jacobson was not alone in holding this opinion. Armen Boyajian, of all people, had his reservations, too.

"I'll never forget Sam's first solo recital. Up to then, most of his performing had been done in costume in opera. To stand alone, and to carry an entire evening on your own, in different languages, is a horse of a different color. Sam hadn't done much with song programs. He had to break one in before performing it on the major concert stages. In other words, he had to come up through the minors. Naturally, because he was comfortable with me, he asked me to play for him. I went on several recital jaunts with Sam but the initial recital was the one that I really had to help him get through. It took place in Colby, and was a 'favorite son returns' kind of thing. You couldn't fly to Colby directly; actually, it was a challenge to get there indirectly. I flew into the closest airport, whose name I can't remember, rented a car, and drove just about across Kansas to get to Colby. Sam and Carrie were already there and I have to say it was a wonderful place to visit. His mother and the others were farm folk, beautiful, quiet, people. I saw the house where Sam was born and the recital itself took place in his high school. It was special for me, who was so involved with Sam, to see where it all came from. Sam was VERY nervous at that recital because it contained a lot of new material. He was most confident with the operatic excerpts and, not surprisingly, got a huge hand when we ended the first half with an aria from *Mefistofele*. He was on home ground with that, but there were Schubert songs to be done and a lot of new words to memorize. We were in the middle of one of the Schuberts when all of a sudden he jumped a whole page. I had to scramble like a madman to catch up with him. Afterwards, I said, 'Sam, you owe me a page.' 'What do you mean?' he asked. I took the music and pointed to the page. 'This,' I said. He looked down, and then looked up, smiled sheepishly, and said, 'Oh yeah.' I did the program with him a number of times and then Warren took over. After that, any time Warren couldn't make a concert, I'd fill in.

"Sam's first Carnegie recital was a big hit but people were expecting a lot from him. They wanted the lieder to be in the same league as the opera stuff. Sam's real home was the opera stage, and though he is a great singer, for me, he wasn't as comfortable on the recital stage. If you compare him to someone like Dietrich Fischer-Dieskau, you'll get what I mean. Fischer-Dieskau deals with words, delves into the poetry, lives with it, and interprets it. There's no question that Sam has the more beautiful voice, but what does Sam know about Schubert that Fischer-Dieskau couldn't write ten books about! And that also goes for someone like Thomas Hampson, who's really deeply into lieder. They're different types. I think the New York recital public was kind of hoping they'd get a combo of those two elements, and it never occurred. He's sensitive, but not that sensitive to words that he would color them in a poetic way; it's not Sam. With his disposition and that voice, he's not going to be a delicate poet. That being said, I gave him credit for simply doing it. I remember thinking at the time that the audience was lucky he even sang a Schubert song. Then he'd come to the end of the program and sing these Cole Porter things, a Rossini aria, and pieces like that. All of a sudden, he'd relax and bring down the house. I have to say he grew into recitals and little by little got better at it, but I don't think the solo recital ever was his home base. It's different today, he's doing concert programs with Flicka von Stade and they're a big hit. No lieder, but lots of showstoppers. Now, as then, he always puts on a damn good show."

Another person who believes that Sam was perhaps not the consummate artist on the recital stage is Sam. "When I started doing the recitals, I was frightened to death. Once I got into it, I enjoyed it, and I still enjoy it, but I was never a great recitalist."

In certain ways, the recital versus opera issue was analogous to the *Boris Godunov* quandary. Yes, Sam could do solo appearances, but they may not have shown him at his best. Yes, Sam could sing Boris, but it might not have been the ideal role for his voice. However, suggesting that Sam Ramey not sing Boris was like urging a .400 hitter to bunt. "Boris Godunov intrigued me because it's a great role for a bass, in some ways, the greatest," mused Sam. "Boris was a bad good guy or a good bad guy who tore up the scenery, just the kind of part I love. It's a role you can sink your teeth into and it calls for heavy-duty acting like King Lear for a Shakespearean. That's why, when the Los Angeles offer came, I was really tempted. I was doing all the beautiful bel canto stuff and other operas with lovely lyric lines, and here was this vocal Mt. Everest to conquer. I wanted to take the challenge, but Armen and Matthew put up a fuss."

The fussing worked. Sam heeded Boyajian and Epstein's advice, which in essence was, put off to tomorrow what you should think better of doing today. After a few exploratory technical sessions with Boyajian, during which his teacher kept at him to "save" Boris for later, Sam turned down the Los Angeles offer. Eventually he would add the tortured Tsar to his inventory performing the role first in Geneva and then, among other cities, in Salzburg, New York, and, in what turned out to be a turning point in his personal life, Chicago. He waited until he was over fifty, fifty-one to be exact, to take it on, and it was a wise choice. Any earlier and it might have interfered with his repertoire. Neither Armen Boyajian nor Matthew Epstein ever fully approved of Sam's choice.

Whatever Sam sang, he always knew what he was singing about and lest that statement sounds anomalous, consider the fact that not every opera singer, even some great ones, did know! Apropos, Anne Midgette, the Washington Post music critic, tells a fitting story about Eileen Farrell, the outstanding dramatic soprano of the mid-twentieth century. Farrell, an Irish Catholic New Englander, was famous for her Medea, a role she sang many times, although in concert versions rather than on the operatic stage. During a recording session of the Cherubini work, the conductor stopped her and said, "Now, when you get to the point where you kill the children...." to which Farrell shrieked, "Kill the children? What kind of shit is this! I'm not going to sing that!"

Sam Ramey's first gimmick, his vocal dexterity, came at the beginning of his professional life and could have been quite enough. But at the height of his operatic career, Sam got his second gimmick, a hot idea that would extend his appeal beyond the portals of the world's opera houses and into the public arena. The inspiration was the brainchild of Matthew Epstein who, long after he stopped being Sam's manager, continued to aid and abet his friend's career. With a few notable exceptions, Silva in *Ernani*, Iago in *Otello*, and Sir John in *Falstaff*, Sam had plumbed the bass canon. He was about as box office as an opera singer can get especially in the roles that called for him to strut his bare-chested stuff. Sam worked out in the gym religiously and was in great physical shape, and much was made of his proclivity for portraying muscle men. His City Opera debut as Attila inspired *The New York Times* to dub him the "Rambo of early Verdi." For Sam, playing yet another robust half naked protagonist was a lark. What't more, Norman Treigle never sang the role, thus no comparisons could be made.

Rambo roles aside, if Sam shone in one particular area, it was as the villain. Devils and devils incarnate became an integral part of his operatic inventory. What amazed everyone who knew him personally was how did a nice easy-going guy like Sam Ramey become so identified with a mean son-of-a-bitch like the Devil? Warren Jones feels that "Sam loves to sing evil people because there's not a single evil bone in his body. It's not that it's a fascination for him so much as it allows him to have a good romp on stage. Giorgio Tozzi was the first Mephistopheles I saw. He had such a good time playing the devil. He enjoyed it from the top to the bottom, clowning around in the light-hearted parts, and then doing the serious moments, like in the garden scene when he turned around and you saw that he was evil through and through. Sam has the same kind of enjoyment about evil." Sam dittoes his friend Warren's appraisal and acknowledges with a smile, "I always enjoyed playing bad guys, they have more fun."

The big, 'bad guy' made his debut in the Old Testament where he was called *ha-satan*. He was a member of the divine court of heaven and roamed the earth gathering information about humankind, and reporting his findings to God. During his global wanderings, *ha-satan* tried to incite seditious behavior among humans in order to discredit mankind. A born troublemaker, he hoped to cause a rift between God and his creatures. *Ha-satan* was re-named "*diabolos*" in the Greek translation of the Bible, and in Latin, the word became *diabolus,* which eventually led to, *devil.* Over the centuries, the Devil has collected countless names, *The Prince of Darkness*, *The Dark Angel*, *The Serpent*, *The Tempter, Beelzebub, Mammon, Lucifer*, et al. He also boasts colloquial aliases such as variations on *Nicolas Scratch* like *Mr. Scratch*, *Old Scratch*, and *Old Nick*. His names are legion, and this list barely scratches the surface, but of all his monikers, the Devil is perhaps most widely identified as

## SAMUEL RAMEY: American Bass

Satan. Like it or not, in whatever manifestation he assumes, the Devil has proven to be far more intriguing than any of his angelic counterparts. You can fear him, hate him, or even deny him, yet he remains peculiarly irresistible. For Sam Ramey he proved to be the perfect vehicle.

In literature and in music, the Devil often turns up as Mephistopheles, and under that name, he is the antagonist in three standard musical stage works: Gounod's *Faust*, Boito's *Mefistofele*, and Berlioz's, *The Damnation of Faust*. Mephistopheles also appears in Ferruccio Busoni's rarely performed *Doktor Faustus*. Although the Gounod, Boito, and Berlioz operas provided Samuel Ramey with defining roles, he also excelled in portraying the Devil in disguise, for example, as Bertram in Meyerbeer's *Robert, le diable*, as Nick Shadow in Stravinsky's, *The Rake's Progress,* and as Lindorf, Coppelius, Dapertutto and Dr. Miracle in Offenbach's *Tales of Hoffman*. The devil in Sam had emerged in the Paterson Lyric Opera production of *Faust* but then took a back seat as Sam moved into his apprenticeship with the New York City Opera. After a relatively brief quietus the devil leaped into the forefront again with Sam's first City Opera Mephistopheles and from there it was full Satan ahead.

In 1995, Matthew Epstein negotiated a contract for Sam to appear with the St. Luke's Chamber Orchestra in New York with Julius Rudel conducting and got together with the singer to figure out the program. Considering Sam's expertise in the satanic repertory and factoring in his huge successes, it was little wonder that Matthew Epstein had a brainstorm as they mulled over selections. Why not create a concert comprised of arias and musical interludes from the works in which the devil dominates? Sam loved the idea. The opportunity to do his (best) thing appealed to Sam primarily because it would allow him to display his vocal skills. And, there was a special perk. Singing in front of an orchestra rather than on an opera stage, gave Sam the opportunity to indulge in the sartorial bent that had been his trademark since white suede shoes days back in Colby. For a country boy, Sam Ramey is curiously fashion conscious, a trait that remained under wraps until financial security enabled him to indulge in haute couture. While it was no surprise to see him on the cover of *Opera News* magazine, it was rather startling to find his smartly clad person featured on the cover of a gentlemen's fashion magazine. The adult fashion phenomenon began when he started carrying a "manbag," those small leather purses for men, and then moved on to embrace his wardrobe. Soon, his clothing became as much a hallmark for Sam as, according to reviewers, 'his mandatory bare-chested appearances' in opera.

"Women artists have to worry so much about what they're going to wear on stage; men just have a choice of black or white tie," Sam explained. "I kind of liked the idea of doing something different and was always on the lookout for special formal wear. And I found it in a magazine article about Gianni Versace. He designed a set of tails and the minute I saw the picture, I wanted to own it. Most tails are open in the front; this set was really very different, closed in front, double breasted, and cut away to the tails in back. I loved those tails and I went right over to Charivari's on 81st Street and Columbus Avenue to get them. They had only one suit left and it was my size. I read it as a sign and bought it on the spot. I immediately began wearing it for my concert appearances. One of the first times I wore it was at a La Scala performance of the Verdi *Requiem*. I was standing in the anteroom when the conductor, Ricardo Muti, walked in. Someone said to him, loud enough for me to hear, 'What on earth is Sam Ramey wearing?' Muti fixed his eyes on me, looked me up and down, then smiled, and said, again, loud enough for me to hear, 'Ah si, nostro Samuel e sempre un po speziale.' ('Oh yes, our Sam is always a little special.')

Now, Sam had his white tie, his top hits, and a showcase. Matthew Epstein chose a number of Satan-inspired arias and orchestral pieces for the musical evening, and came up with an appropriate and catchy title, *A Date with the Devil*. Appropriate to most, that is but not to some fundamentalist Christian groups who found the title, if not the program, blasphemous. "When I did the show in Kansas," recalls Sam, "I was picketed by followers of Reverend Fred Phelps, a homophobic rightwinger. My concert was a double whammy. Not only did it feature the devil, my audience contained a lot of gays. No wonder the Phelps gang stood in front of the hall yelling garbarge."

*A Date with the Devil* came to Avery Fisher Hall in New York on February 7, 1996 with Julius Rudel conducting the Orchestra of St Luke's. Since then, give or take a few arias, Sam continued to present A *Date with the Devil,* both at home and abroad.

Jane Scovell

# An Ending

In the spring of 1997, Sam was singing Mephistopheles in a La Scala production of *Faust*. The Rameys rented an apartment in a residence hotel for the duration of the Milan engagement. Occasionally, they invited friends over for dinner. On one of those evenings, after the company left and Carrie retired, Sam walked around the apartment checking to see that the lights were turned off when, as he describes it, "All of a sudden I felt weird. It's the only way I can describe it, weird, like kind of weak in my head and in my knees. I kept on walking around trying to shake the feeling and then I guess I just passed out. I came to, got up from the floor, and got into bed. Later, I started feeling weird again, even lying in my bed. I had a pain in my left arm and I truly thought I was having a heart attack. Carrie called Nancy Gustafson and Giuseppe Sabatini who were in the same hotel. Giuseppe was the Faust in the Scala production. They came over, took one look at me, and called for an ambulance. The ambulance arrived, and I was taken to a nearby clinic where I spent the rest of the night on a gurney in the hallway. The next day, they started doing a whole bunch of tests. Meanwhile, Nancy called a Milanese friend of hers who was married to a doctor. She told Nancy that the clinic wasn't a good place so they pulled me out of there and moved me to a private hospital. I stayed for a few days and had more tests. Even though they couldn't find anything wrong, I cancelled the rest of the Scala performances, and flew home. I got that same weird feeling on the plane, dizziness and spots in front of my eyes. When we landed in New York a wheelchair was waiting for me and, sick as I felt, I remember thinking this is pretty good, we don't have to wait to get through customs.

"I went to see my doctor and he sent me to all these specialists, neurologists mostly, to figure out if something was wrong. I had cat scans and a bunch of other tests. The neurologists couldn't find anything either, and so I was sent to a heart specialist. Meanwhile, the pain stopped, which was a relief. I'm pretty sure it was the heart doctor who had me take a tilt table test. They laid me out, strapped me down, and put an intravenous into my arm. I was lying flat out and the table was raised up to a position where I was standing but attached to the table. They told me to stay perfectly still and not to move. I said, okay. I'm standing, standing, standing, when all of a sudden I started to feel kind of strange. I passed out. They did a few more tests and then the doctor spoke to me. My problem was diagnosed as an overactive adrenal gland, and I was put on something like a Beta-blocker, which I took for around a year. After I stopped the medication, I never had another problem. But let me tell you, while it was happening, it was pretty scary. I wasn't used to having health problems. That was bad enough, but it exacerbated another problem, a personal one. To be honest, things hadn't been good between Carrie and me for a long time, and this episode was the beginning of the end of our marriage.

"I was supposed to do *Boris Godunov* in Salzburg that summer and while I was having the tests I decided that, whatever the outcome, I needed to take the summer off. Without discussing it with Carrie, I called Joyce Arbib and told her I wanted to cancel. Joyce said not to worry that she'd take care of everything. She called Salzburg and they were fine about it. They were fine but Carrie wasn't. When she found out that I had cancelled, she went ballistic. She was furious at me. Maybe it was because I hadn't talked it over with her before speaking to Joyce, who knows? All I know is, this marked the beginning of the end of our marriage. It was very sad to come to the realization that, after nearly thirth years, we really didn't have anything in common anymore."

The dissolution of the Ramey's marriage did not come as a surprise to friends and associates who long had sensed a strain in the relationship. Still, it was dismaying especially for those who had known them from the beginning. Carrie and Sam Ramey were officially separated but it took years before the marriage ended legally.

"Not long after the separation, I moved to Chicago," recalls Sam, "and I began seeing a soprano, Lindsey Larsen. We were married when my divorce was finalized. Lindsey is the love of my life."

# A New Beginning

Lindsey Rae Larsen Ramey, born in Sioux Falls, South Dakota on April 30, 1964, comes from generations of Lutheran/Scandinavian South Dakotan stock. Tall, blonde, statuesque, her heritage is immediately apparent. Looks aside, Lindsey has the same down-to-earth mid-Western qualities as her husband, and a similarly wry sense of humor. She is, as well, a nurturer. Lindsey always wanted to be a singer and, like her husband, her earliest aspirations were pop-oriented, first rock, then musical theatre. By the time she met Sam, however, she was totally committed to opera and had joined the Lyric Opera of Chicago chorus. More than music, dentistry runs in the Larsen family. Lindsey's father, John David Larsen III, is a dentist, and her mother, Sally Rae Peterson Larsen, daughter of a dentist, is a dental hygienist. It was Sally Rae's mother, Alice Peterson, who broke the mold. At one time the youngest violinist in the South Dakota Symphony orchestra, Alice Peterson was a teacher, conductor, and choral director. Taking her cue from her grandmother, Lindsey focused on music and while at Lincoln High participated in the school's musical events. She did undergraduate work at St. Olaf College in Northfield, Minnesota where she majored in music. During her senior year, her career plans faltered. She began to experience intense performance anxiety resulting in panic attacks whenever she appeared on stage. Auditions were physically and emotionally draining and, even if she managed to get parts, fear hampered her performances. Though she went to psychologists, used relaxation tapes, and tried hypnosis, all efforts were in vain. Frustrated and exhausted, she returned to Sioux Falls where she remained for two years. She lived at home and, "much to the chagrin" of her parents, worked as a bartender. Determined to get back to singing, she moved to Chicago where she enrolled first in the opera program at Northwestern and then at De Paul for postgraduate study.

"I took on three or four part-time jobs to keep afloat. I was a horrible waitress, an okay bank teller, and a good receptionist. I did some church work, including singing in the choir. For some reason, I had no trouble doing solos in church; it just wasn't an issue. To make more money, I auditioned for and got into the Lyric Opera chorus. Donald Palumbo was the chorus director and I learned a lot from him. He's at the Met now. The chorus was great for me because I had a chance to sing and I also got a bird's eye view of great singers at work, singers like Samuel Ramey.

"I first saw Sam in person when Chicago Lyric did *Boris Godunov*. Of course I'd heard of him and I'd seen him on television and, let's face it, I was a fan. During *Boris* rehearsals Sam would come by and chat with the cast and crew. He was always friendly but I couldn't even make eye contact with him. If he glanced my way, I'd look down at the floor. He was a star and I was a lowly chorister. The next year Sam came back for *Faust*. We didn't exchange two words mostly because the women's chorus went onstage just as the men's came off and there was no opportunity to talk. Sam knew a few of the choristers and he'd talk to them. Sometimes I'd be in the group and he'd kind of acknowledge me but that was it. Once, someone took a picture of us; he's smiling and my face is frozen.

"The following year Sam returned for *Don Carlo*. At the same time there was a gala for Ardis Kranik, the director of the Lyric Opera. It was a black tie evening and we choristers were appropriately gowned. I was standing in the wings waiting to go on when I got real thirsty. I went over to the water cooler to get a drink. Sam was standing nearby and as I walked past him he smiled and said, 'You look very lovely.' I was so taken aback I blurted, 'Thank you. So do you.' The minute I said it, I realized how stupid I must have sounded. I was mortified and fled to the cooler. The next season he came for *Nabucco*. Really, that's how I remember my time at the Lyric—by what operas Sam was doing. *Nabucco* was performed in the fall and we ended up standing in the wings on the same side of the stage waiting to go on. He said, 'Hi, how are you, Lindsey?' I was dumbstruck that he actually knew my name. But by then, I was so tongue-tied. While we waited in the wings, we'd exchange a few jokes and stuff like that. That's how we got to know each other. That winter, Sam and his wife split up and he moved to Chicago. He was appearing a lot with the Lyric. I guess he probably wanted a change of pace from New York. Eventually, he decided to make the move to Chicago permanent. One afternoon we ran into each other on Michigan Avenue. We talked a bit and that was that. I was thrilled to see him but it was just a casual meeting. The next day, I came home and found a message on my answering machine saying, "Hello, this is Sam Ramey." I started laughing. I thought someone was playing a joke on me. But then I thought, who could imitate that voice? It's got to be Sam Ramey. He was calling to ask me out on a date and we started going together. I can't say for sure how fast Sam fell in love, but I can tell you he had me at that first telephone call.

"My mother was not happy with the situation. On the one hand, she was very excited because I was seeing SAMUEL RAMEY. On the other hand, although Sam was separated from his wife, my mom thought it was inappropriate for us to be dating before the divorce was final. My family's solid Lutheran and very conservative and this definitely was not standard operating procedure. In time, my mother got over it. She had to because the divorce went on for almost five years. Once it became final, my mom, who despaired of me meeting Mr. Right, said, 'It's like the Lord knew that Sam would come along, eventually.' My dad was okay with it from the beginning. Sam is the only person I dated that my father liked. He never thought the others treated me well enough. Even so, after a couple of years, I remember him saying to me, 'I don't think he's going to get divorced. I don't think it's going to happen.' Well, it did happen but it wasn't easy. The lawyers gave us a date on which the divorce would be granted and told me I could go ahead with the wedding plans. I was traveling with Sam, so my mom had to take over the arrangements. Unfortunately, Carrie Ramey and her lawyer decided not to sign, and the wedding had to be cancelled. Sam and I were both upset. I was unhappy for us and also for my poor mother who'd put the wedding together. My mom was great about it. Sam was an angel. It was a hard time for him but he remained calm and helped me to be that way, too. When things got put on hold, he rarely said anything against Carrie. Sure, he'd get upset initially, but then he'd say, 'This isn't the only side of her personality. She's under a lot of stress. She's a very good person, too.' That's how Sam is, fair. While we waited for the divorce, I spent a few years as Sam's live-in and traveling companion and made the best of it. I wasn't happy that we weren't able to be man and wife but there was nothing I could do about it.

"In many ways it was an exciting time, so many cities to visit and so many people to meet. In general, I was the youngest person in the crowd and the most uncelebrated. It was hard to be casual about being introduced to people like Joan Sutherland, Beverly Sills and Luciano Pavarotti. Sam's colleagues were my idols. One meeting stands out from all the rest. After a performance at the Met, Sam went down the hall to talk to someone, and I stayed in the dressing room. There was a knock on the door. I said, 'Come in' and the next thing I knew, I was face to face with Marilyn Horne. I was terrified.

'Hi,' she said, 'I'm Marilyn Horne.' Like she needed to tell me who she was. I grew up listening to her sing and hearing stories about her. She came over and sat down next to me on the sofa. We chatted for a bit, then she reached over, took my hand in hers, and looked me straight in the eye.

'You take good care of our boy, now,' she said.

'I will, I will,' I answered. I always knew how special Marilyn was to Sam and at that moment I realized how special he was to her."

Lindsey Larsen and Sam Ramey were married on June 29, 2002 in Sioux Falls, South Dakota. While their daily routine scarcely changed, a great sense of relief came with the legitimization of their union. They were happy, and wanted to increase that happiness. Getting the divorce was a struggle, and having a child also proved difficult. Because of fertility challenges, they decided to try in vitro fertilization. They are remarkably candid about what they went through. According to Lindsey, "It was tough on both of us. I had to take all the steroids and Sam had his cross to bear, too. I remember at parties, after a drink or two, he'd tell anybody within hearing distance that he had to have surgery. I heard him say more than once, 'yep, they had to cut open my nuts.'" The Rameys were fortunate that Lindsey got pregnant the first time especially since three subsequent tries were unsuccessful.

"We were so thrilled, it's hard to put into words how we felt. And the fact that we got a hit the first time was amazing. My due date was the end of May and Sam had overseas engagements around that time. He'd had these dates for years. One was at the Paris Opera. He planned to fulfill his scheduled appearances and then fly back for the birth. It was kind of iffy and I was nervous about him *not* being with me. But I didn't say anything. A few months before the due date, Sam and I were in Vienna where we ran into

Bryn Terfel, a terrific guy and a marvelous singer. The conversation centered on music and then drifted into our impending 'blessed' event. Sam said that wherever he happened to be singing, he intended to fly back for the baby's birth. Bryn kind of shook his head. He told us that he'd been on an airplane trying to get home for the birth of one of his children and agonized all the way because he wasn't sure he'd get back in time. He did make it, but the experience was so nerve wracking he vowed never again to play it so close. 'Sam,' he told my husband, 'whatever else, just make sure you'll be there for the birth.' I was so happy Bryn said what he did. I think it kind of helped Sam make his final decision. Rather than jeopardize his chances of being with me Sam cancelled Paris. It was lucky he did, because the baby was two weeks early.

"My mother had planned an extended stay so she was there when it happened. As I recall, I got up to get something and bingo, my water broke. I told Sam to get our suitcases. They tell you to pack an overnight bag so that you can get to the hospital fast. I packed mine when I was in my sixth month. Sam was supposed to pack his, too, and I kept bugging him to do it. He kept saying he would but when I said, "Get the suitcases," he cried out, 'Oh my gosh, I haven't packed.' Okay, I told him, you go pack and I'll put on some make-up. Sam ran up the stairs and after a few minutes came racing down again, took me by the arm, and helped me out the door. I waited on the front step while he ran to the car. He opened the door and ran back to get me, crying, 'Come on, come on.' I got into the front seat. Sam closed the door and chased around to get behind the wheel. Just then my mom walked out of the house. 'Sam,' she called from the front steps, 'you forgot the suitcase you just packed.' Sam stopped dead in his tracks. For a minute he stood there with his eyes closed. Then he said under his breath and very, very slowly and deliberately, 'Okay. I'm fine. Everything's fine. I can do this. I can do this! I've sung at La Scala.' Honestly, it was like something out of *I Love Lucy*. We got to Northwestern Memorial Hospital and I was checked in. Sam slept on a couch in the room while I waited to go into labor. They had to give me a shot of Pitosin and soon we were off to the delivery room with me clutching my stomach and Sam clutching his camera. I didn't want any videos of the birth, just photographs. Our son, Samuel Guy Ramey, was born on May 27$^{th}$ 2003. I was awake for everything. Sam was clicking away on his camera like some crazy paparazzi. I watched as the nurses put Guy on the scales. Sam photographed the weigh-in and was grinning from ear to ear. At the same time, I could see tears running down his cheeks.

"Because of his age Sam was convinced that he wasn't going to have children, and he'd been kind of fearful during the pregnancy. It was such a relief when Guy finally arrived. Becoming a father changed Sam a lot, in a good way. My husband's not a selfish person at all, but when you have children everything is centered on them. Sometimes that's kind of off-putting for a person who's used to getting all the attention. Not Sam. He's so much more settled now and he feels that his life is complete. Sam loved Guy from the minute he was born; it took me a couple of weeks. I was so darned tired. Sam took over, holding him, changing him, and feeding him while I adjusted to motherhood. Sam's the one who carries the pictures and not one or two, it's a whole stack, and he whips them out for everybody. At first, he actually carried a *framed* picture! Sam plunged into fatherhood and I think he enjoyed pushing Guy in his stroller as much as he did singing! There is a downside of course; Sam's got a lot of energy but it's not easy being an older parent. He's been tired ever since we had Guy. Frankly, I think my husband's getting a taste of what it must have been like for his parents when he was little."

Lindsey Larsen became Sam Ramey's wife but she has never stopped being a fan. Although she heard him on stage in many of the roles that made him famous, her great regret is not having seen his Don Giovanni in person. It is Sam's regret as well. While her own career is on hold, ironically, marriage has helped Lindsey deal with the performance anxiety. When Sam and she started living together, she considered auditioning again but then dropped it. She did not want anyone to think that she was using his name to get work. She kept up with singing lessons simply because of her love for music and actually gave a recital in 2005. The concert was a result of her winning the Farwell Award while at De Paul. The award included subsequent solo appearances at the Chicago Cultural Arts Center's Preston Bradley Hall. Somewhat leery of being on her own, Lindsey asked if she could give a duo recital with her husband. Big surprise, the programmers were delighted to present Mr. and Mrs. Samuel Ramey in song. It had been five years since Lindsey had sung in public and she was, understandably, nervous. Sam's presence, and the fact that she knew the audience came to hear him, not her, had a calming effect. They each did their own set and then joined together for one duet, Gershwin's, *Bess, You is My Woman Now*. Lindsey has not sung in public since that appearance; she is too busy being wife and mother. Asked if she would ever sing again, she says she would like to think that sometime in the future, she might do a little recital here or a little concert there, very low key. I'm a dime-a-dozen lyric soprano, and there are zillions of us. Still, she adds with post-feminist confidence, "it's always good to keep your own thing going."

Lindsey and Guy continued to travel with Sam as he fulfilled engagements in the States and abroad. But that freedom ended when Guy began formal schooling. At this stage, it should not rock the boat that much. Sam has said he would like to fully retire at seventy and, allowing that he set that goal a while ago, he has opera and concert engagements that will carry him through the next few years. One particular series, the concerts he has been doing for the past ten years with Frederica von Stade, is close to his heart. Jeffrey Vanderveen put them together, and it was his idea to divide the program into two sections. The first part is semi serious and features classical selections. After the intermission, Broadway and Pop take over. "Flicka and I collaborated on the program," explains Sam. "We picked out our solo stuff and came to an agreement on what to sing together. Funny thing is, it's not that easy to find duet material for mezzo and bass." The two of them have performed with orchestral and piano accompaniement, and these concerts definitely are crowd pleasers. One recital brought Sam back to Bob Jones University, which he found little changed. Sam and von Stade obviously enjoy being with each other, indeed they are old friends; von Stade sang at Sam and Lindsey's wedding. The fact is, if anyone were to say to an opera aficionado of a certain age, "Quick, name the two most liked singers in the profession," odds are that Flicka von Stade and Sam Ramey would top the list. Along with likeability, each is an artist of the highest order. Von Stade, adored in her own right, is outspoken in her admiration and affection for her colleague and thrilled to be working with the man who, in her estimation, is "the greatest male singer of my generation."

"Sam will go on forever, like the Energizer bunny. The first time I sang with him was in the late seventies or early eighties on a recording of Rossini's *Otello*. *Otello* has something like five tenor parts and really good singers were brought in. Then, Sam came in and began singing the bass part. Everybody freaked out. 'God has put this voice in a human being?' was the thought in everyone's head, not just mine. I know Sam was not at the very beginning of his career, but it seems to me that he went from zero to eighty in about three years. I mean most of us have apprentice years where you move slowly and steadily up the ladder but Sam was different. He was sort of periphery and you kept hearing his name and then all of a sudden he was everywhere.

I'd never heard anything like his voice in my life. It was coloratura and he was moving it around like mad. And that sound! It's a core of sound that I really do think comes straight from his heart. Sam and I didn't do that much together on the operatic stage but now we're performing these recitals in the States and Canada and it's a joy. What I love is, I'll call him on his cell phone and he'll say HELLO and that hair-raising depth of sound is like no one else's in the world. I swear it makes me feel like answering, 'Hello God, this is Flicka, how are you?' Really, there *is* godliness in his voice. I can't explain him. What you see and hear is what you get with Sam. And what you get is the pure column of sound and behind that is a pure column of soul. Plus, and this amazes me, he has an incredible sense of fashion. Traveling with him is quite an experience. I'm Mrs. 'StayinEconoLodges,' and I have my reliable little black bag with the necessary items, a few dresses, shoes, toiletries, et cetera. Sam comes on our jaunts carrying the biggest bags you've ever seen, and I still don't know what's in them. We've become good friends, but he does tend to keep to himself, which is fine, because I like to do that, too. We'll sit together in a car for hours and maybe he'll say three words. But whenever I say something like, 'Sam, my friend's coming to dinner. Would you join us? ,' he happily accepts. He loves people but, like I said, he really keeps to himself. Well, with one exception. I spent a lot of time with him in the winter and spring of 2007 and 2008, and I swear he must have called Lindsey at least twenty times a day. And he'd tell her in absolute detail what he was doing. I think he really depends on her and she looks after him, for sure. You can't say he's fragile, but he is fragile in a way because he needs protection or comfort around him. I think because he was so much younger than his siblings, he didn't have close companionship as a child. Oh, I don't want to go on too much about it; let's just say there's no one I'd more rather be 'on the road' with than Sam Ramey."

SAMUEL RAMEY: American Bass

# Ecco il suo Mondo

Sam Ramey's career has been the happy result of luck, pluck, and talent. From the day he decided on his calling, things have had a way of falling into place for him. Professionally, he always has known what he wanted and has known how to get it without stepping on toes. On the personal side, while he is not the kind of man you would expect to have three wives, each of his marriages seems to have been right for its time. The first helped him grow up, the second afforded exactly what he needed for his career and his self-esteem, and the third has provided solace and a son. Not everything has been sugar coated, however, and in the past couple of years there have been some tough blows. The deaths of Beverly Sills in 2007 and then a year later of Edgar Vincent, hit him hard. Still, they were of an older generation and he could accept the appropriate inevitable, something he could not do when his friend and colleague, tenor Jerry Hadley, committed suicide in July 2007. Hadley was fifty-five years old.

"Sam and Jerry were very close," explains Lindsey Ramey. "They had a real rapport. People called them the 'Dean Martin and Jerry Lewis' of opera because they were always kidding around, on and off stage. They were great pals and even when they weren't working together, they kept in touch though e-mail. Jerry had that dark side, though, and drinking was part of it. Still, he was so charming and so upbeat you didn't think it would end so tragically. Sam had such a hard time dealing with Jerry's death. Every now and then he'd start to cry just thinking about it. I've never seen him like that."

Sam has gotten along with friends and associates from his school days right up to the present. Paul Ackerman, his high school chum, was surprised and happy to see Sam at the Colby Community High class reunion in 2000. "We have a reunion every five years but this was the first time Sam was able to make it. We were out at the country club and it was late at night and we're all sitting around visiting and chatting. Now, most of us are modestly successful. I got a Doctorate, but nobody is in Sam's league. You'd never know it by the way he acts, though. He's the same to everybody. Sure, he stands out. He's a star, but he's just plain Sam to all of us. At the reunion banquet, the Bald Eagle Choir sang and Sam joined us. He really doesn't belong in the choir because, unlike most of us bald eagles, he's still got that full head of hair. Well, his voice came booming out over the choir, not because he was showing off, but just because he was singing. Another time, he went to Wichita to sing for the opera company, and a lot of Colby people went to the performance. Everyone wanted to say hi to him and we all got in the reception line. One of the directors of the opera kept coming over to Sam telling him to hurry it up so they could go over and meet with the sponsors. Sam kept saying, 'sure,' but he wouldn't budge till he'd greeted everybody. At one point, he recognized a woman standing back in the line; he broke loose, went right over and gave her a big hug. I didn't recognize her, neither did most of the others, but Sam did. It was Ms. Paterson, his music teacher. Another time, the Kansas opera decided to honor Sam and brought him back for a banquet. A bunch of us decided to go, and we drove up to Kansas City for the big deal in this hotel ballroom. There were about a dozen of us and we had our own Colby table. Sam, of course, was sitting on the dais with all the dignitaries. We were talking and laughing at our table and Sam couldn't take his eyes off of us. You could tell he wanted to know what we were laughing about. It was obvious that he so much more wanted to be sitting with us than all the bigwigs. But that's Sam and that's why we love him."

Sam's colleagues are equally appreciative of his gracious, gentlemanly, conduct and it is well nigh impossible to find anyone with anything to say against him. "Sam's personality is just not the norm for an opera singer," laughs bass-baritone Spiro Malas, a long time colleague at the New York City Opera. 'He's just so laid back. When he told me that he'd seen me as Leporello in the Central City Opera production, I said, 'Why didn't you say hello?' and he said, 'Well, I was in the chorus and you were a star.' And this is from the guy who, as far as I'm concerned, has done some of the greatest bass singing of all time. In the beginning, he watched and listened, and he was very smart. He was very sure about what he did. I remember one *Carmen* rehearsal when Julius stopped the orchestra and called out, 'Sam, you're singing too loud. Do it softer.' Sam said okay, and sang it again. I thought it sounded the same, but Julius said, 'That's it, now you've got it!' Sam told me later, 'I never changed a thing. I sang Zuniga and I sang Zuniga.' One time we were doing a *Don Giovanni* together in Los Palmas and his applause really wasn't what it should have been. I grabbed him afterwards and I said, 'Sam, you have a great smile and you don't smile enough. You tell Zerlina you've got a castle and money, and this and that, but you don't tell her that you've got something *else*. You gotta seduce Zerlina with a little smile. You know, *la ci darem*...a little smile...*la mano*...a smile...*la mi dirai*...another smile. Come on, MILK it, Sam.' Finally he did it, and the applause was twice as much. Another time during a performance of *The Queen of Spades*, Sam all of a sudden, threw in a High G. 'Jesus Christ, Sam,' I said. Where did that come from?' He could do things like that with no effort."

Marlena Malas, a voice teacher at Juilliard, has known

Sam since City Opera days and, like her husband, believes that Sam is in a class all his own. "A lot of the time when Sam sang he was bare-chested. As a teacher, I looked hard at him to see what the hell he was doing. How was he breathing? Was this coming out? Was that working? With Sam you never saw anything amiss, no wrong moves. Everything was done correctly and that's a tribute to the wonderful work he did with Armen Boyajian. Singers nowadays don't want to do the work. They want it yesterday and they're not willing to take the time to do it right. It's funny, we really worry in the theatre, that is, when we're watching an artist perform we think, what's happening here? Is this going to be okay? Will he get the notes? You never got that with Sam. You never worried when Sam was singing; everything was under control. That's old-time singing and that's the way it should be done."

Anne Manson, who conducted the *Boris Godunov* at Salzburg, was impressed both by Sam the singer and Sam the man. "He has incredible coloratura, incredible control, and the resonance of the voice, the edge of the voice in the coloratura, doesn't get lost at all. It has astonishing fire. And he's such a nice man! I got to do the *Boris* in Salzburg because I was Abbado's assistant and replaced Claudio when he was called for another engagement. Everyone in the cast was so kind, especially Sam. He was under a terrible strain because of his marital difficulties, and he still was thoughtful and helpful to me. I know that afterward he recommended me for *Susanna* in Geneva as well as a *Date with the Devil* concert. It was in Geneva that I met Lindsey and I was struck by how happy Sam was, so different from Salzburg. He deserves that happiness."

Lotfi Mansouri, a former general manager of the Toronto and San Francisco Opera companies, admires the manner in which Sam has handled his career in a profession overflowing with inflated egos. "He uses his ego and talent onstage rather than putting on phony-baloney shows in private," says Mansouri. "Sam has a firm sense of self, but he knows where and when to deploy it."

The legendary Montserrat Caballe treasures her appearances with him. "Singing was Sam's job, but he did more than his job. He was one of the most supportive and helpful persons I ever worked with. I get a little nervous before I sing. I would get these problems, mostly in my head, and he would take the time to calm me down. 'Take it easy, Montsie, 'it's all up here,' he'd say, and tap his forehead. 'You'll be just fine.' And his voice was so soothing it made me feel better. Sam is a great singer, everyone knows this, but he is the perfect gentleman, too. That is something everyone also should know."

Colleagues praise him and fans love him. He even has an official fan club; it was created in Vienna some twenty years ago. "It all began in the days when I appeared in Vienna fairly often," reminisces Sam. "Certain ladies always came back after the performances and I chatted with them and signed programs, things like that. I got to know them pretty well. One night, Eva Janauschek, an original member of the group, handed me a sheet of paper, asked me to look it over and tell me what I thought. It was a proposal for a fan club. I said I thought it was fine. In those days, the city of Vienna officially registered fan clubs but required the artist to give written permission for a club to be formed. I was happy to sign the necessary papers, and the Samuel Ramey Fan Club was registered. I don't know if this practice still exists but there were a few fan clubs at the time mine was started. Jose Carreras's was the biggest. He had hundreds in his club while mine was never more than about thirty people. Eva, Mara Schwarz and Lilian Hoffmann were in at the beginning, and, at various times, there've been members from Austria, Germany, Switzerland, Italy, France, Japan and the U.S. They used to travel all over the world to see me, and at least one or two of them, were at any given performance. In 1999, one member, Ursula Eggenberger, published a biography of me in Switzerland. I was quite touched that she put in all that effort. She actually went to Colby! Until now it's been my only biography. It's in French, though, so a lot of people have never read it." Terry Kobel, a New Yorker, became a member of the Sam Ramey Fan Club in 1997, and still manages to get to wherever Sam is singing. "There's a lot of camaraderie among us and because we're a relatively small group we got a chance to really get to know Sam away from the opera house. He's generous with his time and always joins us for coffee klatches, lunches or dinners. The club has gotten smaller, but we're still here!"

While the majority of Sam's professional experiences have been mutually satisfactory and relatively free of strife, there have been exceptions, which he reluctantly acknowledges. "Look, I can remember in those early days thinking, "I'm better than he is, why can't I be singing that?" which is normal. But I never voiced my feelings. And while I'm sure it must have been there, I never noticed any real pettiness or jealousy from the people I worked with. Anyway, it never became obvious. Honestly, over all these years I can only recall a handful of incidents where colleagues behaved in a less than generous manner. One of those times occurred when I did my first Scarpia at the Met. The soprano who'd been hired to sing Tosca did all the rehearsals, including the dress, and then was paid off when it was decided that she wasn't right. So they brought in another soprano who, as the saying goes, shall remain nameless. I couldn't believe it when I learned that she refused to come and rehearse with me. It was my first Scarpia in twelve years and I wanted to iron a few things out in the second act, which is pretty intricate. I get stabbed to death at the end and I wanted to get the staging just right. When apprised of my request, she responded, 'That's his problem. It doesn't do any good for me to come to rehearsals. I do what I feel. I never do it the same way twice and that's how I perform.' I can't imagine a worse attitude. But as I said, it doesn't happen that often."

SAMUEL RAMEY: American Bass

Sam well remembers all that went into the making of his career, the hardships as well as the accomplishments. He had to struggle to make ends meet at the beginning, yet he saw no reason why aspiring young singers should have to worry about finances. To that end, he donated $100,000 to establish the Samuel Ramey Endowed Opera Fellowship at his alma mater, Wichita State University. Each year a worthy opera student is given a $5,000 graduate award. If you ask him why he did it, Sam smiles and says, "Why not? Look, I came very close to giving up singing when I first came to New York. I was trying to support myself, and seeking encouragement, all at the same time. I sure could've used some assistance. Strictly speaking, the bottom line is money. It really helps if you don't have to worry where your next meal is coming from. I just like the idea of helping to make it a little bit easier for kids who are in the position now that I was back then.

"As for me, I don't know what I would have done if my singing career hadn't worked out. It did, and I'm profoundly grateful. I'm grateful too, that my family could share in my success. My mother and my sister came to New York for a *Mefistofele* in 1977, and a *Manon* with Beverly. Mom also was there for a *Rinaldo* at the Met. My brothers were at some concerts but only saw me in an opera, once. We had a family reunion in Santa Fe and it was the one and only time my whole family saw me on the operatic stage. I wish my dad had been around for all the good stuff but I kind of think he knew what might happen way back when he told that junior high school baseball coach that I wanted music.

"The years go by quickly when you enjoy what you're doing. It's hard to believe I've been singing professionally for over three decades, all those years and I still get excited about going on stage. One big clue that I've been around for a while, is that I got heavier than I like to be. We have a gym in the basement of our house and I work out once in a while, nowhere near as much as I used to do. I'm more into power walks, now. I did manage to drop a lot of excess poundage late in 2008 and I'm back to fighting weight. I have engagements lined up, including Met appearances in 2010, a few recitals with Flicka, and an appearance with the Washington Opera.

"My schedule isn't as grueling as it used to be. That's allowed me a bit of freedom, which I never had before. I can do things like go to class reunions with my high school pals. Look, I know I can't go on singing forever and I've pretty much made up my mind I'm going to do more teaching in the future. I've taught some master classes, including one in Hawaii in the summer of 2007, and I'm on the faculty of the Chicago College of Performing Arts at Roosevelt University. So far I haven't had a chance to really dig in and teach with any consistency mostly because I'm still out there performing. I don't know if I'll be any good but I do know that a good teacher instills confidence and makes you feel that you're improving. That can make all the difference to a young singer. It's a little frightening to contemplate, but I'm going for it. It's inspiring to see what Jackie Horne's done for a new generation of singers. She's been teaching and giving master classes for over a decade. Speaking of which, Jackie told me a funny story. She overheard a couple of her male students discussing their participation in opera scenes. Said one to the other, 'At that point I raised my right arm and covered my heart with my left hand, you know, the Ramey Gesture.' Can you beat it? I'm a gesture!

"All in all, my own professional life's been so terrific I just feel I should give something back. Wait, make that I *want* to give something back, and teaching seems a good way to do it. It's awesome to realize you can be an inspiration even after you've retired from the operatic stage. Really, when I think about it, opera's been very, very, good to me."

Opera has been very, very good to Samuel Ramey and he has been very, very good to opera. According to Matthew Horner, a Vice President of IMG's Vocal Division and Sam's American manager, "Sam changed the character of what every bass has to be in the future. In essence, there is no bass who auditions for me or anyone else in this business who doesn't bring some sort of aria that 'moves,' whether it's Rossini, Handel, or whatever virtuosic music. This simply wasn't the case before the singular phenomenon of Sam Ramey. It's not that there weren't great basses; there were sublime basses like Cesare Siepi, Tancredi Pesaro, Ezio Pinza, Jerry Hines, and Norman Treigle, singers that Sam idolized, but they didn't sing this virtuosic music. He transformed the character of his voice type. Truly, the only other singer I can think of who did that was Marilyn Horne. Suddenly, Sam created a category unto himself for which there may never be another advocate. And, he was always humble about his accomplishments. One of the few times Sam ever engaged in self-praise happened after I saw him in *Viaggio a Reims* at Pesaro. I told him I just couldn't imagine anyone else singing it the way he did. Sam paused, thought, and then said, 'Well, probably not.'"

Some two decades ago, a *New York Sunday Times Magazine* article on Samuel Ramey, *A Voice like a Lion's Roar*, recounted the story of the world premiere of Massenet's *Don Quichotte*. Feodor Chaliapin created the role, which Sam successfully essayed over a half a century later. The premiere took place on February 19, 1910 at The Monte Carlo Opera House, a jewel box theatre located inside a casino. Because of the proximity, it was commonplace for opera audience members to wander into the gambling house during intermissions and gather around the tables. At the *Don Quichotte* opening, after Chaliapin did his first turn on the stage, he suddenly appeared in the casino. Throughout the evening the "Ingenuous Knight," dressed in costume, continued to race back and forth from the casino to the theatre, placing his bets at the table, and returning in time for his next entrance. His antic behavior did not affect his performance; it was a triumph. "Chaliapin was unique," observed Sam, who would never behave in such a manner. "He did everything. He was totally theatrical. You know they once asked him what he'd do if he lost his voice and he said right away, 'Oh, I'd become the world's greatest actor.'" Asked what *he* would do if he lost his voice, Sam thought a bit and answered, "I don't know."

That was at the height of his career. Now he knows, and is beginning to look to the next stage. If his future is anything like his past, teaching might turn out to be Samuel Ramey's third gimmick.

# SOUND BITES

## from SAM RAMEY

Jane Scovell

## SAMUEL RAMEY: American Bass

It's been my experience that if you're looking to create a character on stage, you'll find the key in the libretto and the score. Composers know what they're doing and if you trust them, you'll find your interpretation and, as I've explained earlier, I've always tried to follow my own advice. I don't go into productions with preconceived notions. I never went in with the attitude that "this is the way it's going to be," because I knew I had to work with a director who had his ideas as well as with colleagues who had theirs. I've worked with some terrfic directors and, within reason, have welcomed any suggestions they made. However, I sang long enough to find myself in an era when a lot of directors were more concerned about putting their stamp on the material rather than respecting and enhancing it.

Not long ago I had dinner with a singer friend and her husband. He was starting a career as an opera director and we got on the subject of modern productions. I told him I had a real problem with all this "concept" stuff. For one thing, I just don't think that an opera should be updated past the time that the composer lived. How can you, or why would you, put a Mozart opera in the twentieth or twenty-first century? If you do that, you're not respecting the composer's or the librettist's vision. Music should never take second place to the *mise en scene*. When it comes to opera productions, "old fashioned" and "traditional," are not dirty words. If I sound too conservative for some folks, so be it. Bottom line, I think the composer's—not the director's—name should be above the title, and if I sound too conservative for some folks, so be it. With that in mind, I'm going to randomly offer observations on a number of my roles. If my comments seem more casual than clinical, that's also the way I am.

++++++++++++

# Argante & Assur

Argante, in Handel's *Rinaldo*, is a good example of the arrogant, bass bad guy who frequently pops up in *opera seria*. I got to sing him because Marilyn Horne and Matthew Epstein put together the production of Handel's *Rinaldo*. Argante is among my most difficult roles. In fact, it would be right up there with Rossini's Maometto except that it's not as large a part. The hardest singing is right at the beginning, when you have a demanding aria followed by another demanding aria. After that, Argante is pretty much a "whatever happened to my part" kind of guy. Except for a little duet with the soprano, he literally disappears. A bass can only hope his work isn't forgotten by the final curtain.

++

Assur, in Rossini's *Semiramide*, is an equally demanding coloratura role, but he gets to sing throughout the opera. To top it off, he has that incredible mad scene practically at the end. No one's going to forget him.

Jane Scovell

# Attila

In 1972, not long before I joined the City Opera, I read in the paper that the New Jersey State Opera was performing *Attila* with Jerry Hines in the title role. I knew of the opera but I didn't own a score or anything like that so it wasn't something I had a real take on. I was curious about it, though, curious enough to go New Jersey, along with Arman Boyajian and Paul Plishka, to see it. During the performance I remember thinking, as any bass in his right mind might, "Hmmmm, this is an interesting piece." I filed *Attila* away in the back of my head and went on with my career.

After that career took off, Beverly Sills called me into her office at City Opera. "Sam, I want to do something for you," she told me, "and I want it to be something that City Opera hasn't done before." I thought a moment. "How about *Attila*?" I said. "I'll look into the possibility," Bev answered, "and I'll let you know." Like me, Bev knew *of* the opera but she didn't *know* it; she had to check it out before making a commitment. It was my good fortune that the Lyric Opera of Chicago had done a production for Nicolai Ghiaurov. When Bev heard that, she immediately contacted the Lyric and rented their production.

Most of Verdi's early operas were still somewhat in the *bel canto* mode and in those days, at least in my opinion, there wasn't much distinction made between baritones and basses. The tessitura and range are so high, it's as though Verdi wasn't that sure if he was writing for a bass or a baritone. Attila is a perfect example; it's full of high Fs and it's not an easy sing at all. The singing challenge aside, what I found most interesting was the character of Attila himself. He's gone down in history as "the Hun," hardly a sympathetic figure. However, all the bad stuff he did happened before the opera begins so in Verdi's hands, he actually becomes sympathetic. The audience is on his side because the other characters—the soprano, the baritone, and the tenor—are all plotting against him. Despite Attila's reputation, audiences were drawn to him in a positive way and that provided me with a real challenge. In performance, I wanted to try to make him not so likeable, and more like he was historically. I don't think I ever really succeeded. It was almost impossible to do because Verdi was more interested in emphasizing Attila's nice guy qualities than being true to history. I used to get a kick out of having people come back after the performance saying, "Oh, we felt so sorry for you and we were so sad when you got killed."

A big deal was made out of my singing Attila bare-chested; it wasn't my idea. Everybody thought I was keen to take my shirt off all the time but it was for the role not for the beefcake opportunities. It happened like this, Nicolai Ghiaurov was supposed to appear stripped to the waist in one scene of the Chicago production, but he didn't want to do it. So Hal George, the costume designer, made him a tunic. During the Chicago run, Ghiaurov got the hiccups, couldn't get rid of them, and had to cancel a few performances. Jerry Hines took over. I saw production pictures, and Jerry was definitely bare-chested. When it came time for me to do *Attila* at City Opera, they gave me a choice of wearing the tunic or not. I opted for the latter because it was already set in the production.

I did *Attila* twice at City Opera and then I was asked to do it in Venice. This was a particular thrill for me because *Attila* premiered at La Fenice. The theatre's archives contained all of the original designs, including sets and costumes, and it was decided to recreate the original production. By the time of the Fenice production, I'd become fairly well known in Italy because of all I had done at the Rossini Festival and at La Scala. I had quite a following. On opening night I sang my big dramatic aria, *Mentre gonfiarsi l'anima parea*, at the end of Act One. In it, Attila tells about a nightmare he's had and then it goes into a big ensemble and confrontation scene ending with a great two-verse *cabaletta*, all of which is typical of early Verdi. It's one of the most difficult arias in my repertoire, but it's one of my favorites. That evening, I finished the aria and strode downstage brandishing a sword over my head. I couldn't believe the roar that came from the audience. Honestly, the applause wouldn't stop. I didn't know what to do. It just went on and on and on. Finally I motioned to the conductor and we did a *bis,* repeat, of the *cabaletta*. Actually, we ended up doing a *bis* for three or four performances. In the past, repeats happened with some regularity, but they rarely occur anymore, even in Europe.

Jane Scovell

SAMUEL RAMEY: American Bass

# Basilio, Mustafa, & Selim

Rossini's got great comic roles and I got to do few of them during my career. Basilio, the music master in *Il Barbieri di Siviglia,* is perhaps the best known. I sang Basilio in my second season with the New York City Opera in a refurbished version of an old production. Arnie Voketaitis was the Basilio and I was the cover. Arnie had a conflict and another singer was scheduled to do the last performance. Out of the blue, the replacement cancelled, and I was put into the production. Basilio was my first larger role at City Opera and it's one of the few comic roles that stayed in my repertoire. The last time I did it was at the Met in 2007 and I'm doing it again in 2010. I've been singing Basilio for nearly forty years. It's a lot of fun and I love doing it but, truthfully, he's not a character of much dimension. Basilio is almost a cameo part. He's not integral to the opera and more a caricature than a character. Audiences love him, though, because he provides a real comic turn. And what singer could scoff at a role that contains one of the greatest comic arias ever written, *La calunnia.*

++

I began singing Mustafa in *L'Italiana in Algeri,* while touring with the National Opera Company. I think I was the first Mustafa who actually sang the part as written. Previously, it had been done by buffo basses who faked the coloratura, perhaps because nobody asked them to sing all the notes. I didn't wait to be asked. I just sang them because they were there.

++

Selim in *Il Turco in Italia,* is fun to do, but certainly not a favorite of mine. He doesn't really have an aria of his own, just a series of duets, which is not exactly a selling point for taking on the role. The drawing is of me as Selim, but it could just as well be Mustafa since they're both turbaned guys

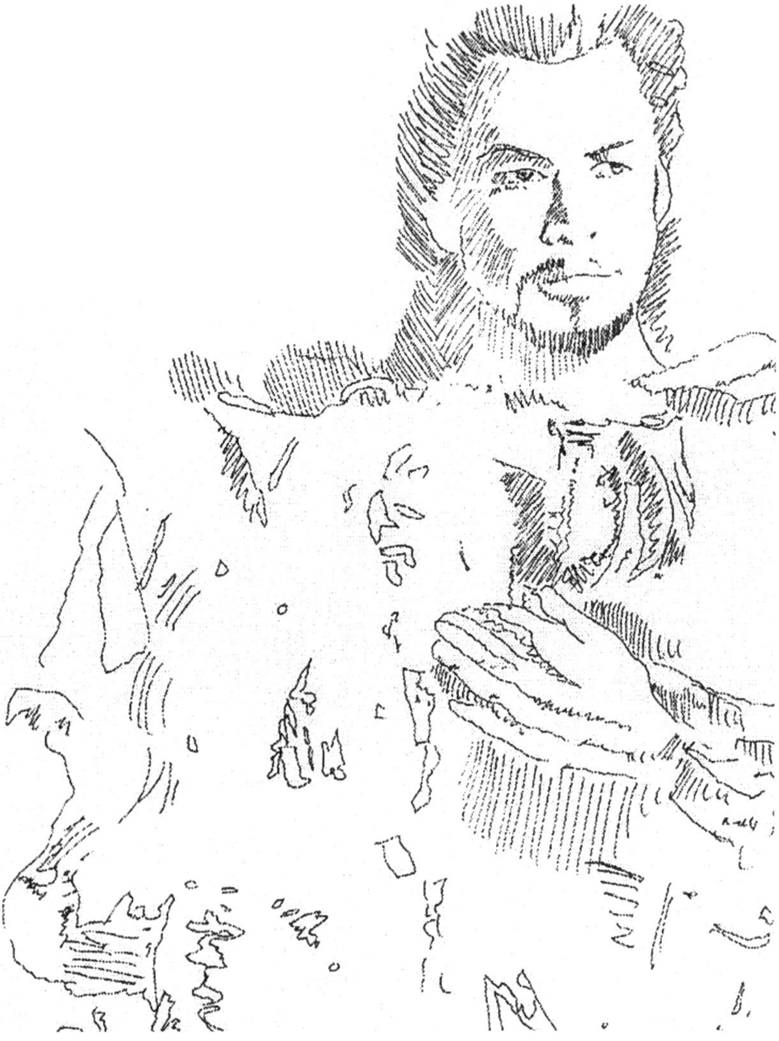

# Bertram

In the early eighties, I was singing the French version of Rossini's *Moise* in Paris. During the run, I had a meeting with the directors of the Opera House. They wanted to do a special series featuring operas that had premiered at the old Paris Opera House and Meyerbeer's *Les Huguenots* was under consideration. They asked if I would be interested in doing it. I said that if they were thinking of Meyebeer, and, if they wanted me involved, how about *Robert Le Diable*? I really didn't know the opera at all but I'd read an interview with Nicolai Ghiaurov in which he said that *Robert le Diable* contained a great bass part, Bertram, which he was hoping to do. (He never got to do it, but I never forgot what he said.) The Paris Opera House directors thought I had a good idea. *Huguenots* was still in the repertoire but *Robert* would be something different. So they did it, and I got to sing Bertram for my one and only time in performance. (In 1988, I sang a concert version at Carnegie Hall for Eve Queler's Opera Orchestra of New York.) Bertram isn't the Devil; he's an emissary of the devil who's been sent to recruit Robert. Robert is saved and Bertram goes back where he came from, but before he goes he gets to sing several lovely arias. Ghiaurov was right; it is a great part.

Jane Scovell

SAMUEL RAMEY: American Bass

# Bluebeard & Gianni Schicchi

While these two gentlemen would seem to be strange bedfellows, I sang them as part of a double bill in Los Angeles, and then in Washington, D.C. Schicchi wasn't a part that I ever really thought that much about doing. When I first arrived in New York City I was told that the Metropolitan Opera Studio was going to do the opera, so I learned Schicchi's big aria. But nothing came of it. No learned aria goes to waste, though. Years later, the L. A. Opera wanted to do Bartok's, *Duke Bluebeard's Castle* and Puccini's *Gianni Schicchi* together. By then, I'd sung Bluebeard at the Metropolitan and was familiar with the role; but aside from that aria, I didn't know Schicchi at all. When the opportunity to sing both of them presented itself, I realized that coupling *Schicchi* with *Bluebeard* would make for a pretty interesting double bill. So I signed on.

When I did *Bluebeard* at the Met in 1988, the production was in traditional dress and I wore a long wig. At the end of the opera, there was a dramatic moment where I tore off the wig to expose a baldhead. I'd been wearing a bald cap but I had a lot of trouble with it during performances. The glue came undone, and the cap would come off with the wig. If there's one thing I'm not, it's bald, so tearing off a wig to expose my full head of hair looked ridiculous. We couldn't get it right, and it was worrisome because *Bluebeard* was scheduled for a live telecast. You can't cover up any glitches on TV with the cameras in your face. Just before the broadcast, I got a phone call from Peter Gelb, who was head of the Met's video department at the time. "Sam," he said, "I think I know what your answer will be to this, but I'm going to ask you anyway. Would you shave your head for the telecast?" (You can guess my answer.)

Duke Bluebeard is a very sad, very lonely man, and a serial killer. He's truly one of the most unusual characters in my repertoire—make that, the entire operatic repertoire. His persona is defined by this terrible loneliness. He just can't connect and when he does, it ends disastrously for his wives. The ladies have to know what's going on, and still they marry him. At the end of the opera, after he's gotten rid of his latest bride, Judith, he says, "Here I am in my lonely empty castle again." What else is new? It's a somber opera and what a stroke of genius to couple it with a romp like *Gianni Schicchi*.

++

The Hollywood director, William Friedkin, perhaps best known for *The Exorcist*, was hired to direct the Bartok/Puccini double bill. Early in rehearsals, he invited the cast over to his house for lunch, and at one point, pulled me aside. "I've got something on video that I want to show you," he said. "It's an idea I have for your character." We went upstairs and watched a bit of the classic Humphrey Bogart film, *The Treasure of the Sierra Madre*, directed by John Huston and co-starring his father, Walter. Bill and I looked at the famous scene where the Walter Huston character does a quirky little dance after they discover the treasure. "That's what I want Schicchi to do," Friedkin told me, pointing to the dancing Huston on the screen. And when it came time for Schicchi to do his little jig, that's exactly what I did.

## SAMUEL RAMEY: American Bass

Jane Scovell

SAMUEL RAMEY: American Bass

# Godunov & Kutuzov

My excursions into the Russian repertory were limited to Boris in Moussorgsky's *Boris Godunov*, Pimen, also in the same opera, and Kutuzov in Prokofiev's *War and Peace*. (Oh, I guess I should include an English language version of Tchaikovsky's *Pique Dame* and a German version of *Eugene Onegin*.)

In the late 1980s and early 1990s, I sang a lot with the opera in Geneva. Huges Galles was the General Director; later, he became General Director of the Paris Opera. While I was performing in Geneva, we had a meeting to discuss future projects. He asked if there was something I would like to do for the first time. I mentioned *Boris Godunov*. He agreed but added that he specifically wanted to do the <u>first</u> version of the opera. Again, it was something I <u>knew</u> of, but had never heard, or seen. That first version was not a success, in part, because there was no prima donna role. Consequently, there was no love music. Moussorgsky then wrote a second and longer version, which included a love story and an extended duet for a mezzo- soprano and tenor in the so-called, Polish Scene. The music is beautiful but I prefer the first and shorter version. I loved the first version, musically and dramatically, the moment I looked at it; it really focuses on Boris's story without the distraction of a superimposed love scene.

Boris Godunov's character is based in reality and is probably the most emotionally involving role in my repertoire.

Boris supposedly had a hand in the murder of Tsar Ivan's son and heir, but actual proof of this was never found. Whether he was involved or not, Boris carries a lot of guilt. He has a huge monologue, which boils down to a mad scene, plus, an especially moving death scene. During the latter, he speaks to his young son, the Tsarevich, telling him of his own trials and tribulations and the burdens of leadership. I have to say, after I had my son, Guy, that scene got to me more than it ever had before. Generally speaking, *Boris* is produced along traditional lines at least in terms of costumes. I was in an updated version in Salzburg where, along with a period coronation cape and crown, I wore a three-piece suit and a tie. I found it a bit unsettling. It's hard to feel like Boris Godunov if your costume takes you totally out of character. I had a stage mishap during that *Boris*. When the prologue began, I was standing onstage behind a huge bell that was resting on a dais. The bell was supposed to be raised and I was to step forward, stand underneath it, and sing my opening number. Well, the bell didn't budge, and I realized I had to do something fast. So I high-tailed it around the dais and stopped in front of the immobile bell, as the bemused conductor, Anne Manson, gave me my cue.

I performed the first version of Boris in 1993 in Geneva and repeated that version several times. The Lyric Opera of Chicago borrowed the production for me to open their 1994 season. Then, in 2005, David Gockley arranged for me to do it with the Houston Grand Opera to celebrate my thirtieth anniversary with that company. And, when David moved on to become General Director of the San Francisco Opera, he brought me, and the production, to San Francisco in 2008, where I celebrated my thirtieth anniversary with <u>that</u> company. David always has been a steadfast supporter of my art and I so appreciate his loyalty I want to thank him, in print.

++

Kutuzov, the commander of the Russian forces fighting

Napoleon, is a wise man and a clever strategist. He knew the French army would have a hard time with the Russian winter. He also knew that the Russians' ability to stick it out would be the key to their ultimate triumph. Kutuzov is a down-to-earth kind of man and a real leader. If he swapped his Russian uniform for a U.S. Cavalry officer's, he could step right into a John Ford western. I sang the role at the Met in the 2002 season, and repeated it again in 2007-08.

# Don Giovanni & Leporello

Mozart's Don Giovanni is probably the most arrogant role I ever sang. What an ego! And what a libido! I sang my first *Don Giovanni* with City Opera in 1974. I did it in Salzburg with von Karajan and that's where I met Ferruccio Furlanetto who played Leporello. Later, at the Met, Ferruccio and I would do a *Don Giovanni* with a twist. The twist was that we alternated singing the two roles. The idea behind that began in 1982 when Beverly Sills did a new production of *Don Giovanni* for me. Justino Diaz was brought in to sing Leporello. One day, Bev called me in to her office.

"You know, Sam," she said, "we're thinking about you and Gus Diaz switching roles for a few performances. Would you do it?" I said sure. So Gus and I swapped back and forth a few times. That's how I got to sing my first Leporello. Make no mistake, even though he's Giovanni's servant, Leporello is a main character, not a secondary role.

When Ferruccio and I did the Zeffirelli production at the Met, we pulled the same Giovanni/Leporello switcheroo City Opera had featured. I was the Don for the first five performances and Leporello for the last four. It was fine with me for many reasons. Although Don Giovanni is the title part and a great <u>acting</u> role, I don't think his music is nearly as interesting as Leporello's. Leporello's *Catalogue Aria*, is one of the most famous bass solos in all opera. I learned it in college, and I've been singing that aria for a long, long, time.

What I enjoyed most in the Don's music was the recitatives. (It goes back to the summer of 1974 and my work with Luigi Ricci.) My favorite Giovanni recitative occurs at the beginning of Act Two. After a Giovanni/Leporello duet, Leporello asks, "Why don't you just leave women alone? All you do is get into trouble." Don Giovanni replies, "For me women are more necessary than the bread I eat." But he doesn't stop there. He goes on to say, "I can't just love one; if I only loved one then I would be denying all the others what they could have." Like I said, what an ego! Look, I'm not going to second-guess da Ponte and Mozart, but I've always been troubled by that particular moment in the opera. I think that Don Giovanni's recitative should lead into a solo but it's just a recitative leading into a trio. As far as the vocal range, Don Giovanni doesn't go very high and doesn't go very low. It's all sort of middle voice and has been sung by baritones, bass-baritones, and basses. It's a matter of taste. I prefer hearing a bass-baritone or bass do it, but that's a personal prejudice.

When it comes to operatic characters, the right costume has an effect on performance. My experience with a Zeffirelli production of *Don Giovanni* is a good example. I went in for a fitting and they had a whole set of costumes made just for me, at least three different ones. I tried them all on and then Zeffirelli came in. He took one look at them, turned to the costume lady with whom he always worked, and said, "No, no, this design is not good. You can do better. We're not going to use these costumes at all. We're going to start all over." The costume lady's face fell to the floor. But, they remade the costumes, and you know what? Zeffirelli was absolutely right. I could really strut my stuff in those outfits.

SAMUEL RAMEY: American Bass

Jane Scovell

# Don Quichotte

Massenett's *Don Quichotte* is another opera I discovered while in college. I bought an old European recording with nobody famous on it, at least nobody I had ever heard of. (I also bought another LP with Chaliapin singing Quichotte's arias; you don't get more famous than that.) I became interested enough in the opera to write to Patelson's Music Store in New York City and order a score. Not so long ago, I was sad to read in the *New York Times* that Patelson's, a family-owned music store, and a New York institution, was closing after six decades. It's another victim of high tech and high rents. According to the *Times* reporter, "It would have been hard to study music seriously in New York without Patelson's." Believe me, Patelson's influence went way beyond New York's city limits. It certainly meant a lot to me out in Kansas.

The first time I got to sing *Quichotte* was kind of a fluke. In 1979, I made my Paris Opera debut and in the process got a French agent, Claude Stricker. She called me out of the blue and asked if I knew *Don Quichotte*. I told her I was familiar with it but had never done it. "Would you like to do it?" she asked. I said, sure. That's how I came to sing Quichotte in Rouen with Gabriel Bacquier as Sancho Panza. The production was a big success but I didn't get to do the opera again till the City Opera gave me the 1986 production.

Quichotte is a challenging part because there are moments when he's very bold and then lots of other moments where he's very introspective. He goes back and forth between these extremes. Vocally, there are lots of colors and that wide range makes it difficult to sing, especially at the end. His death scene is the hardest of all to put across. It's an intimate setting—just Don Quichotte and Sancho Panza—and contains really beautiful music. You have to do it exactly right. All in all, I find the opera extraordinarily moving and when I sang the part I tried to capture its nuances. It was challenging but worth it because *Don Quichotte* is an opera I truly love. And I was fortunate enough to do it quite a bit. I sang it in New York, Chicago, San Francisco; the last time was in Paris in the early 2000s.

SAMUEL RAMEY: American Bass

Jane Scovell

# Escamillo

When I was in Europe, I saw real bullfights on television and I was struck by the way the matadors project this super macho kind of thing. That's Escamillo. He's an alpha male and his character doesn't go much beyond that. He's not very deep. Consequently, he's not very interesting. He swaggers and flirts, but, basically, he's two-dimensional. And, once he's done his big aria and sung his duets with Carmen, that's it.

Escamillo is a bass-baritone role that's more frequently done by baritones. I sang it for the first time in Santa Fe in 1971 and although I've sung it in many opera houses, I can't say it was one of my favorites.

Jane Scovell

SAMUEL RAMEY: American Bass

# Figaro

From college days on, Mozart's Figaro was one of my favorite roles. I was called a "natural" Figaro by critics and audiences. I think it's because his character is the closest to my own. Our personalities are alike. Figaro sometimes seems like an oaf, but he's actually a very clever guy. I think of myself as more astute than clever. Figaro's a fun loving guy, too, but he stands up for himself when he's challenged, even if it means facing down his superior, the Count. Musically, I prefer singing Figaro to Don Giovanni. Figaro has three great arias, and one of them takes place within the final minutes of the opera, satisfying the Jackie Horne rule for selecting roles, which is 'always check to see where your character is at the end.'

Figaro was my first big lead role at City Opera. In my second season in the fall of 1973, I was covering Basilio in a new production of *Barber*. At the last performance, whoever was singing Figaro cancelled, and I was thrown in. I did okay. That's when Matthew Epstein started pushing me to get a publicist. I met with some, but I resisted seeing Edgar Vincent because I didn't think I was on his level. In time, we got together and, as you've read, he represented me until his death in 2008. I did the old *Figaro* production at City Opera a couple of times and again in 1976 after it was refurbished. I've sung Figaro all over the world.

I love to sing Mozart and I sang a lot of him in roles that

also included Don Alfonso in *Cosi Fan Tutte*. I recorded the role of Sarastro in *The Magic Flute*, but I never sang it onstage. When you come right down to it, Mozart's probably my favorite composer. The second act finale of *Figaro* is a perfect example of his brilliance. Listening to it, or singing in it, it's a sublime experience to follow the way the music weaves in and out, touching each character and defining each personality, and then bringing it all together in one miraculous whole. That's genius.

## SAMUEL RAMEY: American Bass

Jane Scovell

# Giorgio & Zaccaria

Giorgio, in Bellini's *I Puritani*, is one of those graybeard characters that Matthew Epstein wanted me to avoid at the beginning of my career. It's a fairly big part, but aside from his aria and *suoni la tromba*, a duet with the baritone, it's a pretty conventional and boring role. Both the baritone and the bass parts are easy enough to sing, but relatively unrewarding. Even though *suoni la tromba* can bring down the house, the opera belongs to the soprano and the tenor. By the way, the tenor can steal the whole show with his big aria.

I first sang Giorgio with a small company in New York called Bel Canto Opera; it was right before I joined the City Opera. Bel Canto performed in the basement of a church and I probably don't have to add that they didn't pay. At one time, close to a hundred opera workshops like the Bel Canto company flourished in New York City. There's barely a handful left.

++

The second graybeard is Zaccaria from Verdi's *Nabucco*. I made my debut in the role with the Paris Opera in 1995. *Nabucco* was Verdi's first big success and it established him as a leading composer. Zaccaria is the High Priest of Jerusalem. He's got a big aria in the first act in which he tells his people, who've been defeated by Nabucco, the King of Babylon, to keep their faith in God. It's a good solid role and I sang it for a good solid length of time.

Jane Scovell

SAMUEL RAMEY: American Bass

# Gounod's, Berlioz's, & Boito's Devil

For a pair of devils, Gounod's and Berlioz's Mephistopheles are pretty well rounded characters. They share similar traits, both are fun loving and charming, and, while they do get a bit nasty at times, they're not overly mean. In that respect, they're quite different from Boito's Mefistofele, who's much more dramatic, and really in your face. One thing all three devils share is a sardonic sense of humor, which makes them all the more interesting.

Although I always used to say my favorite role was whatever I was doing at the time, I've already confessed that if push came to shove, I'd have to go with Gounod's Mephistopheles. *Faust* also contains what may be my favorite aria, Mephistopheles's serenade, *Vous qui faites l'endormie*. I always sang it for auditions and I usually got the jobs. So it became a lucky piece for me. In fact, if I were told that I could sing only one aria, that's the one I'd choose. I've also said that Frank Corsaro's production of *Faust* at City Opera has remained my favorite. That production emphasized Mephistopheles's multi-dimensional qualities. And it's got a light touch. Mephistopheles is suave, elegant, and very cavalier. While the same can be said of Berlioz's devil, Boito's Mefistofele stands apart from the other two.

Aside from the garden scene in which he appears as a cavalier, Boito's devil is totally satanic, and in keeping with his nature, he's pretty frightening. Charlie Elson did my make up for the City Opera production. Charlie and I were apprentices together in Santa Fe and he went on to become the best make-up guy around. Charlie worked free-lance and when they brought *Mefistofele* back, he was called in and designed a whole new look. He built a terrifying prosthetic mask for me. Talk about Boris Karloff getting into his monster face in *Frankenstein*! I had to go through a similar, though far less grueling process. I lay down on a couch and was told to relax. Straws were stuck up my nostrils so I could breathe while the plaster was piled on my face. I was flat on my back for at least an hour till it hardened. What could be more relaxing? I think they have better techniques now, at least I hope they do. Anyway, they made a bust of me from the plaster mold and used that to build the mask.

I came close to singing another devil role, the one in Anton Rubinstein's, *The Demon*. A Russian coach at the San Francisco Opera took me through it but both of us felt that the upper range was a bit too daunting. Basically it was a bass-baritone role with the accent on baritone. Not my satanic cup of tea.

In January 2008, I sang Mephistopheles with the Wichita Grand Opera. I had come full circle to sing my favorite role right in my own back yard.

# SAMUEL RAMEY: American Bass

# The Grand Inquisitor

The Grand Inquisitor is the big daddy of *graybeard* roles and one that I did not assume until late in my career. It's kind of natural for a bass to slide into it after he's sung King Philip, which is how I did it. Nicolai Ghiaurov reversed the order. He made his Scala debut as the Grand Inquisitor to Boris Christof's Philip, and then took on the role of the King. I sang the Grand Inquisitor twice, both times at the Met. The first occasion was during a gala evening of opera scenes honoring Alfredo Kraus, Mirella Freni, and Nicolai Ghiaurov, each of whom was celebrating twenty-five years at the Met. They did the second act of *Faust* for Kraus, the last act of *Butterfly* for Freni, and the *Don Carlos* Cabinet Scene for Ghiaurov. I had the honor of singing the Grand Inquisitor to Nicolai's Philip.

The Grand Inquisitor is grand indeed. His appearance is both majestic and forbidding He has key scenes with the King and, although Philip is the larger part, the Inquisitor has the upper hand. He knows the King is under his thumb and Philip knows it, too. After their duet, the King's last line is, "So the throne always has to give way to the altar."

Jane Scovell

SAMUEL RAMEY: American Bass

# The Hoffman Villains

The Hoffman villains—Lindorf, Coppelius, Dappertutto and Dr. Miracle—are some of the most unsympathetic characters in my repertoire. You might think that my devil characters, Mephistopheles, Mefistofele, Nick Shadow, etc., would be the least sympathetic but, while they are evil incarnate, they have <u>charm.</u> That's something a devil should have in order to work his wiles. With one possible exception, the Hoffman boys are pretty charmless.

I bought my first recording of the *Tales of Hoffman* when I was in college and it's still in my library. The album is the soundtrack from the 1951 Michael Powell and Emeric Pressburger film. The movie emphasized dancing and, except for Robert Rounseville and Ann Ayers who both sang and acted Hoffman and Antonia, dancers played the main parts with singers dubbing their voices. Moira Shearer was Olympia and Bruce Darganel, a Welsh bass, sang the villains, while Robert Helpman danced them. Hoffman is Lindorf's potential rival for Stella's affections.

Lindorf is the chief bad guy and I've always thought of the others as his alter egos. Lindorf is out to get Hoffman and achieves his goal through the other three. Coppelius has supplied the eyes for the doll, Olympia and sells Hoffman magic glasses which make the doll appear human. Dappertutto is a slick fellow and oozes a kind of charm. He has a relationship with Giulietta and gets to sing the *Diamond Aria*, one of my favorites. While I have a special fondness for Dr. Miracle because he was my first full operatic role, he's an unqualified SOB, which brings up an important point.

All four Hoffman villains are facets of one person and that's why I believe it is really important for one singer to do all the roles. To me, it doesn't make sense to have different singers doing them. At the opera's 1881 premiere, all the roles were sung by Emile-Alexandre Taskin, a bass-baritone. After that, the roles began to be divvied up between two or more singers. In earlier days at the Met, they never had one singer do them all. I know Pinza sang a couple of the parts, Lindorf and Dr. Miracle, but I'm pretty certain it was Norman Treigle at City Opera who revived the tradition and made it fashionable to do all four. Jim Morris, Michael Devlin, Gus Diaz, and Ruggiero Raimondi, among others, have tackled them. I was the first singer to do all four roles at Covent Garden when I appeared in John Schlesinger's production.

It's a bit different for the female quartet—Stella, Olympia, Giulietta, and Antonia. Like the four villains, the four ladies were sung at the premiere by one soprano, Adele Isaac. (Actually, at the last minute, the Giulietta sequence was dropped, so she wound up doing a trifecta.) Off hand, I can't recall anyone besides Beverly Sills and Joan Sutherland who have done it in modern times. In my opinion, it's much more of a challenge than doing the bass parts because it ranges from coloratura soprano down to mezzo. The mezzo Giulietta is the hard one and I'm pretty sure that's the role Bev least enjoyed doing. At one point, Natalie Dessay said she was going to do it. I asked her about it recently and she said she never did. Those Hoffman ladies are a pretty big sing. We bass baritones love to sink our chops into the male parts, but most sopranos are happy doing just a couple of the female counterparts.

SAMUEL RAMEY: American Bass

Jane Scovell

# Maometto II

I was in Treviso in late May of 1980 doing a recording of *L'Italiana* with Jackie Horne when the people from the Pesaro Rossini Festival called me. They wanted me to come in August and do *La Gazza Ladra*. I had to say no because I was too busy and besides, I knew nothing about that opera. Then they asked if I could come the following summer and do *L'Italiana*; I said it was a possibility. I told Matthew Epstein and he went to the Festival to check the place out. It passed Matthew's muster and he gave me the go ahead. I went to Pesaro in 1981 and was there for five straight summers. I was gone for a few years and went back in 1989 to do *La Gazza Ladra*. The last time I sang at Pesaro was in 1992 when I did Lord Sydney in *Viaggio en Reims*.

Pesaro was a good place to be. We had a core group of singers who were there every summer in the Festival's formative years and we had great fun. The officials tried hard but for a while it was a shoestring operation. You were never quite sure if you'd be paid. I was offered Maometto in the summer of 1985. Despite the difficulties, I was drawn to it because, well, it's the title role, which never hurts. The Pesaro *Maometto II* was a Pier Luigi Pizzi production. Pizzi pulled out all the stops for my entrance aria. (The aria is really difficult; to look at all those black notes on the score is blinding.) I was carried in on a chair held by these pretty boy bodybuilders Pizzi always had hanging around, and who inevitably wound up in his productions. While I was seated, I sang the short opening *Sorgete, sorgete,* after which the musclemen lowered the chair to the floor. Then they got down on all fours in front of me. I stepped off the chair and started walking on their backs up onto the shoulders of three or four standing guys. I held on to the extended arms of some extras to maintain balance while I sang the wickedly difficult *Duce di tante eroi*. I know that's how it happened because it's on *YouTube*, but even watching it, it's hard to believe I actually did it. Anyway, it's one of the two best entrances in my repertoire; the other was in *Rinaldo*.

Brief though our acquaintanceship was, I made a recording but I only performed it in Pesaro, Maometto was a showcase role I loved doing. It's probably the most vocally difficult of all the Rossini roles. And since Rossini is the most difficult composer to sing, that makes Maometto the most difficult of all my roles.

SAMUEL RAMEY: American Bass

SAMUEL RAMEY: American Bass

# Nick Shadow

Nick is another one of those roles that's been done by basses, bass-baritones, and baritones. Like Don Giovanni, it doesn't go very high and it doesn't go very low; it's all sort of middle voice. Any bass clef voice can sing it but, personally, and perhaps prejudicially, I think it's much better with a bass or bass-baritone. *The Rake's Progress* is a very clever adaptation of the Faust legend based on Hogarth's etchings and paintings. Stravinsky and W.H. Auden fashioned a wonderfully inventive piece; modern music done in the neo-classic style, with harpsichord recitatives, and set in eighteenth century England.

Nick is the devil in disguise and I first sang him in the David Hockney production in Glyndebourne. Nick's got his charm but he's a pretty insidious guy. Whenever I sang in *The Rake's Progress,* I always thought of the English movie, *Bedazzled*. Peter Cook and Dudley Moore wrote their version of the Faust legend, dropping it into London's swinging sixties. Moore's Faust is a short order cook at a Wimpy Burger who's infatuated with a waitress named Margaret. Cook's character, the devil, is called George Spiggot. Raquel Welch was also in the cast. The film is really smart and funny and made a big impression on me. I can't tell you why, but whenever I sang Nick Shadow I somehow made a connection to the movie.

# Olin Blitch

*Susanna* is another of those operas that I became aware of while in college. (I sent to Patelson's for the score.) Arthur Newman, my college voice teacher, was in the original production at the City Opera. Norman Treigle created the role of Blitch. The first time I did *Susanna* was in San Diego. Carlisle Floyd, the composer, staged it and we became friends. Blitch is a combination of piety and lust. In most productions he has his eye on Susanna from the very beginning. In the first scene he immediately asks the Elders, "Who's that pretty girl over there?" and ends up dancing with her. In other words, he's right in there. In that respect, he could be portrayed as a sort of predator, but I didn't see him that way. I tried to make him a conflicted person, a preacher who can't control himself, like the Reverend Davidson in Somerset Maugham's *Rain*.

Jane Scovell

# Philip II

I waited a long time to sing this great Verdi role. Lots of basses take it on at a much earlier age. My first was in Brussels for Gerard Mortier in the fall of 1983 when I was 41 years old. Philip is a graybeard role but one with real heft. He's a tortured man in his public and private lives. He's unsure of his subjects' loyalty and of his (much younger) wife's love, not to mention the fact that Carlo, his son and heir, is part of an insurgency movement, and is in love with his stepmother, the Queen.

I did Philip many times. One of the most memorable productions of *Don Carlos* took place at La Fenice theatre in Venice. It was a weird one. The sets were bizarre, sort of futuristic, and I believe the designer also was the director. He didn't have much experience as a director, which I immediately discovered. When I arrived in Venice, I went directly to the rehearsal. The other cast members were already there so I joined them onstage. I went right into a scene between Philip and the Inquisitor and began walking around the set as we sang. No one told me what to do; I was just blending in till I got my stage directions. We finished and the director came up on stage, I thought, to give me instructions. Instead, he smiled and cried, "Perfetto!" I looked at him and said, "Really?" And that was it. Later, after the costume fittings, I asked, "Don't you want me to put gray in my hair?" "Oh no, no, no," he said. "It's perfect. You look wonderful." I honestly kept trying to get him to let me whiten up but he wouldn't budge.

The reason I made a fuss came right from the libretto. I've mentioned the big age discrepancy between the King and his wife, and in his aria, *ella giammai m'amo*, Philip says, "I know she doesn't love me. I can tell by the way she looks at my white hairs." If you talk about white hairs and you don't have them, it doesn't make sense. You need authenticity to help you feel the character. Not everyone is as much of a stickler as I. I know of one bass in his early thirties who flatly refused to gray his hair. I didn't have white hair when I began singing Philip, but I put it in to be true to the text. What's more, I continued to do so until I had my very own.

By the way, Philip and the Grand Inquisitor and Don Giovanni and Leporello are the only instances where I played two different characters in one opera. I did Baron Douphol and Dr. Grenville in *Traviata*, but they're not main protagonists.

SAMUEL RAMEY: American Bass

Jane Scovell

# Scarpia

After I'd been studying with Armen Boyajian for a while, we began discussing the role of Scarpia. Armen thought it was right for me, and so did I. I think the Met made an offer, but I wanted to do it somewhere else first. So I jumped at the chance when Covent Garden contacted me. In 1991, I appeared in the old Zeffirelli production, the one that Tito Gobbi sang with Maria Callas, and I had a huge success. I was very pleased when the reviews said I was the best Scarpia since Gobbi. Oddly, over a decade would pass until I appeared as Scarpia at the Met. That was in 2004, and right after that, I returned to sing it again at Covent Garden. In 2006, Covent Garden mounted a new production and, once more, I was asked back. The final score? .... Covent Garden, 3, The Met, 1. But I sang it in lots of other places including Vienna, Paris, Chicago and Los Angeles. I sang the last one in January 2009 in Vienna.

Scarpia was a role that I had had in the back of my mind for a long time. I sang Angelotti in *Tosca* in my college days and in the early days at City Opera. Angelotti is a bass part and Scarpia is considered to be more a baritone, but baritones are not real happy doing it. Scarpia doesn't have any great high notes and a lot of it is on the low side. On the other hand, most basses find Scarpia a touch on the high side. I thought I'd be comfortable with it because I had the highs and the lows. Scarpia is a very interesting character, a fascinating man in that he's not a stock villain. He's a police chief who thinks nothing of lying, torturing, murdering, and seducing but he's also very suave and a shrewd judge of character. He likes what he likes (Tosca) and he wants what he wants (Tosca) and he pulls out all the stops to get her. He's a lot of fun to play, especially when you've got a first class Tosca singing opposite you.

I sang a very special Scarpia in March 2007. Believe it or not, it was my <u>professional</u> opera debut in Kansas. The Wichita Grand Opera had been trying to get me there for years, and I finally made it.

++++

Well, there you have it; short takes on a long career. Talking about my roles is like reminiscing about old pals. It's a bittersweet pleasure because most of them are gone now. But a few are still around, and we get together occasionally. What's more, I've made some new musical friends, like Gianni Schicchi, who have been good companions in these last years. Old or new, I'll never forget any of them, and I will always be grateful that they were part of my life.

# Epilogue

On April 24, 2009, twenty-five years after his Met debut, Samuel Ramey sang Leporello in the Metropolitan Opera production of *Don Giovanni*. At intermission, he was honored on stage for his quarter of a century milestone. During the brief ceremony, General Manager Peter Gelb presented him with an antique score of *Don Giovanni* encased in a fragment from the old Met's curtain. The gift is inscribed: *For Samuel Ramey in celebration of the twenty-fifth anniversary of your Metropolitan Opera debut with admiration and friendship from your colleagues.*

"Since his debut in *Rinaldo* in 1984," said Gelb, "Sam has appeared in 29 roles in 291 performances, including this evening's. On this stage he has ruled supremely over all those roles." The audience interrupted and applauded roundly. Sam smiled, and bowed his head in a typically "Aw shucks," manner.

"Sam has been in some great productions," Gelb continued, adding rather candidly, "and some that were not as great. But whatever the production, Sam was perhaps comforted by his own acting credo which he recently revealed. 'In rehearsals,' he confessed, 'I do what the directors want; in performances, I do what I want.'"

# Selected Bibliography

Eggenberger, Urula. Samuel Ramey: *Un Diable a Plusiers Visages*. Chapelle-sur-Moudon, Suisse. Editions Ketty & Alexandre. 1998

Gossett, Philip. *Divas and Scholars: Performing Italian Opera*. Chicago and London. The University of Chicago Press, 2006

Horne, Marilyn; Scovell, Jane. *Marilyn Horne: The Song Continues*. Fort Worth. Baskerville Publishers, Inc. 2004

Morgan, Brian. *Strange Child of Chaos: Norman Treigle*. New York, Lincoln, and Shanghai. Universe, Inc. 2006

Sokol, Martin L. *The New York City Opera: An American Adventure*. New York and London. Macmillan Publishing Co., Inc. 1981

Opera Magazine Ltd. *Basses in Opera: Profiles of Thirteen Great Basses*. Great Britain. Simpson Drewett, Richmond, Surrey. 2005

# Chronology

| | |
|---|---|
| **1969** | National Opera Company, Raleigh, NC (Toured Southeastern US), *La Périchole*: Don Pédro; *Don Pasquale*: Don Pasquale; *L'italiana in Algeri*: Mustafa<br>Little Orchestra Society, Alice Tully Hall (New York debut, semi-staged concert), *The Prodigal Son* (Britten): The Elder Son |
| **1970** | Opera Orchestra of New York, Avery Fisher Hall (concert performance), *Rigoletto*: Monterone |
| **1971** | Paterson Lyric Opera, Paterson, NJ, *Faust*: Méphistophélès; *La boheme*: Colline; *Anna Bolena*: Enrico VIII |
| **1972** | Paterson Lyric Opera, NJ, *Pique Dame*: Tomsky<br>Providence Opera, RI, *Aida*: Il Re<br>Metropolitan Opera Auditions, New York, NY, National Finalist<br>Boston Opera, MA, *La traviata*: Dr. Grenvil<br>Harford Opera Theatre Association, MD, *La boheme*: Colline; *Il trovatore*: Ferrando |
| **1973** | Bel Canto Opera Company, New York, NY, *I Puritani*: Giorgio<br>New York City Opera (spring season, debut), *Carmen*: Zuniga; *Cosi fan tutte*: Don Alfonso New York City Opera at Kennedy Center, *Carmen*: Zuniga<br>Harford Opera Company, MD, *Rigoletto*: Sparafucile<br>New York City Opera (fall season), *Les Contes d'Hoffmann*: Crespel; *Anna Bolena*: Rochefort; *Ariadne auf Naxos*: Trufaldino; *La Traviata*: Baron Douphol; *Il barbiere di Siviglia*: Don Basilio; *I Puritani*: Walton; *Roberto Devereux*: Sir Gualtiero Raleigh<br>Dayton Opera Association, OH, *Manon*: Comte des Grieux<br>Toledo Opera, OH, *Manon*: Comte des Grieux |
| **1974** | Opera Theatre of New Jersey, *La Gioconda*: Alvise<br>New York City Opera (spring), *Carmen*: Zuniga; *La boheme*: Colline; *I Puritani*: Walton; *Ariadne auf Naxos*: Trufaldino; *Anna Bolena*: Rochefort; *Il barbiere di Siviglia*: Don Basilio; *Medea*: Creon<br>New York City Opera (fall), *Anna Bolena*: Enrico VIII; *Medea*: Creon; *Faust*: Méphistophélès; *L'incoronazione di Poppea*: Seneca; *Tosca*: Angelotti; *Don Giovanni*: Don Giovanni<br>Philadelphia Lyric Opera, PA, *La boheme*: Colline |

# Chronology

**1975** Omaha Opera Company, NB, *Lucia di Lammermoor*: Raimondo
Florentine Opera Company, Milwaukee, WI, *Lucia di Lammermoor*: Raimondo
New York City Opera (spring), *Le nozze di Figaro*: Figaro; *Salome*: First Nazarene; *Anna Bolena*: Enrico VIII; *Turandot*: Timur; *Il barbiere di Siviglia*: Don Basilio; *Faust*: Méphistophélès; *I Puritani*: Giorgio
Santa Fe Opera, NM, *Carmen*: Escamillo
Artpark Opera, Niagra, NY, *Le nozze di Figaro*: Figaro
New York City Opera (fall), *Les Contes d'Hoffmann*: Four Villains; *Turandot*: Timur; *Salome*: First Nazarene
Houston Grand Opera (debut), TX, *Rinaldo*: Argante
Fort Worth Opera, TX, *Pique Dame*: Tomsky
Philadephia Lyric Opera, PA, *Anna Bolena*: Enrico VIII

**1976** Vancouver Opera, Canada, *Pique Dame*: Tomsky
New York City Opera (spring), *Le nozze di Figaro*: Figaro; *Turnadot*: Timur; *La boheme*: Colline; *Il barbiere di Siviglia*: Don Basilio; *Carmen*: Escamillo
Bob Jones University, Greenville, SC, *Mefistofele*: Mefistofele
Amigor Canarios de la Opera Gran Canaria, Spain, *Don Giovanni*: Don Giovanni
Milwaukee Symphony, WI, *La Damnation de Faust*: Méphistophélès
Glyndebourne Festival Opera (European Debut), England, *Le nozze di Figaro*: Figaro
New York City Opera (fall), *Turandot*: Timur; *Carmen*: Escamillo; *Il barbiere di Siviglia*: Don Basilio; *Le nozze di Figaro*: Figaro

**1977** Grand Théâtre de Bordeaux, France, *Don Giovanni*: Don Giovanni
New York City Opera (spring), *Il barbiere di Siviglia*: Don Basilio; *Mefistofele*: Mefistofele; *Carmen*, Escamillo
Florentine Opera Company, Milwaukee, WI, *Faust*: Méphistophélès
New Jersey State Opera, Garden State Arts Center, *Aida*: Ramses
Glyndebourne Festival Opera, England, *The Rake's Progress*: Nick Shadow
New York City Opera (fall), *Mefistofele*: Mefistofele; *Le nozze di Figaro*: Figaro; *La boheme*: Colline; *Manon*: Comte des Grieux

**1978** Netherlands Opera, Amsterdam, Holland, *Les Contes d'Hoffmann*: Four Villains
New York City Opera (spring), *Mefistofele*: Mefistofele; *Il barbiere di Siviglia*: Don Basilio; *Le nozze di Figaro*: Figaro; *La boheme*: Colline
Tulsa Opera, OK, *I Puritani*: Giorgio
Hamburg Staatsoper, Germany, *Il barbiere di Siviglia*: Don Basilio; *Pelléas et Mélisande*: Arkel
Glyndebourne Festival Opera, England, *The Rake's Progress*: Nick Shadow

# Chronology

**1979**
New York City Opera (fall), *Le nozze di Figaro*: Figaro
San Francisco Opera (debut), CA, *La Boheme*: Colline
Hamburg Staatsoper, Germany, *La Boheme*:Colline; *Le nozze di Figaro*: Figaro; *Il barbiere di Siviglia*: Don Basilio
New York City Opera (spring), *Faust*: Méphistophélès; *Mefistofele*: Mefistofele
Opéra Nationale de Paris (debut), France, *La Boheme*: Colline
Aix-en-Provence Festival, France, *Le nozze di Figaro*: Figaro
New York City Opera (fall), *Faust*:Méphistophélès; *Le comte Ory*: Le Gouverneur
Lyric Opera of Chicago, IL, *La Boheme*: Colline

**1980**
Pittsburg Opera, PA, *Don Giovanni*: Don Giovanni
Tonhalle Konzerthaus, Zurich, Switzerland, *Mefistofele*: Mefistofele
New York City Opera (spring), *Le comte Ory*: Le Gouverneur; *Don Giovanni*: Don Giovanni; *Carmen*:Escamillo; *Les Contes d'Hoffmann*: Four Villians; *La Boheme*: Colline
Hamburg Staatsoper, Germany, *Eugene Onegin*: Gremin
Aix-en-Provence Festival, France, *Semiramide*: Assur
New York City Opera (fall), *Anna Bolena*: Enrico VIII; *Don Giovanni*: Leporello
Théâtre des Arts, Rouen, France, *Don Quichotte* (Massenet): Don Quichotte
Hamburg Staatsoper, Germany, *Macbeth*: Banquo
Netherlands Opera, Amsterdam, *Le nozze di Figaro*: Figaro

**1981**
New York City Opera (spring), *Don Giovanni*: Don Giovanni; *Don Giovanni*: Leporello; *Attila*: Attila; *Anna Bolena*: Enrico VIII
Teatro alla Scala (debut), Milan, Italy, *Le nozze di Figaro*: Figaro
Vienna Staatsoper (debut), Austria, *Carmen*: Escamillo; *Le nozze di Figaro*: Figaro
New York City Opera, Wolftrap, VA, *Attila*: Attila
Rossini Opera Festival (debut), Pesaro, Italy, *L'italiana in Algeri*: Mustafa
Vienna Staatsoper, Austria, *Don Giovanni*: Don Giovanni
San Diego Opera, CA, *Susannah*: Olin Blitch
Théâtre Nationale de Paris, France, *Carmen*: Escamillo; *Semiramide*: Assur

**1982**
New York City Opera (spring), *Le nozze di Figaro*: Figaro; *L'amore dei tre re*: Archibaldo; *Susannah*: Olin Blitch
Tulsa Opera, OK, *Il barbiere di Siviglia*: Don Basilio
Teatro alla Scalla, Milan, Italy, *Le nozze di Figaro*: Figaro
Festival Ottawa, Canada, *Rinaldo*: Argante
Rossini Opera Festival, Pesaro, Italy, *L'italiana in Algeri*: Mustafa
New York City Opera (fall), *L'amore dei tre re*: Archibaldo; *Le nozze di Figaro*: Figaro; *Susannah*: Olin Blitch; *Mefistofele*: Mefistofele
Royal Opera House Covent Garden (debut), London, England, *Le nozze di Figaro*: Figaro

# Chronology

**1983** Carnegie Hall (concert), New York, NY, *Semiramide*: Assur
Pittsburg Opera, PA, *Faust*: Méphistophélès
Edmonton Opera, Canada, *Les Contes d'Hoffmann*: Four Villains
Winnipeg Opera, Canada, *Les Contes d'Hoffman*: Four Villains
Hamburg Staatsoper (concert), Germany, *Semiramide*: Assur; *Les Contes d'Hoffmann*: Four Villains
Opernhaus Zurich, Switzerland, *La Damnation de Faust*: Méphistophélès
Deutsche Oper Berlin (concert), Germany, *Semiramide*: Assur
Royal Opera House Covent Garden, London, *Don Giovanni*:Don Giovanni
Teatro alla Scala (concert), Milan, Italy, *La Damnation de Faust*: Méphistophélès
Rossini Opera Festival, Pesaro, Italy, *Il turco in Italia*: Selim; *La donna del lago*: Douglas
Théâtre Nationale Opéra de Paris, France, *Il barbiere di Seviglia*: Don Basilio
Théâtre Royal de la Monnaie, Brussels, Belgium, *Don Carlo*: Filippo II
Hamburg Staatsoper, Germany, *Don Carlo*: Filippo II

**1984** Metropolitan Opera (debut, Jan 19), New York, NY, *Rinaldo*: Argante
Carnegie Hall (concert), New York, NY, *Chérubin* (Massenet): Le philosophe
Teatro la Fenice (debut), Venice, Italy, *L'italiana in Algeri*: Mustafa
Lyric Opera of Chicago (concert), IL, *Rinaldo*: Argante
Rossini Opera Festival, Pesaro, Italy, *Il viaggio a Reims*, Lord Sydney
San Francisco Opera, CA, *La sonnambula*: Rodolfo
New York City Opera (fall), NY, *Mefistofele*: Mefistofele
Chicago Symphony (concert), IL, *Boris Godunov*: Pimen
Deutsche Oper Berlin, Germany, *Les Contes d'Hoffmann*: Four Villains; *Semiramide* (concert): Assur; *Le nozze di Figaro*: Figaro
Carnegie Hall (concert), New York, NY, *Semele*: Cadmus, Somnus
Royal Opera House Covent Garden, London, England, *Il barbiere di Siviglia*: Don Basilio
Hamburg Staatsoper, Germany, *Semiramide* (concert): Assur; *Don Carlo*: Filippo II
Théâtre Nationale de l'Opéra de Paris, France, *Robert le diable*: Bertram
New York City Opera (summer), NY, *Attila*: Attila
Rossini Opera Festival, Pesaro, Italy, *Maometto II*: Maometto
Teatro alla Scala, Milan, Italy, *Il viaggio a Reims*: Lord Sydney
Teatro Comunale di Firenze, Florence, Italy, *Faust*: Méphistophélès
Hamburg Staatsoper, Germany, *Faust*: Méphistophélès

**1986** Royal Opera House Covent Garden, London, England, *Faust*:

# Chronology

|      | |
|------|---|
|      | Méphistophélès; *Les Contes d'Hoffmann*: Four Villains; *Semiramide* (concert): Assur<br>Tulsa Opera, OK, Faust: Méphistophélès<br>Hamburg Staatsoper, Germany, *Faust*: Méphistophélès; *Don Carlo*: Filippo II<br>Teatro la Fenice, Venice, Italy, *Attila*: Attila<br>Hamburg Staatsoper, Germany, *Mefistofele* (concert): Mefistofele<br>New York City Opera (summer), NY, *Don Quichotte*: Don Quichotte<br>San Francisco Opera, CA, *Le nozze di Figaro*: Figaro<br>Metropolitan Opera, New York, NY, *I Puritani*: Giorgio |
| 1987 | Teatro la Fenice, Venice, Italy, *Attila*: Attila<br>Metropolitan Opera, New York, NY, *Carmen*: Escamillo<br>Salzburg Easter Festival, Austria, *Don Giovanni*: Don Giovanni<br>Tulsa Opera, OK, *Don Carlo*: Filippo II<br>Teatro alla Scala, Milan, Italy, *Le nozze di Figaro*: Figaro<br>Salzburg Festival, Austria, *Don Giovanni*: Don Giovanni<br>Hamburg Staatsoper, Germany, *Don Giovanni*: Don Giovanni<br>Lyric Opera of Chicago, IL, *Faust*: Méphistophélès; *Le nozze di Figaro*: Figaro |
| 1988 | Metropolitan Opera, New York, NY, *Macbeth*: Banquo<br>Vienna Staatsoper, Austria, *Il viaggio a Reims*: Lord Sydney<br>Opera Orchestra of NY (concert), Carnegie Hall New York, NY, *Robert le diable*: Bertram<br>Hamburg Staatsoper, Germany, *Don Giovanni*: Don Giovanni<br>Grand Théâtre de Genève, Switzerland, *Don Carlo*: Filippo II<br>Lyric Opera of Chicago, IL, *Don Giovanni*: Don Giovanni<br>Metropolitan Opera, New York, NY, *Carmen*: Escamillo |
| 1989 | Metropolitan Opera, New York, NY, *Bluebeard's Castle*: Bluebeard<br>Théâtre Nationale de l'Opéra de Paris (concert), France, *Mefistofele*: Mefistofele<br>Royal Opera House Covent Garden, London, England, *Don Carlo*: Filippo II<br>Vienna Staatosper, Austria, *Il viaggio a Reims*: Lord Sydney<br>London Symphony (concert), England, *La Damnation de Faust*: Méphistophélès<br>Rossini Opera Festival, Pesaro, Italy, *La Gazza Ladra* Podesta<br>San Francisco Opera, CA, *Mefistofele*: Mefistofele<br>Lyric Opera of Chicago, IL, *Don Carlo*: Filippo II |
| 1990 | Vienna Staatsoper, Austria, *Faust*: Méphistophélès; *Le nozze di Figaro*: Figaro<br>Metropolitan Opera, New York, NY, *Don Giovanni*: Don Giovanni; *Don Giovanni*: Leporello; *Il barbiere di Siviglia*: Don Basilio; *Semiramide*: Assur<br>Barbican Hall (concert), London, England, *Mefistofele*: Mefistofele<br>Maggio Musicale Festival, Florence, Italy, *Don Giovanni*: Don Giovanni |

# Chronology

**1991**
Bayerische Staatsoper (concert), Munich, Germany, *Semiramide*: Assur; *Le nozze di Figaro*: Figaro
Salzburg Festival, Austria, *Don Giovanni*: Don Giovanni
San Francisco Opera, CA, *Don Quichotte*: Don Quichotte
Metropolitan Opera, New York, NY, *Faust*: Méphistophélès; *Le nozze di Figaro*: Figaro
Dallas Opera, TX, *Faust*: Méphistoplélès
Royal Opera House Covent Garden, London, England, *Tosca*: Scarpia
Teatro alla Scalla, Milan, Italy, *Attila*: Attila
Salzburg Festival, Austria, *Don Giovanni*: Don Giovanni
Lyric Opera of Chicago, IL, *Mefistofele*: Mefistofele; *Le nozze di Figaro*: Figaro
San Francisco Opera, CA, *Don Giovanni*: Don Giovanni; *Attila*: Attila

**1992**
Teatro la Fenice, Venice, Italy, *Don Carlo*: Filippo II
Metropolitan Opera, New York, NY, *Don Giovanni*: Don Giovanni; *Il barbiere di Siviglia*: Don Basilio; *Don Carlo*: Filippo II
Royal Opera House Covent Garden, London, England, *Les Contes d'Hoffmann*: Four Villains
Houston Grand Opera, TX, *Mefistofele*: Mefistofele
Grand Théâtre de Genève, Switzerland, *Attila*: Attila
Aix-en-Provence Festival, France, *The Rake's Progrss*: Nick Shadow
Rossini Opera Festival, Pesaro, Italy, *Il viaggio a Reims*: Lord Sydney
Metropolitan Opera, New York, NY, *Les Contes d'Hoffmann*: Four Villains
Berlin Philharmonic, Germany, *Il viaggio a Reims*: Lord Sydney
Teatro alla Scala, Milan, Italy, *Don Carlo*: Filippo II

**1993**
Teatro alla Scala, Milan, Italy, *Don Carlo*: Filippo II
Teatro La Fenice, Venice, Italy, *Faust*: Méphistophélès
Royal Opera House Covent Garden, London, England, *Le Damnation de Faust*: Mephistopheles; *Attila*: Attila
Grand Théâtre de Genève, Switzerland, *Boris Godunov*: Boris Godunov
Salzburg Festival, Austria, *Bluebeard's Castle*: Bluebeard
Lyric Opera of Chicago, IL, *Boris Godunov*: Boris Godunov
Metropolitan Opera, New York, NY, *I Lombardi*: Pagano, Ermito

**1994**
Teatro alla Scala, Milan, Italy, *Maometto II*: Maometto
Valencia, Spain (concert), *Mefistofele*: Mefistofele
Metropolitan Opera in Frankfurt (concert), Germany, *I Lombardi*: Pagano, Ermito
San Francisco Symphony, CA, *La Damnation de Faust*: Méphistophélès
Salzburg Festival, Austria, *Boris Godunov*: Boris Godunov
Lyric Opera of Chicago, IL, *Boris Godunov*: Boris Godunov; *The Rake's Progress*: Nick Shadow

# Chronology

**1995**
San Francisco Opera, CA, *Mefistofele*: Mefistofele
Teatro alla Scala, Milan, Italy, *Mefistofele*: Mefistofele; *Les Contes d'Hoffmann*: Four Villains
Grand Théâtre de Genève, Switzerland, *Faust*: Méphistophélès
Houston Grand Opera, TX, *Attila*: Attila
Paris Opera-Bastille, France, *Nabucco*: Zaccaria
San Francisco Opera, CA, *Faust*: Méphistophélès; *Don Giovanni:* Don Giovanni
Vienna Staatsoper, Austria, *Jerusalem* (Verdi): Roger, Ermit

**1996**
Lyric Opera of Chicago, IL, *Faust*: Méphistophélès
Washington National Opera, Washington, DC, *Mefistofele*: Mefistofele
Royal Opera House Covent Garden, London, England, *Nabucco*: Zaccaria
Houston Grand Opera, TX, *Susannah*: Olin Blitch
Vienna Staatsoper, Austria, *Jerusalem* (Verdi): Roger; *Don Carlo*: Filippo II; *Don Giovanni*: Don Giovanni
Santander Festival, Spain, *Nabucco*: Zaccaria
Lyric Opera of Chicago, IL, *Don Carlo*: Filippo II
San Francisco Opera, CA, *Les Contes d'Hoffmann*: Four Villains

**1997**
Opéra de Paris Bastille, France, *Faust*: Méphistophélès; *La Damnation de Faust*: Méphistophélès
Vienna Staatsoper, Austria, *Mefistofele*: Mefistofele
Opernhaus Zurich, Switzerland, *Faust:* Méphistophélès
Metropolitan Opera, New York, NY, *Faust*: Méphistophélès
Teatro alla Scala, Milan, Italy, *Faust*: Méphistophélès
Lyric Opera of Chicago *Nabucco:* Zaccaria, Chicago, IL
Metropolitan Opera, New York, NY, *Il barbiere di Siviglia*: Don Basilio; *The Rake's Progress*: Nick Shadow; *Boris Godunov*: Boris Godunov

**1998**
Metropolitan Opera, New York, NY, *Boris Godunov*: Boris Godunov; *The Rake's Progress*: Nick Shadow
Marinsky Theatre, St. Petersburg, Russia, Chaliapin Commemoration concert, Basses, *Don Carlo* and *Mefistofele* arias
Royal Opera House Covent Garden (concert), London, England, *Mefistofele*: Mefistofele
Opéra de Paris-Bastille, France, *Don Carlo*: Filippo II
Lyric Opera of Chicago, IL, *Mefistofele*: Mefistofele

**1999**
Washington National Opera, Washington, DC, *Boris Godunov*: Boris Godunov
Metropolitan Opera, New York, NY, *Susannah*: Olin Blitch; *Mefistofele*: Mefistofele
Houston Grand Opera, TX, *Mefistofele*: Mefistofele
Vienna Staatsoper, Austria, *Les Contes d'Hoffmann*: Four Villains
Teatro Colon, Buenos Aires, Argentina, *Mefistofele*: Mefistofele
San Francisco Opera, CA, *Louise*: Le père

**2000**
Los Angeles Opera, CA, *Faust*: Méphistophélès
Metropolitan Opera, New York, NY, *Mefistofele*: Mefistofele

# Chronology

|      |   |
|------|---|
|      | Opéra de Paris-Bastille, France, *Les Contes d'Hoffmann*: Four Villains; *Don Quichotte*: Don Quichotte<br>Houston Grand Opera, TX, *Nabucco*: Zaccaria<br>Metropolitan Opera at Carnegie Hall, New York, NY, *Bluebeard's Castle*: Bluebeard<br>Grand Théâtre de Genève, Switzerland, *Susannah*: Olin Blitch<br>Opernhaus Zurich, Switzerland, *L'amore di tre re*: Archibaldo<br>Lyric Opera of Chicago, IL, *Attila*: Attila |
| 2001 | Metropolitan Opera, New York, NY, *L'italiana in Algeri*: Mustafa; *Nabucco:* Zaccaria<br>Houston Grand Opera, TX, *Don Carlo*: Filippo II<br>San Francisco Opera, CA, *Simon Boccanegra*: Fiesco<br>Teatro Colon, Buenos Aires, Argentina, *The Rake's Progress*: Nick Shadow; *Attila*: Attila<br>Opéra de Paris-Bastille, France, *Attila*: Attila<br>Lyric Opera of Chicago, IL, *Billy Budd*: Claggart |
| 2002 | Metropolitan Opera, New York, NY, *Don Carlo*: Filippo II; *War and Peace*: Kutuzov<br>Los Angeles Opera, CA, *Bluebeard's Castle*: Bluebeard; *Gianni Schicchi*: Schicchi<br>Lyric Opera of Chicago, IL, *Susannah*: Olin Blitch<br>Los Angeles Opera, CA, *Les Contes d'Hoffmann*: Four Villains |
| 2003 | Vienna Staatsoper, Austria, *Don Carlo*: Filippo II<br>Opernhaus Zürich, Switzerland, *Don Carlo*: Filippo II<br>Metropolitan Opera, New York, NY, *Nabucco*: Zaccaria; *The Rake's Progress*: Nick Shadow<br>Opera Orchestra of New York Carnegie Hall, New York, NY, *Attila*: Attila<br>Cleveland Orchestra (concert), OH, *Don Carlo*: Filippo II<br>Arena di Verona, Verona, Italy, *Nabucco*: Zaccaria; *Carmen*: Escamillo<br>Los Angeles Opera, CA, *La Damnation de Faust*: Méphistophélès<br>Lyric Opera of Chicago, IL, *Faust*: Méphistophélès |
| 2004 | Metropolitan Opera, New York, NY, *Tosca*: Scarpia; *Nabucco*: Zaccaria; *I vespri siciliani*: Procida<br>Opéra de Paris-Bastille, France, *La Damnation de Faust*: Méphistophélès; Bluebeard's Castle (concert): Bluebeard<br>Royal Opera House Covent Garden, London, England, *Tosca*: Scarpia<br>Washington National Opera, Washington DC, *Billy Budd*: Claggart |
| 2005 | Lyric Opera of Chicago, Tosca, Scarpia Chicago, IL<br>Metropolitan Opera, *Don Carlo,* Grand Inquisitor New York, NY<br>Don Giovanni Leporello<br>Opéra de Paris-Bastille, *Boris Godunov,* Boris Godunov, Paris, France<br>Teatro Carlo Felice, *Billy Budd:* Claggart, Genoa, Italy |

# Chronology

|      |  |
|------|--|
| | Vienna Staatsoper, *Tosca:* Scarpia, Vienna, Austria |
| | Houston Grand Opera, *Boris Godunov:* Boris Godunov, Houston, TX |
| | Los Angeles Opera, *Tosca:* Scarpia, Los Angeles, CA |
| **2006** | Teatro San Carlo, Naples, Italy, *Attila*: Attila |
| | Metropolitan Opera, New York, NY, *La forza del destino*: Padre Guardiano |
| | Opera Orchestra of New York, Carnegie Hall, New York, NY, *L'amore dei tre re*: Archibaldo |
| | Royal Opera House Covent Garden, London, England, *Tosca*: Scarpia |
| | Washington National Opera, Washington, DC, *Bluebeard's Castle*: Bluebeard; *Gianni Schicchi*: Schicchi |
| | Metropolitan Opera, New York, NY, *Don Carlo*: Grand Inquisitor; *Il barbiere di Siviglia*: Don Basilio |
| **2007** | Houston Grand Opera, TX, *Faust*: Méphistophélès |
| | Wichita Grand Opera, KS, *Tosca*: Scarpia |
| | Metropolitan Opera, New York, NY, *Il barbiere di Siviglia*: Don Basilio; *War and Peace*: Kutuzov |
| | Chicago Opera Theatre, IL, *Bluebeard's Castle*: Bluebeard |
| | Gran Teatro del Liceu, Barcelona, Spain, *Manon*: Comte des Grieux |
| | Terme di Caracalla, Rome, Italy, *Nabucco*: Zaccaria |
| | Teatro Real, Madrid, Spain, *Boris Godunov*, Boris Godunov |
| | Opéra de Paris-Bastille, France, *Tosca*: Scarpia |
| **2008** | Vienna Staatsoper, Austria, *Les Contes d'Hoffmann*: Four Villians |
| | Wichita Grand Opera, KS, *Faust*: Méphistophélès |
| | Opéra de Paris-Bastille, France, *Il barbiere di Siviglia*: Don Basilio |
| | Gran Teatre del Licuo, Barcelona, Spain, *Luisa Miller*: Wurm |
| | Ravinia Festival, Chicago, IL, *Don Giovanni*: Leporello |
| | San Francisco Opera, CA, *Boris Godunov*: Boris Godunov |
| | Vienna Staatsoper, Austria, *Tosca*: Scarpia |
| | Metropolitan Opera, New York, NY, *La Rondine*: Rambaldo |
| **2009** | Vienna Staatsoper, Austria, *Tosca*: Scarpia |
| | Metropolitan Opera, New York, NY, *La Rondine*: Rambaldo; *Don Giovanni*: Leporello; *Turandot*: Timur |
| **2010** | Metropolitan Opera, New York, NY, *Attila*: Pope Leo; *Il barbiere di Siviglia*: Don Basilio |

# DISCOGRAPHY

The recordings are CDs, with the exception of those labeled as LP (33s).

Abbreviations
* live, p* partially live, Leg.: Legendary, Leg.*: Legendary (LP),
LOC: Lyric Opera of Chicago, MM: Mondo Musica, Serenis.: Serenissima

Information listed by composer in the following order:
Title of Work (*Role*), Year Recorded, Conductor, Other Cast Members, Label

**COMPLETE WORKS**

BACH
Cantatas BWV 80 & 140, 1981, Leppard, Ameling, Finnie, Baldwin, Philips
Mass in B Minor, 1977, Marriner, Marshall, Baker, Tear, Philips

BARTOK
Bluebeard's Castle (*Bluebeard*), 1987, Fischer, Marton, CBS, Sony

BEETHOVEN
Ninth Symphony, 1989, Marriner, Mattila, von Otter, Araiza, Philips

BELLINI
Norma (*Oroveso*), 1984, Bonynge, Sutherland, Caballe, Pavarotti, Decca

BERNSTEIN
On the Town (*Pitkin, First Workman, Announcer*), 1992*, Tilson Thomas, Von Stade, McLaughlin, Hampson, Lear, Daly, DG

BIZET
Carmen (*Escamillo*), 1995, Sinopoli, Larmore, Gheorghiu, Moser, Teldec

BLITZSTEIN
Regina (*Horace Giddens*), 1991, Mauceri, Ciesinski, Réaux, Greenawald, Decca

BOITO
Mefistofele (*Mefistofele*), 1988, Patane, Marton, Domingo, Sony

# Discography

Mefistofele (*Mefistofele*), 1989*, Bartoletti, Dessi, Cupido, Serenis
Mefistofele (*Mefistofele*), 1995*, Muti, Crider, La Scola, RCA

## BRAHMS
A German Requiem, 1986, Previn, M. Price, Teldec

## BRUCKNER
Te Deum, 1980, Baremboim, Norman, Minton, Rendall, DG (LP)

## DONIZETTI
Anna Bolena (*Henry VIII*), 1975*, Rudel, Scotto, Marsee, Kolk, Legato
Anna Bolena (*Henry VIII*), 1987, Bonynge, Sutherland, Mentzer, Hadley, Decca
Caterina Conaro (*Andrea Cornaro*), 1973*, Silipigni, Gencer, Campora, Taddei, Morris, Legato
Lucia di Lammermoor (*Raimondo*), 1976, Lopez-Corbos, Caballe, Carreras, Sardinero, Philips
Lucia di Lammermoor (*Raimondo*), 1990, Marin, Studer, Domingo, Pons, DG
Messa di Gloria, 1983*, Gelmetti, Susovsky, Savastano, CBS (LP)

## FLOYD
Susannah (*Olin Blitch*), 1993-94, Nagano, Studer, Hadley, Chester, Virgin

## GOUNOD
Faust (*Méphistophélès*), 1993, Rizzi, Hadley, Gasdia, Agache, Teldec

## HANDEL
Ariodante (*The King of Scotland*), 1978, Leppard, Baker, Mathis, Burrowes, Bowman, Philips
Rinaldo (*Argante*), 1975*, Foster, Horne, Mandac, Rogers, Walker, Voce (LP)
Rodelinda (*Garibaldo*), 1985, Bonynge, Sutherland, Nafe, Rayam, Decca
Semele (*Cadmus, Somnus*), 1985*, Nelson, Battle, Horne, Blake, Leg.
Semele (*Cadmus, Somnus*), 1990, Nelson, Battle, Horne, Aler, DG
Messiah, 1986, Davis, Battle, Quivar, Aler, EMI

## HAYDN
Armida (*Idreno*), 1978, Dorati, Norman, Ahnsjö, Rolfe Johnson, Philips

## LEIGH and DARION
Man of La Mancha (*The Inkeeper*), 1990, Gemignani, Migenes, Domingo, Hadley, Sony

## MASSENET
Chérubin (*Le philosophe*), 1984*, Lewis, Von Stade, Putnam, Masterson, Voce (LP)
Chérubin (*Le philosophe*), 1991, Steinberg, Von Stade, Anderson, Upshaw, RCA

## MEYERBEER
Robert le Diable (*Bertram*), 1985*, Fulton, Anderson, Lagrange, Vanzo, Donati, Legato

# Discography

**MOUSSORGSKY**
Boris Godounov (*Boris Goudounov*), 1993*, De Waart, Rolfe Johnson, Tomlinson, Begley, Serenis.
Boris Godounov (*Pimen*), 1993, Abbado, Kotcherga, Lipovsek, Larin, Langridge, Sony

**MOZART**
Don Giovanni (*Don Giovanni*), 1985, Karajan, Tomowa-Sintow, Baltsa, Battle, Wingerg, Furlanetto, DG
Don Giovanni (*Leporello*), 1990, Muti, Shimell, Studer, Vaness, Mentzer, Lopardo, EMI
Le nozze di Figaro (*Figaro*), 1981, Solti, Te Kanawa, Popp, von Stade, Allen, Decca
Die Zauberflöte (*Sarastro*), 1989, Marriner, Te Kanawa, Studer, Araiza, Philips

**OFFENBACH**
Les Contes d'Hoffmann (*Lindorf, Coppélius, Miracle, Dapertutto*), 1987-89, Tate, Lind, Norman, Studer, Araiza, Philips

**PONCHIELLI**
La Gioconda (*Alvise*), 1987, Patané, Marton, Lamberti, Milnes, CBS

**PUCCINI**
La boheme (*Colline*), 1995, Pappano, Vaduva, Swenson, Alagna, Hampson, EMI
Tosca (*Angelotti*), 1974*, Rudel, Nilsson, Carreras, Fredricks, Legato
Tosca (*Angelotti*), 1976, Davis, Caballe, Carreras, Wixell, Philips
Tosca (*Scarpia*), 1990, Sinopoli, Freni, Domingo, DG

**RODGERS and HAMMERSTEIN**
Carousel (*Billy Bigelow*), 1987, Gemignani, Rendall, Brightman, Forrester, MCA

**ROSSINI**
Il barbiere di Siviglia (*Basilio*), 1982, Chailly, Horne, Barbacini, Nucci, Dara, CBS-Sony
Il barbiere di Siviglia (*Basilio*), 1992, Gelmetti, Mentzer, Hadley, Hampson, Pratico, EMI
Il barbiere di Siviglia (*Basilio*), 1992, Lopez-Corbos, Larmore, Gimenez, Hagegard, Corbelli, Teldec
La donna del lago (*Douglas d'Angus*), 1983, Pollini, Ricciarelli, Valentini Terrani, Gonzales, CBS-Sony
La gazza ladra (*The Podesta*), 1989, Gelmetti, Ricciarelli, Manca di Nissa, Matteuzzi, Furlanetto, Sony
L'Italiana in Algeri (*Mustafa*), 1980, Scimone, Horne, Battle, Palacio, Zaccaria, Erato
Maometto II (*Maometto*), 1983, Scimone, Anderson, Zimmermann, Palacio, Philips

# Discography

Maometto II (*Maometto*), 1994*, Ferro, Gasdia, Scalchi, Ford, Serenis.
Moïse et Pharaon (*Moïse*), 1983*, Prêtre, Gasdia, Verrett, Lewis, Lafont, Legato
Otello (*Elmire*), 1978, Lopez-Corbos, Von Stade, Carreras, Fisichella, Philips
Semiramide (*Assur*), 1980*, Lopez-Corbos, Caballe, Horne, Araiza, Legato
Semiramide (*Assur*), 1980*, Lopez-Corbos, Caballe, Horne, Araiza, HRE (LP)
Semiramide (*Assur*), 1992, Marin, Studer, Larmore, Lopardo, DG
Il Signor Bruschino (*Gaudenzio*), 1991, Marin, Battle, Lopardo, Desderi, DG
Il turco in Italia (*Selim*), 1981, Chailly, Caballe, Palacio, Nucci, Dara, CBS-Sony
Il viaggio a Reims (*Lord Sidney*), 1984, Abbado, Ricciarelli, Gasdia, Araiza, Raimondi, DG
Il viaggio a Reims (*Lord Sidney*), 1992*, Abbado, Studer, Serra, McNair, Matteuzzi, Raimondi, Sony
Messa di Gloria, 1992, Marriner, Jo, Murray, Araiza, Gimenez, Philips
Petite Messe Solenelle, 1983, Scimone, Ricciarelli, Zimmermann, Carreras, Philips

SAINT-SAENS
Samson et Dalila (*Un vieillard hébreu*), 1991, Chung, Meier, Domingo, Fondari, Courtis, EMI

STRAUSS
Elektra (*Orest*), 1995, Sinopoli, Schwarz, Marc, Voigt, Jerusalem, DG

STRAVINSKY
The Rake's Progress (*Nick Shadow*), 1984, Chailly, Pope, Walker, Langridge, Dean, Decca
The Rake's Progress (*Nick Shadow*), 1995, Nagano, Upshaw, Hadley, Lloyd, Bumbry, S. Cole, Erato

THOMAS
Hamlet (*Claudius*), 1993, De Almeida, Anderson, Graves, Hampson, Kunde, EMI

VERDI
Aida (*Ramfis*), 1990, Levine, Millo, Zajick, Domingo, Morris, Sony
Attila (*Attila*), 1989, Muti, Studer, Shicoff, Zancanaro, EMI
Don Carlo (*Filippo II*), 1992*, Muti, Pavarotti, Dessi, d'Intino, Coni, Anisimov, EMI
Don Carlo (*The Grand Inquisitor*), 1992, Levine, Silvester, Millo, Zajick, Chernov, Furlanetto, Sony
I due Foscari (*Loredano*), 1976, Gardelli, Ricciarelli, Carreras, Cappuccilli, Philips
I Lombardi (*Pagano*), 1996, Levine, Anderson, Leech, Pavarotti, Decca
Macbeth (*Banco*), 1986, Chailly, Nucci, Verrett, Luchetti, Decca
I Masnadieri (*Massimiliano*), 1982, Bonynge, Sutherland, Bonisolli, Manuguerra, Decca
Oberto (*Oberto*), 1996, Marriner, Guleghina, Urmana, Neill, Philips
Rigoletto (*Sparafucile, Monterone*), 1978, Rudel, Milnes, Sills, Dunn, Kraus,

# Discography

EMI
Rigoletto (*Sparafucile*), 1993, Rizzi, Agache, Vaduva, Larmore, Leech, Teldec
Messa da Requiem, 1987*, Muti, Studer, Zajick, Pavarotte, EMI

WEILL
Street Scene (*Frank Maurrant*), 1989,90, Mauceri, Barstow, Reaux, Hadley, Decca

WRIGHT and FORREST
Kismet (*The Poet*), 1990, Gemignani, Swenson, Migenes, Hadley, Sony

RECITALS AND CONCERTS

*The Sensational Samuel Ramey*: Le Caïd, Ernani, Don Carlo, Le comte Ory, Il barbiere di Siviglia, Rinaldo, Semiramide, Semile and excerpts from musicals, 1974-81*, various conductors, Leg.

*Mefistofele and Other Villains*: Mefistofele, Attila, Les Contes d'Hoffmann, Don Giovanni, Robert le diable, Faust, 1978-85*, various conductors, Leg.*

*Recital*: Arias by Carissimi, Scarlatti, Legrenzi, Mozart, Vaughan Williams, Dougherty and excerpts from Simone Boccanegra, Ernani, Les Contes d'Hoffmann, Le Caïd, Faust, Show Boat, 1980*, Laurence Scrobacs, pianist, Leg.*

*Amadeus*: Figaro arias (film sound track), 1982, Marriner, Carrere

*Opera Arias*: Attila, Nabucco, Mefistofele, La sonnambula, Semiramide, Don Giovanni, L'amore dei tre re, Rinaldo, 1986, Renzetti, Philips

*Music for Life*: excerpts from Don Carlo, 1987*, Levine, DG

*Rodgers and Hammerstein*: various selections, 1988, Matz, EMI

*Operatic Arias*: Ernani, Le comte Ory, Simone Boccanegra, Nabucco, Les Vêspres siciliennes, La Damnation de Faust, Robert le diable, Il barbiere di Siviglia, Don Carlo, Lucrezia Borgia, 1988, Delacôte, EMI

*La Grande Notte a Verona*: excerpts from Attlia, 1988*, Franci, Polyphon

*French Opera Arias*: Carmen, Faust, Le Siège de Corinthe, Les Huguenots, Les Contes d'Hoffmann, Le Caïd, La Jolie Fille de Perthe, Grisélidis, Le Jongleur de Notre-Dame, Don Quichotte, 1989, Rudel, Philips

*Carols of Christmas*: Christmas carols with Sarah Vaughan, 1989, Bagley, Hallmark

# Discography

*Copland & Ives*: Old American Songs, 1990, Warren Jones, pianist, Decca

*Rossini Arias*: Il viaggio a Reims, Stabat Mater, La Cenerentola, L'Italiana in Algeri, Semiramide, Alle Voci della Gloria, 1991, Ferro, Teldec

*Tucker Gala XVI*: Susannah, 1991*, Conlon, RCA

*Rossini Gala*: Le Siège de Corinthe, Il viaggio a Reims, 1992*, Norrington, EMI

*Bicentenary of La Fenice*: Attlia, Semiramide, 1992*, Prêtre, MM

*Samuel Ramey on Broadway: So in Love*, 1993, Stratta, Teldec

*Marilyn Horne: The Men in My Life*, 1993, Gemignani, RCA

*Marilyn Horne: 60th Birthday*: excerpt from Show Boat, 1994*, James Levine, pianist, RCA

*Ev'ry Time We Say Goodbye*: Barber, Foster, Griffes, Gershwin, Bowles, Porter, 1995p*, Warren Jones, pianist, Sony

*Metropolitan Opera Gala*: excerpts from Faust, 1996*, Levine, DG

*Ardis Krainik Celebration Gala*: Attila, Show Boat, 1996*, Bartoletti and Tweeten, pianists, LOC

*No Tenors Allowed*: Duets by Cimarosa, Donizetti, Bellini, Verdi with Thomas Hampson, 1997, Gomez-Martinez, Teldec

*Date with the Devil*, Arias from Faust, La Damnation de Faust, Mefistofele, Rudel, Naxos

VIDEOS AND DVDs

BERNSTEIN
On the Town (*Pitkin, First Workman, Announcer*), 1992, Tilson Thomas, Von Stade, McLaughlin, Hampson, Lear, DG

BIZET
Carmen (*Escamillo*), 1987, Levine, Baltsa, Mitchell, Carreras, DG

BOITO
Mefistofele (*Mefistofele*), 1989, Arena, Benackova, O'Neill, Pioneer

HAYDN
Die Schöpfung (The Creation), 1990, Muti, Popp, Araiza, Bär, Sony

# *Discography*

MASSENET
Manon (*Comte des Grieux*), 1977, Rudel, Sills, Price, Hale, Pioneer

MOZART
Don Giovanni (*Don Giovanni*), 1987, Karajan, Tomowa-Sintow, Varady, Battle, Winbergh, Furlanetto, Sony

ROSSINI
Il barbiere di Siviglia (*Basilio*), 1976, Caldwell, Sille, Titue, H. Price, Pioneer
Semiramide (*Assur*), 1990, Conlon, Anderson, Horne, Olsen, Polygram

STRAVINSKY
The Rake's Progress (*Nick Shadow*), 1978, Haitink, Lott, Goerke, van Allen, Pickwick

VERDI
Attila (*Attila*), 1991, Muti, Studer, Kaludov, Zancanaro, Pioneer
Don Carlo (*Filippo II*), 1992, Muti, Pavarotte, Dessi, d'Intino, Coni, Anisimov, EMI

*Karajan in Salzburg*: excerpts from rehearsals of Don Giovanni, 1987, Karajan, DG

*La Grande Notte a Verona*: Attlia, 1988, Franci, Polygram

*Metropolitan Opera Gala 1991*: The Impossible Dream, 1991, Levine, DG

*Rossini Gala*: Le Siège de Corinthe, Il viaggio a Reims, 1992, Norrington, EMI

*Metropolitan Opera Gala 1996*: Faust, 1996, Levine, DG

# Publisher's Note:

Opera is the art that encompasses all others. Some call it the supreme art. The talent, commitment, and charisma of those who bring it to life should be respected and honored. That is what we attempt to do in the Great Voices Series. We have been at this rewarding task for fifteen years. At this juncture it is important to recognize those who have lent their skills and devotion to the Series.

I thank Jane Scovell for, not only writing two of the books, but also for introducing us to many people in various aspects of opera, all of whom consider her a friend. What a pleasure to deal with the elegant Nora London, the fabulously talented and gentlemanly Placido Domingo, the steel will, quick wit and incomparable voice of Marilyn Horne, the open graciousness of Samuel Ramey, who spins out Rossini and Verdi as child's play. I remember the quiet dignity of Renata Tebaldi, the patient counsel of Edgar Vincent, and the thrill of listening for the first time to the never before released tracks on our CD of Mario Lanza, which Domingo says, "grabs one with astonishing force."

I offer sincere thanks to Dick Kriegbaum for his patient labor, Paul Gruber for valuable advice, Mark Moore for many splendid book covers, Van Cliburn winner, Jose Feghali, who insisted on taking time from his career to master many of the CDs, and Bill Park who for 15 years helped us assemble many of them. And to Fanchee Ann Whitaker who cheerfully, steadfastly and without fail has seen to it that all the pieces come together. Thanks to all unmentioned, but deeply appreciated, friends of The Great Voices Series.

Ronald E. Moore
Publisher

# INDEX
## OF NAMES APPEARING IN TEXT

**A**

Abbado, Claudio 118
Academic Press 43
Ackerman, Paul 12, 184
Ali, Muhammed 35
Anna Bolena 62, 99
Arbib, Joyce 110, 142, 171
Astaire, Fred 56
Ashe, Arthur 141

**B**

Bartered Bride 28
Bernstein, Leonard 118 f
Bing, Rudolf 42, 11, 125
Blackman, Harry 141
Blake, Rockwell 131
Bliss, Anthony 140
Bolen, Vicky 25 ff
Bonynge, Richard 118
Boris Godunov 119
Boughton, Harrison 22
Boyajian, Armen 49 ff, 74, 84, 101, 147, 162, 186
Brooks, Patricia 83, 93, 115
Burcheladze, Paata 119
Burrows, Stewart 68

**C**

Caballe, Montserrat 116, 117, 120 f, 187

Caldwell, Sarah 65 ff
Callas, Maria 74 f
Capobianco, Tito 93, 102
Carmen 70, 78
Carreras, Jose 116
Caruso, Enrico 2, 99
Chailly, Riccardo 118
Chaliapin, Feodor 2, 16, 149, 191
Christie, John 111
Christof, Boris 2
Clinton, Bill 140
Coronation of Poppea 148
Corsaro, Frank 138
Cosi fan tutte 24
Crosby, John 30

**D**

Damnation of Faust 167
Davis, Colin 118
Devlin, Michael 112
Diaz, Justino 105
Doktor Faustus 167
Domingo, Placido 42, 99, 120
Don Carlo 174
Don Giovanni 99, 103, 116
Don Quichotte 85, 150, 191

**E**

Ellis, Brent 63, 73
Epstein, Matthew 36, 71f, 94,

*275*

*Index*

106, 123, 126 ff, 142, 147, 149, 167
Estes, Simon 121

**F**

Falstaff 25, 34 f
Farrell, Eileen 165
Faust 57, 99, 100, 150, 154, 167
Fischer, William 18
Fischer – Deskau, Dietrich 163
Fletcher, A. J. 35 ff
Florez, Juan Diego 132
Francis, Muriel 88 ff

**G**

Galvany, Marisa 60, 99
Gelb, Peter 144
Gergiev Valery 119
Ghiaurov, Nicolai 2, 127
Gibbs, Raymond 83
Glossop, Peter 68
Gossett, Phillip 117, 130
Graham, Tom 105 ff, 121, 133, 153
Grimaldi, Nicolo 129

**H**

Hadley, Jerry 183 f
Hampson, Thomas 163
Harrison, Phil 12
Hale, Robert 80
Hedden, Steve 11
Helms, Jesse 37
Heston, Charlton 141
Hines, Jerome 3
Horne, Marilyn 2, 30, 71, 75, 117, 124 ff, 128 ff, 138 ff, 147, 152, 154, 159, 177, 190 f
Horner, Matthew 191
Hurok, Sol 90

**I**

I Due Foscari 116
I Puritani 81, 120
Il Trovatore 64
Il viaggio a Reims 117, 191
Infidelity Foiled 24
Ingpen, Joan 127

**J**

Jones, Warren 157, 161, 166
Julius Caesar 79

**K**

Karajan, Herbert von 116 f
Kerschenbaum, Lois 84
Killebrew, Gwendolyn 73
Klaus, Wally 43
Krause, Alfredo 116

**L**

La Boheme 62, 64
La Giaconda 74
La Traviata 67, 83
Lancaster, Burt 146
Le Comte d'Ory 126
Lee, Christopher 146
Leinsdorf, Eric 98 f
Lefort, Bernard 126
Levine, James 119, 123, 134

# Index

L' Italiana in Algiers 130, 134, 152
Loch, Ron 20
London, George 3
Lucia de Lamermoor 81, 116
Lunsway, Sam 20, 26, 28

## M

Maazel. Lorin 118
Malas, Marlena 185 ff
Malas, Spiro 21, 185
Manon 81, 189
Manson, Anne 186
Mansouri. Lofti 186
Maometto 147
Maples, R. L., Wilma 28
Mariner, Neville 118
Marriage of Figaro 99, 111, 133
Marsee, Suzanne 115
Medea 81
Mephistofole 100, 113, 144, 146, 167, 189
Meredith, Morley 28
Merritt, Chris 131
Midsummer's Night Dream 24
Mikado 28
Mildmay, Audrey 111
Milnes, Sherril 5, 21, 116
Morelli, Giuseppe 110
Morris, James 3, 127, 135
Mortier, Gerard 126
Muti, Ricardo 118 f, 168

## N

Nabucco 175
Newman, Arthur 32 ff, 74
Norma 120

## O

Oklahoma 28
Ozawa, Seiji 118

## P

Paterson, Kay 12, 17, 184
Pavarotti, Luciano 66, 120
Pinza, Ezio 2, 19, 88, 114, 149
Pique Dame 76
Plishka, Paul 49, 56, 127
Pretre, Georges 118
Previn, Andre 118
Princess Diana 141
Prodigal Son 56

## R

Raimi, Sam 5
Raimondi, Ruggiero 127
Rake's Progress 112
Ramey, Carrie 46 f, 76, 109, 170 ff
Ramey, Darlene 4, 7 f
Ramey, Grace Irene Mallory 5, 9 f, 18, 26, 38
Ramey, Joseph 4, 7 f
Ramey, Leonard 4, 7, 38
Ramey, Lindsey 6, 172 – 180, 183
Ramey, Lolly 5
Ramey, Robert 5, 9, 10, 16, 18
Ramey, Samuel Guy 179 f
Ramey, Vicky 25 – 31
Reiss, Janine 95
Ricci, Luigi 94 f
Ricciarelli, Katie 116
Rigoletto 116
Rinaldo 79, 128, 134, 138, 189

*Index*

Rudel, Jules 69 f, 77, 86, 91, 97 f, 100 ff, 114, 147, 169
Rutenberg, Craig 158

**S**

Salome 45, 81
Scimone, Claudio 118
Secrest, Vicky 13, 121
Semiramide 26, 117, 120, 129
Severinson, Doc 142
Sherman, Bob 59
Shicoff, Neil 155
Siepi, Cesare 2, 19, 110, 127
Siciliani, Francesco 133
Sills, Beverly 33, 42, 52, 68, 77, 79, 82, 92, 96 f, 99, 105, 116, 122, 128, 138, 150, 183
Sinopoli, Giuseppe 118
Smith, Erik 109 ff, 116
Soviero, Diana 127
Sperber, Herta 44, 48
Spielberg, Stephen 5
Stevens, Rise 138
Strehler, Giorgio 152
Streisand, Barbara 145 f
Susannah 92
Sutherland, Joan 66, 74, 120 f, 125

**T**

Tales of Hoffman 24, 62, 81, 99
Terfel, Bryn 178
Tosca 28, 81, 116, 120, 141
Tozzi, Georgio 19, 116
Triegle, Norman 21, 33, 70, 78 ff, 84, 91 f, 96 f, 101, 114 f, 124, 136
Turandot 81

**U**

Urbani, Valentino 129
Ustinov, Peter 141
Vance, John 67, 69 f
Van Dam, Jose 127
Vanderveen, Jeffrey 155 ff, 181
Vincent, Edgar 85 ff, 114, 138, 143, 183
Volpe, Joseph 144
Von Stade, Frederica 181 f

**W**

War and Peace 144
Weidinger, Christine 63 f

**Z**

Zefferelli, Franco 152
Zimbalist, Efrem Jr. 90